Health System Redesign

Joachim P. Sturmberg

Health System Redesign

How to Make Health Care Person-Centered,
Equitable, and Sustainable

 Springer

Joachim P. Sturmberg
University of Newcastle
Wamberal, NSW, Australia

ISBN 978-3-319-87833-1   ISBN 978-3-319-64605-3   (eBook)
DOI 10.1007/978-3-319-64605-3

Printed on acid-free paper

This Springer imprint is published by Springer Nature
The registered company is Springer International Publishing AG
The registered company address is: Gewerbestrasse 11, 6330 Cham, Switzerland

This book is dedicated to my patients for their patience in educating me about the true nature of health. I am indebted to their generosity in sharing with me their experiences of what it means to "be in good health," and how one maintains the "experience of good health" by adapting to the consequences of disease.

Foreword

Notes from the New World

Over the past few years, our work at the Lown Institute has been focused on the deep problems of delivering the right medical care to all. Since our first annual conference in 2012, there has been growing recognition of the failure of modern health systems to deliver needed and wanted care while avoiding unnecessary care. The serious consequences of these twin problems, both in harms to patients and in costs to communities, are staggering.

Our recent series of papers in the *Lancet* attempted to move these issues to a more prominent place in the global health agenda, alongside the traditional focus on communicable and noncommunicable diseases and the newer one on universal health coverage. Fortunately, we are now in the early stages of a worldwide movement to address poor care. However, the more I have reflected on our work, the more I have become convinced that we will not be successful unless we face a key fact: the problems of overuse and underuse are not mere aberrations of an otherwise healthy system, but instead arise from the very fabric of modern medicine and its current paradigm.

The old medical world is in turmoil, turmoil unprecedented in the past century. The issues and problems are piling up faster than solutions are being found. Across the globe, patients are feeling a need for care that is not being met and becoming sceptical of tests and procedures that could bankrupt them. While ageing populations and rising technology costs are core drivers of concerns regarding the efficiency of healthcare delivery, clinicians worldwide are also feeling something more emotional: a sense of loss as care has become more and more transactional and less and less relational. A lot of this is a consequence of the neoliberal era out of which we are emerging, but I am convinced that something deeper is going on.

The evidence is accumulating that the scientific paradigm of the last hundred years has run its course and that we are now encountering dilemmas in every direction. One consequence is that the explosion of technology has made it harder and harder to have an integrated view of the human being at the heart of medicine's purpose. In moments like these, we need to completely reexamine our worldview and revise it to conform to the stubborn reality that confronts us.

The author of this book, Joachim Sturmberg, is one of the many extraordinary people I have encountered in the course of my work in recent years. He is someone whom I know only through the magic of the internet—we are on various listservs together and are connected by a shared passion for reimagining healthcare systems.

Dr. Sturmberg is a remarkable physician, a family practitioner with on-the-ground experience caring for people in rural settings who is also a consummate systems thinker focused on models of integrated care for the individual patient. His capabilities and passion have led him to become an international leader in applying complexity theory to healthcare.

In this capacity, Joachim Sturmberg is clearly a pioneer, an explorer of a new world.

In this book, Sturmberg rightly identifies scientific reductionism as a central problem of our current paradigm. Reductionism deconstructs a complex process, such as the workings of a clock, into its component parts to enable better comprehension of its underlying mechanisms. We have harvested the fruit of this method in the past century with spectacular, almost magical advances in vaccination, antibiotics, surgical techniques and devices. Our knowledge of the intricate molecular components and processes involved in all aspects of health and illness has exploded.

But reliance on a reductionist paradigm is now exposing its disadvantages as continued pursuit of novel, targeted therapies is yielding slower advances at greater and greater cost, as a plethora of examples in cancer and cardiovascular care can attest. This is due in no small measure to the fact that biological systems are highly interconnected and non-linear. The search for a "silver bullet" like penicillin for conditions with complex biology such as cancer or heart disease or behavioural illness is unlikely to succeed.

Beyond biological reductionism, a similar lack of systems thinking is ubiquitous in attempts by health systems to address problems of high costs and poor outcomes, which have so far yielded meagre results. Despite rhetorical flourishes, the real effort is usually small, primarily because new incentives, processes and technology are still largely embedded in the old system.

This is unsurprising because our current healthcare systems focus on transactions rather than relationships. To realise a system that is truly relationship based, we would need to remove transactions—and in fact change everything about the clinical encounter: payment models, delivery models, the technology platform and most importantly the culture. Sturmberg quotes Max Planck, the German physicist who said "When you change the way you look at things the things you look at change".

In Sturmberg's view current health systems have reached a tipping point and are no longer reformable. We must change everything. His book is a welcome contribution to showing us the way forward.

Sturmberg calls for a change in mindset, or worldview. He defines mindset as "a set of assumptions, methods or notions held by one or more people or groups of people which is so established that it creates a powerful incentive within these people or groups to continue to adopt or accept prior behaviours, choices or tools".

The new paradigm that he recommends is complexity theory, a relatively new branch of science that no longer sees the world as mechanistic, linear and predictable, but instead sees it as interconnected, non-linear and adaptive. Over the last 20 years, mathematical frameworks have emerged that help us understand the behaviour of complex systems: network theory, agent-based modelling, scaling theory, the theory of scale-free networks, non-equilibrium statistical mechanics and non-linear dynamics. This mathematics is as important for medicine and healthcare as the calculus was for physics.

Complexity theory allows us to model systems in which the sum of the parts interacts in novel ways far beyond what one might predict from reductionist models. When the interactions between elements are non-linear the behaviour of complex systems is more unpredictable. Sturmberg's point that good and poor health are particularly non-linear and hard to predict is a fundamental truth that explains many of the failures of current approaches.

This framework answers some mysteries in healthcare reform efforts: Sometimes very small inputs may result in very large ("chaotic") responses, but at other times, large inputs may result in no change whatsoever. Moreover, changes in one part of the health system can easily result in deterioration in another.

He points out that the word complexity comes from "complexus" meaning interwoven and show how this framework allows us to completely reorient ourselves in our thinking about health and healthcare. This applies to basic elements like the gnosology of disease and the rendering of a diagnosis as well as to the health system itself. It also invites us to see healthcare as a narrow subsystem within the health system.

Sturmberg's framework allows us to traverse and understand the necessary configurations across the many levels of organisation required in the pursuit of a seamlessly integrated health system. More importantly, this framework allows us to view the experience of health by the person as the principle outcome measure of care.

His approach also sets the stage for a comprehensive programme for the redesign of health systems and allows him to focus attention on all levels of organisation. His paradigm gives local health services permission to self-organise in such a way that achieves the goal of meeting the needs of their people. In Sturmberg's view a sustainable health system principally arises from the local level, which is then influenced by the inputs of regional, state and national levels. Reciprocally, local level health system outcomes influence regional, state and national system functions. He emphasises that managing health system redesign must focus on coherent communication across the system.

One of the critical consequences of this view of healthcare delivery as a complex adaptive system is the empowering of the local care delivery network. His ideal is a local network that constantly improves its services by listening to people's feedback and understanding their needs, then explaining the changes being made in response to their feedback and finally communicating the organisation's successes in delivering what people requested.

Sturmberg also offers some intriguing practical implications of the complex systems approach: How a causal loop diagram of a patient encounter gives the primary care clinician new insights into the patient's illness experience and how it opens a new narrative approach to help the patient make sense of his illness, identify new intervention points and explore alternative treatment approaches in order to modify his illness experience?

I believe everyone in healthcare would benefit from engaging with the ideas presented in this book. The paradigm we seek and that Sturmberg offers holds the promise of a synthesis that liberates us from multiple constraints, greatly advancing our search for a unified image of health. It also restores relationship to the heart of healing.

I share Sturmberg's fundamental worldview, which I see as essential to medicine for the twenty-first century. That he and I have come upon it independently is, I believe, a hopeful sign that we are discovering important intellectual principles in the midst of turmoil, transition and new beginnings.

This book provides a framework for thinking about the new landscape we are entering and I expect that we will be refining and extending its themes and topics for many years to come. As such it is an essential explorer's handbook providing a comprehensive tour of the new world.

President   Vikas Saini
Lown Institute
Cambridge, MA, USA
September 2017

Preface

The recent *Lancet* series *Right Care* (http://www.thelancet.com, January 2017) highlighted that people in high- as well as low- and middle-income countries alike often do not receive the *care they need*. People are either over- or undertreated based on one or a combination of social, economic, political and psychological factors. These factors can be grouped into three domains—*money and finance*; *knowledge, bias and uncertainty*; and *power and human relationships*. Importantly, these factors affect the health system across and between all levels of organisation—global, national, regional and local. In addition, the health system—as opposed to its biomedical healthcare *subsystem*—lacks a clear definition of its specific purpose, goals and values. The dynamic behaviours of these factors amongst and between levels of organisation result in the observable behaviour of a country's health system. Not fully understanding the configurations and relationships amongst the system's agents limits the possibilities for successful health system change.

Health System ReDesign

Our health systems need to be redesigned; in their **current forms, they are no longer fit for purpose** nor are they **financially sustainable** beyond the very near term. Note the emphasis here is on the **health system** rather than the narrow subsystem part that comprises the *healthcare* system. Health system activities entail all aspects that affect human health—education, work, food supply, social and environmental infrastructures besides of the specific health services.

How then do we achieve a *health system* that is fit for purpose, equitable and financially sustainable? To that end, consider Economics Nobel Prize laureate Herbert Alexander Simon's observations:

> Engineering, medicine, business, architecture, and painting are concerned not with the necessary but with the contingent—not how things are but how they might be—in short, with design .... Everyone designs who devises courses of action aimed at changing existing situations into preferred ones.

This book takes its readers on a journey towards a *preferred health system*. Such a system *redesign goes beyond prevailing approaches to healthcare reform*—redesign approaches issues with a **new mindset**, re-examining the fundamental basis of the system, its purpose, specific goals, core values and its core drivers or operating principles (aka "simple rules"). In doing so, it considers the configurations and relationships of its agents across and between its various levels of organisation in the pursuit to achieve a seamlessly integrated health system.

Health system redesign thus is a *process* that requires input from all. As Julio Frenk emphasised, we are all agents of the health system in various ways:

- As patients, with specific needs requiring care
- As users, with expectations about the way in which they will be treated
- As taxpayers/service purchasers and therefore as the ultimate source of financing
- As citizens who may demand access to care as a right
- As co-producers of health through care seeking, compliance with treatment and behaviours that may promote or harm one's own health or the health of others

Taking a *whole of system* perspective, all users (*ought to*) play a key role in determining the purpose, goals and values of the health system. As users have different needs in different contexts, the emerging configurations of local health systems will rightly vary in their specifics while fully embracing its overarching aims. Those emerging local health services will be the "best adapted" given local needs as well as restraints. Therefore, this book cannot—and does not pretend—to provide *easy answers* to the problem; rather, it aims to allude to important issues that underpin the health system redesign process. The book will address three key themes:

- Understanding complexity—what are complexity sciences, and how does complexity thinking shape our understanding of health
- Envisioning a "best adapted" health system—what would it require, examples that point in this direction and ways that might help us to get there
- Achieving a person-centred, equitable and sustainable health system—how can we translate the principles of systems and design thinking in practice, what can we learn from examples that have used these principles and how can we translate this learning towards the goal of achieving person-centred, equitable and sustainable health systems

Diversity of Views

Designing a preferred health system in the first instance will require all with vested interest to openly and transparently address the many issues that underpin the *status quo*. As highlighted above, the health system is conflicted on issues of money and finance; knowledge, bias and uncertainty; and power and human relationships. Will we be able to acknowledge amongst others that:

- The pathways to good and poor health are non-linear and hard to predict
- Health is *personal* and the product of complex dynamic relationships amongst biological, social, emotional and cognitive determinants
- To meet all of a person's health needs requires the engagement with those able to manage the underlying social determinants of health
- Health systems are expected to manage people's needs, not their demands
- Healthcare needs are inversely related to socio-economic status
- Healthcare is a service, not a commodity
- Efficient healthcare goes hand in hand with effective social care
- Health is a human right to be maintained on an equitable basis
- Powers and responsibilities within the health system are distributed amongst all its agents
- The health system provides a security system in case of need, especially for the most vulnerable in our communities
- A mutual approach to healthcare financing—regardless of public or private funding arrangements—is of benefit to *society as a whole*
- The greatest health gains may arise from investments into services outside the health system, e.g. draining standing waters to prevent mosquito-borne diseases, or building community food gardens in poor neighbourhoods

Moving Forward

This book is extensively referenced to allow readers to follow up on familiar as well as unfamiliar or contentious sounding statements. The addition of addenda provides the interested reader amongst others with excerpts from influential thinkers and practitioners covering an epistemology of systems sciences; adaptive leadership and change management; differing perspectives on what constitutes "value in healthcare"; and a brief introduction to understanding the "role and value of social service" for health and well-being.

I would hope that we can start an ongoing conversation about health system redesign. To that end, I have initiated a *LinkedIn Group*—https://www.linkedin.com/groups/13553062—with the aim of creating a movement that can influence the renewal of health systems around the world.

Holgate, NSW, Australia   Joachim P. Sturmberg
May 2017

Acknowledgements

This book arose from ongoing discussions with friends and colleagues from around the globe. I am particularly thankful for helpful comments from Di O'Halloran, Bruno Kissling, Curt Lindberg, Carmel Martin, Beverley Ellis, Marcus Thygeson, Geoff McDonnell, Chad Swanson, Paul Spicker, and Len Gainsford.

Contents

**Part IV   Person-Centred, Equitable, and Sustainable Health
            Systems: Achieving the Goal**

Chapter 1
We Need a Systemic Approach for the Redesign of Health Systems

> *Dealing successfully with complex problems requires an understanding that every problem is interconnected to a large number of other issues, and an appreciation of the inevitable time delay between actions and results [1].*

Navigating the challenges of the present health system crisis calls for a *mindset shift*, one that:

- Embraces *system thinking* as the principle way to understand the problems and design solutions
- Regards the *needs of the person/patient* as the sine qua non for health service delivery
- Views the *experience of health by the person* as the principle outcome measure

This book outlines a systems-based approach to explore the crisis of health systems around the world and outlines how applying systems thinking approaches can result in a *seamlessly integrated, person-centred, equitable, and sustainable health system* (Fig. 1.1).

The core arguments in support of a systems-based approach to the redesign of the health system are as follows:

- Complex adaptive systems are defined by their core focus, changing the health system requires a change of the core focus—*from disease to health*
- The emphasis should be on the *health system* rather than *healthcare system*, the latter representing one of many "health system subsystems"

  - *The health system focuses on the health and well-being of the person*
  - *The healthcare system focuses on the diseases of the person*

- A focus on the "*health of the person*" would demand the *reconfiguration of the external factors* impacting on a person's health, like education, housing, work, social and public infrastructure

J.P. Sturmberg, *Health System Redesign*, DOI 10.1007/978-3-319-64605-3_1

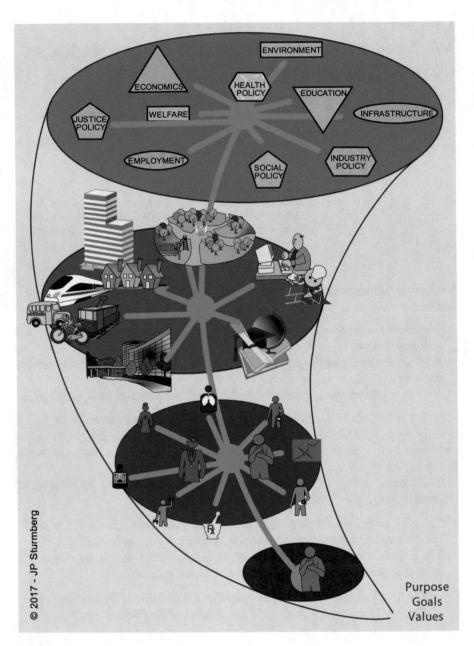

Fig. 1.1 A seamlessly integrated health system. The constraints of the local environment will determine the configurations and relationships that allow the necessary adaptation at every organisational level to make the system seamlessly integrated to *meet the needs of the person/patient*

1.1 Mindsets/Worldviews

Mindsets or worldviews are defined as "a set of assumptions, methods or notions held by one or more people or groups of people which is so established that it creates a powerful incentive within these people or groups to continue to adopt or accept prior behaviours, choices or tools".

Our mindset/worldview reveals itself by the way we engage with problems[1]

- The beliefs and mental attitudes
- The ways we express our thoughts and project our outlooks
- The behaviours we exhibit in the debates

1.1.1 A Complexity Mindset

A complexity[2] mindset sees the world as *interconnected and interdependent*, and it sees the behaviour of the world as the result of the dynamic nonlinear interactions amongst its agents.

A complexity thinking approach accepts that changes to the structure or the function of a complex adaptive system, like the health system, are not precisely predictable. It also accepts that the outcomes of a change at the top levels of organisations may result in locally different outcomes. A complexity mindset appreciates these outcomes as mutually agreeable; each outcome reflects the "best adapted solution" in light of unique local circumstances (Chap. 2).[3]

---

[1]Our mindsets/worldviews are shaped by different perspectives like:

- individualism (i.e. valuing independence and self-reliance) or collectivism (i.e. valuing social inclusiveness, equality and equity)
- fixed (i.e. rule based) or adaptive (i.e. situational and environmental awareness) thinking strategies
- political persuasions like

    - libertarianism (i.e. embracing decentralised government and individual choice and freedom)
    - conservatism (i.e. embracing the preservation of traditional institutions like church and monarchy)
    - liberalism (i.e. embracing choice, private property and equality)
    - socialism (i.e. embracing a belief in the social ownership and control of the means of production and thus a society that provides an economic safety net that protects citizens in case of unemployment, sickness, poverty, and old age)
    - capitalism (i.e. embracing private ownership of the means of production and personal profit maximisation)
    - neo-liberalism (i.e. embracing privatisation, fiscal austerity, deregulation, free trade, and the reduction in the seize of government)

[2]From Latin: *complexus* meaning interwoven.

[3]Chapter references have been added for the key points introduced in this chapter.

Consider the following examples:

- The rapidly growing obesity epidemic, while having many contributing factors, is predominantly the result of the consumption of high sugar containing foods [2, 3]. Public health advocates demand stricter regulation of the addition of sugar during the food production process as part of a multi-pronged approach against obesity [4], sugar producers see it as an attack against their livelihood [5], the food industry argues against such a measure on the basis of increasing production costs and that, anyway, it is not a problem of the foods but rather the consumer's choice [6]. And consumers are in a bind as many of the highly processed foods are very much cheaper than fresh foods [7, Chap. 11]
- Australian patients continuously complain about poor access for semi-urgent surgical procedures in the public hospital system. To ensure transparency of access health departments have established waiting-list rules that proclaim to guarantee that no one has to wait more than 12 months for any procedure [8]. However, as recently transpired, this policy has had "unintended consequences" (Chap. 8); the only way for hospital administrators to achieve this goal is to pressure their surgeons not to place patients on the waiting list—the only way to comply with that demand is not to see uninsured patients until a new waiting list vacancy becomes available [9]

Both of these examples—one a macro, the other a micro-level problem—highlight the interdependencies inherent in each problem. They also highlight the consequences of not appreciating the complex nature of the problem, and the resulting failures associated with inertia in the case of the obesity crisis, or simplistic regulation in the case of managing political expediency and public expectations [10].

Fully appreciating "today's problems" requires the recognition that they are the results of decisions made in response to previous problems having *insufficiently considered their impact on the "system as a whole"* [11, Chap. 9].

1.1.2   Systems and Complexity Thinking in Health and Healthcare

Systems thinking and systems-based approaches to problem solving have had an impact in many domains, yet, they have not been widely applied to health system problems. It is important to distinguish complex systems from complex adaptive systems, and systems thinking from complexity thinking (Table 1.1).

A few attempts have been made to emulate systems approaches from other industries (Table 1.2). However, many industry approaches are of limited value in managing a **health system as a whole** as they are **not** dealing with the **adaptive and emergent dynamics** inherent in **complex adaptive systems**. Not appreciating the complex adaptive nature of the health system leaves healthcare policy makers, managers, and health professionals constantly surprised about the unexpected

Table 1.1 Disambiguation—systems vs complexity

Complex systems—complex systems are system composed of many components that interact with each other
Complex adaptive systems—complex adaptive systems (CAS) are complex systems whose elements (agents) learn and adapt their behaviours to changing environments
Complex and complex adaptive systems both have the characteristic of self-organisation without external control and exhibit feedback resulting in newly created, i.e. emergent (at times unforeseen), behaviours
Systems thinking—exploring the structural relationships and their implications between the elements of a system (understanding the parts in relation to the whole)
Complexity thinking—a mental approach that appreciates the interconnected nature of problems and their nonlinear relationships and dynamics; a mental approach that sees solutions arising from the continual engagement and adaptation of its stakeholders

outcomes resulting from their decision-making. Systems science thinking aims to better understand how *small catalytic events*—typically separated by proximity and time—can explain (and anticipate) complex (adaptive) change in a system. What might be an improvement in one part of the health system can easily result in deterioration in another. The emphasis in managing health system redesign therefore must focus on *coherent communication across the system*. Failing to achieve a coherent redesign of the *system as a whole* will further cement the prevailing *silo effect*.[4]

1.2   Health System Redesign: More than Health System Reform

Reform is typically an endeavour of government to solve a problem in a policy area. As experience shows, most policy decisions fail to improve the problems they were intended to solve. Part of the reason resides in the nature of policy making.

Policy making is a cyclical and iterative process, first described in 1956 by Harold Laswell as the "policy cycle" [30]. This cycle has remained largely unchanged and principally includes the steps of "agenda setting or problem identification", "policy formulation, incorporating issue analysis", "implementation",

---

[4]The term *"functional silo syndrome"* was coined in 1988 by Phil S. Ensor [12]. He observed that managers have a mental model of maintaining information in silos causing divergence of goals between different units of an organisation. Predictors for the occurrence of silos are:

- Number of employees
- Number of organisational units within the whole organisation
- Degree of specialisation
- Number of different incentive mechanisms

Table 1.2 System thinking tools—roles and limitations (citations [12–28] are solely provided as a reference to examples that illustrate a particular technique)

Systems thinking approaches in different sectors	Implications for healthcare
Systems engineering	**Limitations from a *whole system* perspective**
• Design, operate, and measure complex systems over their life cycles • Analyse and improve efficiency, productivity, quality, and safety • Archetype: Apollo programme	• Health is not a product that can be produced; it is a personal experiential state that emerges from within the person's biological, social, emotional, and cognitive context [13, 14] **Potential benefits** • Health system components, like building a new hospital, can be designed using system engineering; however, the running of the new hospital requires the skills of managing complex adaptive dynamics arising from the interactions between staff, patients, and community demands
Business analytics	**Limitations from a *whole system* perspective**
• Performance assessment based on data and statistical methods • Applying metrics to assess business performance • Predictive modelling • Knowledge management • Fact-based decision-making • Artificial intelligence • Visualisation	• Cannot take account of the unique features of a person's illness and care needs—the *raison d'être* of health care • Health service delivery for the largest extent is not transactional but transpersonal **Potential benefits** • Business analysis tools can help to understand the financial flows in the health system; however, the appropriateness of the use of resources remains a clinical judgement. Identifying variation in resource use patterns can facilitate discussions about the appropriateness of resource use in the clinical context

Rule-based approaches	Limitations from a *whole system* perspective
• Systems thinking is used to conceptualise adverse events • Insights are used to formulate rule-based responses for all envisaged scenarios • Archetype: airline industry	• Healthcare for all intents and purposes requires adaptive thinking and responses that negate potential benefits from rule-based approaches. That said they have value, e.g., in theatre to identify the right person and the right procedure being performed Potential benefits • Development of team-based learning: increases situational monitoring, situational awareness, and shared mental models [15] • However, rule-based errors and rule violations increase with complexity and uncertainty in cognitive operators [16]
Decision support systems (DSS) include health information systems, artificial intelligence (machine learning) • DSSs serve the management, operations, and planning levels of an organisation • Help people make decisions about problems that may be rapidly changing and/or are not easily specified in advance • Help decision makers compile useful information from a combination of raw data, documents, personal knowledge, and/or business models to identify and solve problems	Limitations from a *whole system* perspective • DSS in theory offers benefits to medical care, however, studies indicate at best marginal benefits [17, 18] Potential benefits • DSS can help for small scale issues like antibiotic prescribing and critical care protocols [18] • DSS can help to evaluate the impact of different resource allocation strategies [19] • AI can help to identify patterns associated with the particular health outcomes

(continued)

Table 1.2 (continued)

Geographical information systems	Limitations from a *whole system* perspective
• Distribution of agents and their connections • Spatial relationships	• High risk of over-interpretation of local issues without taking account of the embedded global factors
	Potential benefits
	• Early identification of environmental causes of disease [20] • Identification of "hot spots" allows the reallocation of resources for those in greatest need [21] • Helpful in identifying sources of health inequality [22]
Agent-based modelling and other simulation tools [23, 24]	Limitations from a *whole system* perspective
	• Modelling the problem[a] of "how to achieve a seamlessly integrated health system", especially with a focus on meeting the person's needs, has not yet been attempted
	Potential benefits
	• Understanding spread of disease in a community [25, 26] • Understanding patient flow in an emergency department [27] • Optimising operating room utilisation [28] • Testing of policy assumptions [29]

[a]The maxim in simulation modelling is to model problems, not systems

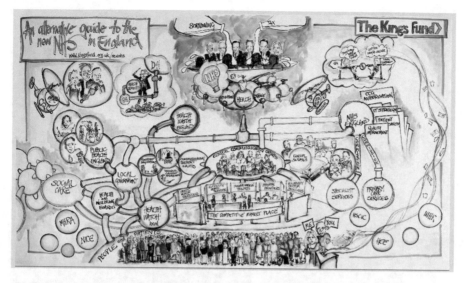

Fig. 1.2 An alternative guide to the new NHS in England (reproduced with permission from the King's Fund)

and "evaluation". While the cyclical nature of policy making varies slightly from country to country, outcomes are typically very similar. Addendum 1 shows some of these variations and details the stages, aims, processes, and potential weaknesses of the policy cycle in greater detail [31].

Despite the "well-defined process", policy making rarely achieves the outcomes initially envisaged. How "*well intentioned*" and "*ambitious*" health policy reform achieves an even "*greater mess*" has been visually summarised (Fig. 1.2) by the King's Fund in relation to the 2012 NHS reform in the UK.[5]

A more productive way to solve complex health system problems might be a design thinking approach [32, Chap. 13].

Design thinking—as a strategy—deliberately involves all affected stakeholders in an iterative problem-solving process. Its approach **combines** insights from SCIENCE (finding similarities among things that are different), ART (finding differences among things that are similar), **and** DESIGN (creating feasible "wholes" from infeasible "parts") in ways that are best suited to find solutions to complex ("*wicked*") problems [33] in the realm of uncertainty.

Design thinking is particularly useful in *the design of complex systems or environments for living, working, playing, and learning. ...this area has also expanded and reflects more consciousness of the central idea, thought, or value that expresses the unity of any balanced and functioning whole. This area is more*

---

[5]For those interested, the King's Fund released a short YouTube video entitled **An alternative guide to the new NHS in England**—https://www.youtube.com/watch?v=8CSp6HsQVtw.

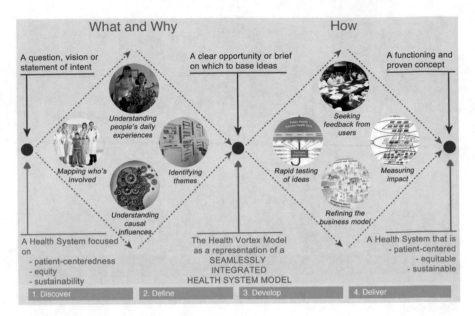

Fig. 1.3 The process of designing a patient-centred, equitable and sustainable health system (adapted from "The Design Council (UK)")

and more concerned with exploring the role of design in sustaining, developing, and integrating human beings into broader ecological and cultural environments, shaping these environments when desirable and possible or adapting to them when necessary [33].

Design thinking follows a solutions-based approach, it starts by defining *how things ought to be* [32]. Working towards the solution (*how things ought to be*) follows a process described by "The Design Council (UK)" as the four distinct divergent and convergent phases of design: *Discover, Define, Develop, and Deliver.* These four steps are illustrated in relation to a *seamlessly integrated, person-centred, equitable, and sustainable health system* redesign as outlined in this book (Fig. 1.3).

The distinction between a policy reform approach reflecting a "*complicated control-based approach*" and an "*emergent approach of redesign*" is illustrated in Addendum 2 (Obamacare health system reform) and Addendum 3 (Canterbury Health District (NZ) system redesign).

1.3 *Designing* a *Complex Adaptive* Health System

Current health systems have reached a tipping point—they are no longer reformable. The notion of reform entails change within the current framework (aka tinkering), i.e. reforms in the long term can only achieve "more of the same". The notion of redesign a priori starts with a "blank sheet" approach, it opens the "space of possibility" to move to a new framework—as suggested here, moving from a focus of "fixing disease" to one of "creating health".[6] Redesign has a "whole of system" focus. It is a process that requires committed leadership and the engagement of all stakeholders.

This book takes its readers on the challenging journey of health system redesign and it does so with a systems and complexity mindset. It describes a system-based pathway for redesign, but it neither pretends nor intends to provide "an easy or definitive answer".

Readers are encouraged to reflect on their experiences in and with their health systems before engaging with the "new ideas" put forward. Each chapter provides a brief "plain English" summary followed by a detailed exploration of the topic. As many readers may engage with these ideas for this first time, this book is highly illustrated, and key ideas are expanded in footnotes and addenda.

While the book, by necessity, had to start with an introduction to the theory, it is not a "theory book". Great care has been taken to provide readers with *real world* examples from around the world to demonstrate how *complexity mindsets* have solved intractable problems at various levels of health system organisation.

References

1. Sturmberg JP (2007) Systems and complexity thinking in general practice. Part I - clinical application. Aust Fam Physician 36(3):170–173
2. Frieden TR, Dietz W, Collins J (2010) Reducing childhood obesity through policy change: acting now to prevent obesity. Health Aff (Millwood) 29(3):357–363
3. Lusk JL, Ellison B (2013) Who is to blame for the rise in obesity? Appetite 68:14–20
4. Hawkes C, Jewell J, Allen K (2013) A food policy package for healthy diets and the prevention of obesity and diet-related non-communicable diseases: the NOURISHING framework. Obes Rev 14:159–168
5. Zonca C (2016) Queensland cane growers take campaign against sugar tax to Canberra. ABC Rural. Available at: http://www.abc.net.au/news/2016-04-22/canegrowers-campaign-against-sugar-tax/7351424, 22 Apr 2016
6. Nixon L, Mejia P, Cheyne A, Wilking C, Dorfman L, Daynard R (2015) We're part of the solution: evolution of the food and beverage industry's framing of obesity concerns between 2000 and 2012. Am J Public Health 105(11):2228–2236

---

[6]"Creating health" entails health promotion and prevention as well as the restoration of health by treating "troublesome" diseases.

7. Wallinga D (2010) Agricultural policy and childhood obesity: a food systems and public health commentary. Health Aff (Millwood) 29(3):405–410
8. NSW Health (2012) Waiting time and elective surgery policy. Sydney: available at: http://www0.health.nsw.gov.au/policies/pd/2012/PD2012_011.html
9. Australian Medical Association (2016) AMA Public Hospital Report Card 2015. Australian Medical Association, Contract No.: available at: https://ama.com.au/sites/default/files/documents/160415%20-%20AMA%20Public%20Hospital%20Report%20Card%202015.pdf
10. Baker P (2014) Fat nation: why so many Australians are obese and how to fix it The Conversation, 6 Mar 2014. Available at: http://theconversation.com/fat-nation-why-so-many-australians-are-obese-and-how-to-fix-it-23783
11. Sturmberg JP, Martin CM (2009) Complexity and health - yesterday's traditions, tomorrow's future. J Eval Clin Pract 15(3):543–548
12. Ensor P (1988) The functional silo syndrome. AME Target: 16. http://www.ame.org/sites/default/files/target_articles/88q1a3.pdf. Retrieved 02 July 2016
13. Sturmberg JP (2013) Health: a personal complex-adaptive state. In: Sturmberg JP, Martin CM (eds) Handbook of systems and complexity in health. Springer, New York, pp 231–242
14. Sturmberg JP (2009) The personal nature of health. J Eval Clin Pract 15(4):766–769
15. Mann S, Marcus R, Sachs B (2006) Grand rounds: lessons from the cockpit: how team training can reduce errors on L&D. Contemporary OB/GYN 51(1):34–42, 7p
16. Clewley R, Stupple EJN (2015) The vulnerability of rules in complex work environments: dynamism and uncertainty pose problems for cognition. Ergonomics 58(6):935–941
17. Moja L, Kwag KH, Lytras T, Bertizzolo L, Brandt L, Pecoraro V et al (2014) Effectiveness of computerized decision support systems linked to electronic health records: a systematic review and meta-analysis. Am J Public Health 104(12):e12–e22
18. Nachtigall I, Tafelski S, Deja M, Halle E, Grebe MC, Tamarkin A et al (2014) Long-term effect of computer-assisted decision support for antibiotic treatment in critically ill patients: a prospective 'before/after' cohort study. BMJ Open 4:e005370
19. Aktaş E, Ülengin F, Önsel Şahin Ş (2007) A decision support system to improve the efficiency of resource allocation in healthcare management. Socio Econ Plann Sci 41(2):130–146
20. Wang Y, Zhuang D (2015) A rapid monitoring and evaluation method of schistosomiasis based on spatial information technology. Int J Environ Res Public Health 12(12):15843–15859
21. McGrail MR, Humphreys JS (2015) Spatial access disparities to primary health care in rural and remote Australia, Geospatial Health 10:358
22. Bürgi R, Tomatis L, Murer K, de Bruin ED (2016) Spatial physical activity patterns among primary school children living in neighbourhoods of varying socioeconomic status: a cross-sectional study using accelerometry and global positioning system. BMC Public Health 16:282
23. Brailsford CS, Harper RP, Patel B, Pitt M (2009) An analysis of the academic literature on simulation and modelling in health care. J Simul 3(3):130–140
24. Barton M, Berger S, Bolt T, Brailsford S, Clarkson J, Connell C et al (2009) Modelling and simulation techniques for supporting healthcare decision making a selection framework. Engineering Design Centre, University of Cambridge, Cambridge
25. Xiao Y, Brauer F, Moghadas SM (2016) Can treatment increase the epidemic size? J Math Biol 72(1):343–361
26. Rutherford G, Friesen MR, McLeod RD (2012) An agent based model for simulating the spread of sexually transmitted infections. Online J Public Health Inform 4(3):ojphi.v4i3.4292
27. Neighbour R, Oppenheimer L, Mukhi SN, Friesen MR, McLeod RD (2010) Agent based modeling of "crowdinforming" as a means of load balancing at emergency departments. Online J Public Health Inform 2(3):ojphi.v2i3.3225
28. Bhatt AS, Carlson GW, Deckers PJ (2014) Improving operating room turnover time: a systems based approach. J Med Syst 38(12):1–8
29. Esensoy AV, Carter MW (2015) Health system modelling for policy development and evaluation: using qualitative methods to capture the whole-system perspective. Oper Res Health Care 4:15–26

30. Jann W, Wegrich K (2007) Theories of the policy cycle. In: Fischer F, Miller GJ, Sidney MS (eds) Handbook of public policy analysis: theory, politics, and methods. CRC Press, New York, pp 43–62
31. Chapman A, McLellan B, Tezuka T (2016) Strengthening the energy policy making process and sustainability outcomes in the OECD through policy design. Adm Sci 6(3):9
32. Simon HA (1969) The sciences of the artificial. MIT Press, Cambridge
33. Buchanan R (1992) Wicked problems in design thinking. Des Issues 8(2):5–21
34. The University of Texas at Austin (2016) The public policy process. http://www.laits.utexas.edu/gov310/PEP/policy/index.html
35. Althaus C, Bridgman P, Davis G (2012) The Australian policy handbook, 5th edn. Allen and Unwin, Sydney
36. HM Treasury (2011) The green book: appraisal and evaluation in central government. HM Government Printer, London
37. Government of Newfoundland and Labrador (2016) The policy cycle. PolicyNL. http://www.policynl.ca/policydevelopment/policycycle.html.

Addendum 1

Policy Making Cycles in Four Countries [34–37]

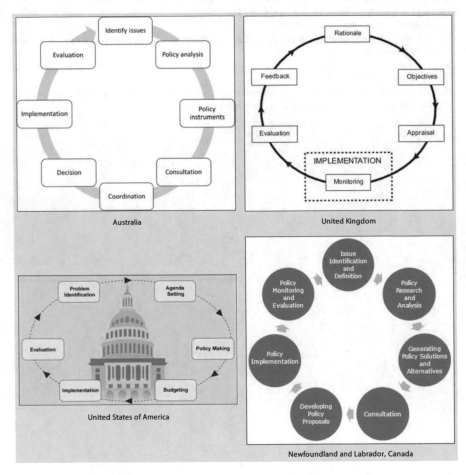

Modified from Chapman A, McLellan B, Tezuka T. Strengthening the energy policy making process and sustainability outcomes in the OECD through policy design [31]

Policy making process table compiled from: Chapman A, McLellan B, Tezuka T. Strengthening the energy policy making process and sustainability outcomes in the OECD through policy design [31]

Stage of cycle	Aims	Processes	Weaknesses

Agenda setting or problem identification	Recognition of a policy problem	• Inherently political
		• Not in the direct control of any single actor
		• Can occur in a bottom-up or top-down fashion
		• Actors actively promote policy issues important to them in order
		  – to have them promoted to the policy agenda
		  – to remain prominent within the political debate
			• Unclear how successfully public opinion influences policy identification
			• Limited capacity within society and political institutions to address all possible policy responses

Policy formulation, incorporating issue analysis	Identification of policy proposals in order to resolve identified issues	• Occurs within government ministries, interest groups, legislative committees, special commissions, and policy think tanks
		• Precedes decision-making
		• Undertaken by policy experts who assess
		  – potential solutions
		  – prepare solutions to be codified into legislation or regulation
		  – initial analysis of feasibility
		  – initial analysis of political acceptability
		  – initial analysis of costs and benefits
		• Consultation with wider society policy is presented to decision makers, usually cabinet, ministers, and Parliament, for consideration prior to implementation	

(continued)

Implementation	The preceding planning activity is put into practice	• Resource allocation • Departmental responsibilities • Development of rules and regulations • By bureaucracy • Creates new agencies • Translation of laws into operational procedures	• "Street-level" bureaucrats need to interpret guidance from central authorities whilst providing everyday problem-solving strategies in order to ensure a successful implementation structure
Evaluation	Policy outcomes are tested against intended objectives and impacts	• Determine any unintended consequences of policies • Establish whether a policy should be terminated or redesigned according to shifting policy goals or newly identified issues • Involves governmental and societal actors in order to influence a reconceptualisation of policy problems and solutions	• Administrative (managerial and budgetary performance) • Judicial (judicial review and administrative discretion) • Political (elections, think tanks, inquiries, and legislative oversight) • A combination of all three

Addendum 2

Obamacare Health System Chart

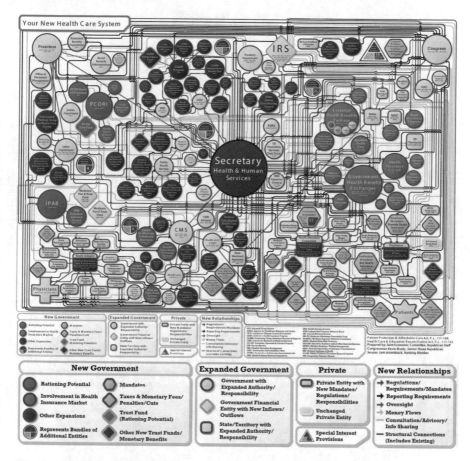

The chart highlights the structural conception behind the policy response. Whilst the details can be better viewed in the online version, the thought processes are clearly evident from the enlarged legend below the chart (a large version of this image is available at http://www.jec.senate.gov/public/index.cfm/republicans/committeenews?ID=bb302d88-3d0d-4424-8e33-3c5d2578c2b0)

Addendum 3

Canterbury Health District (NZ) Health System Redesign Chart

The chart demonstrates the organic and interconnected nature of health care. (A large version of this image is available at http://www.cdhbcareers.co.nz/All-About-Us/How-We-Do-What-We-Do/) (reproduced with permission from the Canterbury and West Coast District Health Boards)

Part I
Complexity and Health: Challenging the Orthodoxy

*The world we see that seems so insane is the result of a belief
system that is not working. To perceive the world, we must be
willing to change our belief system, let the past slip away,
expand our sense of now, and dissolve the fear in our minds.*

William James (1842–1910)
American philosopher, psychologist and physician

Complexity and Health

Complex adaptive system sciences have transformed most science fields with
the exception of medicine and health services. It is freely acknowledged that an
initiation into complex adaptive systems thinking can at first appear abstract, highly
conceptual and even "un-usable". Unsurprisingly tensions arise when applying complex systems thinking in the "real world" of clinical care, healthcare organisations,
or health system design.

In some literature, complexity theory and complex adaptive systems frameworks
use highly specific language to explain the functioning of systems as a whole. It
explicitly opposes reductionism—the assumption that breaking down a system into
its parts is useful to explain and improve its functioning as a whole—and speaks
to the *core driver* of a system that "*determines*" its long-term direction. In other
literature, "systems thinking" or "complexity approaches" are used in quite specific
application, such as mapping relationships, identifying feedback loops, finding gaps
in knowledge, or explaining particular successes/failures. While the underlying
principles are common in both bodies of literature, it is apparent that the conceptual
and the applied can sometimes appear to not speak to each other, or even conflict.
Whether the interest is the *core driver* of a system or a system's long-term direction
or being able to address a specific problem with a systems view, it is necessary to
have a solid grounding in both theoretical and applied approaches.

Understanding complex systems and their behaviour has to become a required
skill to solve the many problems facing health systems. As the Institute of Medicine
pointed out:

Health care is complex because of the great number of interconnections within and among small care systems ... Health care systems are adaptive because unlike mechanical systems they are composed of individuals - patients and clinicians who have the capacity to learn and change as a result of experience. Their actions in delivering health care are not always predictable, and tend to change both their local and larger environment (Institute of Medicine, 2001: 63–64).

Key points to navigate enablers and barriers to system change include:

- Complex adaptive systems theory can help identify the big picture, common drivers of our health system, where and when they limit the ability to change and where leadership and advocacy may be targeted
- Systems thinking can help us understand problems and identify potential solutions to these problems that are not obvious—because they lie in the connections of the system, rather than in specific parts of the system
- Adopting complex systems approaches can bring to light how events, or change, in one part of the system affects other parts of the system
- While complex adaptive system thinking cannot provide "easy answers" [1] it provides a fertile ground to think about and evaluate many different possible solution in context which avoids the "common unintended mishaps" resulting from enforcing linear "expert solutions"

This section aims to provide readers with the necessary philosophical and technical background to systems sciences, the nature of health, and health system organisation and their dynamics. The chapters explore:

- The nature of systems sciences
- The visualisation of complex systems based on Capra's vortex metaphor [2]
- An understanding of the co-existence of different degrees of complexity and their dynamics within complex adaptive organisations based on Kurtz and Snowden's Cynefin model [3]
- The nature of health as a "complex adaptive experiential state"

References

1. Heifetz R (1994) Leadership without easy answers. Harvard University Press, Cambridge, MA
2. Capra F (1996) The web of life. Harper Collins Publishers, London
3. Kurtz CF, Snowden DJ (2003) The new dynamics of strategy: sense-making in a complex and complicated world. IBM Syst J 42(3):462–483

Chapter 2
Complexity Sciences

Overview. Complexity sciences, in plain English, are the *sciences of interconnectedness*.

The aim of complexity sciences is to understand the many different facets of phenomena. Complexity sciences employs a variety of different methodological approaches to describe and to analyse multifaceted phenomena like health, the economy or environmental systems.

- Basically, a system consists of a number of parts that are connected to each other. Systems differ depending on the nature of their connectedness. Simple systems have one-to-one relationships and their behaviour is precisely predictable. Complicated systems have one-to-many relationships with mostly predictable behaviours

- This book deals with *complex adaptive systems* with many-to-many relationships. Their many-to-many relationships make their behaviour emergent, hence their outcomes are unpredictable. Complex adaptive systems have a special characteristic, the members of the system can *learn* from feedback and experiences. The relationships in complex adaptive systems change constantly allowing the system to evolve over time in light of changing demands. However, a system's overall behaviour, despite its adaptation to changing circumstances, remains relatively stable within boundaries, but occasionally, its behaviour may change abruptly and dramatically for no apparent reason

One can compare the behaviour of complex adaptive systems to that of a family; most of the time a family stays together despite ups and downs, but occasionally a family can abruptly break apart to the surprise of its members and its surroundings.

- Another important characteristic of complex adaptive systems is its nonlinear behaviour to change, i.e. the magnitude of change in one member of the system shows a disproportional change in that of others. As experience shows, small changes in the behaviour of a system member often show dramatic changes in

J.P. Sturmberg, *Health System Redesign*, DOI 10.1007/978-3-319-64605-3_2

the behaviour of the whole system, whereas a major change in the behaviour of that member typically results in little or no change

Studying complex adaptive systems aims to understand the relationships and the dynamics between the members of the systems. This understanding allows for better responses when the system as a whole is challenged by constraints and/or unfamiliar challenges.

A special characteristic of *social systems* is their "goal-delivering" nature. In organisational terms these are codified by their purpose, goals and values statements.

Points for Reflection

- What do you understand by the terms "complex/complexity"?
- What do the terms "complex health system", "complex disease", and "complex patient" mean to?
- How do you explain the nature of this "complexity"?
- How do you suggest to best manage this "complexity"?

Systems thinking is a discipline of seeing whole.

– Peter Senge

Everyone has experienced the complexities of the health system, irrespective of their particular role along the continuum of being a patient, working in grass roots care delivery to having overarching policy and financing responsibilities. We are all part of many different systems within the entire health system. We all have observed and experienced the at times surprising behaviours inside our "immediate working system" and the system as a whole. Most of us would have forwarded hunches why a particular system outcome may have occurred. Some of us may well have been involved in analysing "system failures", but did we do so from an understanding of the interconnected behaviours of complex adaptive systems?

Some preliminary considerations:

- "Complexity sciences" still is an emerging field of scientific endeavour (Addendum 1) and entails a number of different methodological approaches like system dynamics, agent-based modelling, or network analysis
- The *colloquial* meaning of complex/complexity needs to be distinguished from its *scientific* meaning. The colloquial meaning of complex/complexity as "difficult to understand" or "complicated" must be distinguished from the scientific meaning of "*the property arising from the interconnected behaviour of agents*"
- "Complexity sciences" defines a worldview that no longer sees the world as mechanistic, linear, and predictable. Rather it sees the world as interconnected. The interactions between elements being nonlinear make the behaviour of complex systems unpredictable (Fig. 2.1)
- Paul Cilliers outlined the philosophical foundations of complexity sciences, parts of which are quoted in more detail in Addendum 2
- The "complexity science framework", like any other scientific framework, provides a mental mind model ABOUT the world, i.e. *The truth of a theory is in your mind, not in your eyes*—Albert Einstein [1]
- Mental models (or worldviews) necessarily have to reduce the real complexity of any phenomenon being described [2, 3]. Useful models, as Box [3] stated,[1] are those that *describe the observed causal relationships* in the real world[2] [4]
- "Complexity" in its scientific understanding refers to "*the nature of the problem not* [emphasis added] *the degree of difficulty*" [5]. The systems theorist David Krakauer illustrates this aspect in relation to Ebola and is quoted in detail in Addendum 3
- "Complexity" exists at every scale, be it at the laboratory or the whole of society level
- The way we look at "things" determines what we see and how we understand. Understanding "things" at the **small scale** results in *greater certainty BUT loss*

---

[1]*Essentially, all models are wrong, but some are useful.* Box, George E. P.; Norman R. Draper (1987). Empirical Model-Building and Response Surfaces [3, p. 424].

[2]However, there are also many unobserved causal relationships (latent variables).

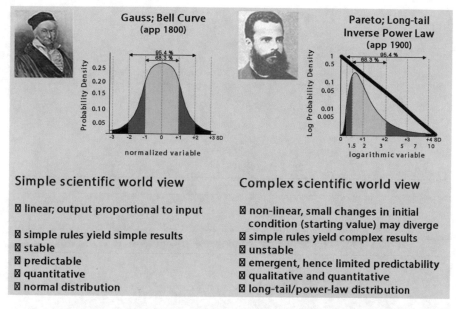

Fig. 2.1 Comparison of the characteristics of the simple scientific and complex scientific world views

of context, whereas understanding "things" at the **large scale** results in *greater uncertainty AND loss of detail* (Fig. 2.2)

2.1   Complex Systems Are …

Systems are described in terms of their structure and relationships (Fig. 2.3). The interactions between the system's agents create an emergent order resulting in the formation of patterns—the process is entirely self-organising [6].

2.2   The Essence of Systems Thinking

As Gene Bellinger put it so succinctly: the *Essence of Systems Thinking* is *Understanding Relationships and Their Implications.*[3]

Systems thinking is an approach to solve problems, where problems are the gap between the existing state and a desired state. Solution narrows or overcomes that gap. Understanding the complexities of a complex adaptive problem in their entirety and finding the *best* solution to overcome such a problem requires (1) the

---

[3]https://www.linkedin.com/pulse/essence-systems-thinking-gene-bellinger.

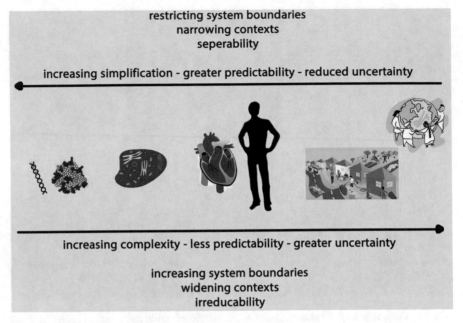

Fig. 2.2 The scale relationship and its impact on complexity and context. At the small scale we have greater certainty but loose context, at the large scale we see the greater context but lose detail

appreciation of the linkages between the elements of the problem and (2) how changes to the behaviour of one element might affect the problem in its entirety. Will an intervention solve the problem, or will it result in unintended consequences making the problem worse or will it create entirely new problems (Fig. 2.4)?

2.3   Complex Systems Theory: An Overview

Complex systems theory has arisen from two main schools of thought—general systems theory and cybernetics. As a theory it provides a ***model of reality NOT reality itself***. However, models provide a useful frame to solve many common problems.

We can use systems theory to distinguish between different types of systems. Along a continuum, they can be classified as simple, complicated, complex (dynamic), and complex adaptive systems (differences are summarised in Table 2.1). Systems theory provides a means to help us make sense of our "wicked" world.

In *simple systems*, elements of the system interact in one-to-one relationships producing predictable outcomes. Simple systems can be engineered and controlled. They are closed to and therefore not influenced by their external environment.

Complicated systems display some of the same characteristics of simple systems in that interactions between elements in the systems are predictable, although

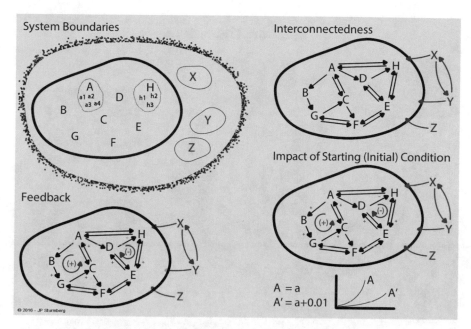

Fig. 2.3 Key features of complex systems. A complex system's structure describes the collection of agents (A–H) contained within a permeable or *fuzzy boundary* (*black circle*), where each agent represents a smaller subsystems (a1–a4) and is part of a larger supra-system (*dotted line*) (*top left*). Agents are interconnected in multiple ways (*top right*), and interconnection often result in *feedback loops* that either *reinforce* (+) or *self-stabilise* (−) the system's dynamic behaviour (*bottom left*). The dynamic behaviour of a complex system can vary greatly with even small changes in a variable's *starting (initial) condition* (*bottom right*). Whilst systems are bounded they receive inputs from and provide outputs to other systems (X–Z) within a larger supra-system

any one element of the system may interact with multiple other elements of the system. Relationships are still linear and outcomes remain predictable. Generally speaking, "complicated" refers to systems with sophisticated configurations but highly predictable behaviours (e.g. a car or a plane)—the whole can be *decomposed* into its parts and when reassembled will look and behave again exactly like the whole. They are also closed to and therefore not influenced by the external environment.

Complex dynamic systems have two key characteristics, they *self-organise* without external control and exhibit *feedback* resulting in newly created, i.e. *emergent* (at times unforeseen), behaviours. **Complexity** is the *dynamic property of the system*; it results from the interactions between its parts. The more parts interact in a nonlinear way in a system the more complex it will be. Complex systems are also open, loosely bounded, and influenced by their environment. Such *fuzzy boundaries* entail some arbitrariness in defining a system.

While any one system as a whole may be defined as a complex system, inevitably subunits are also complex systems in their own right. Thus any defined complex system has to be thought of as being simultaneously a subsystem of a larger system

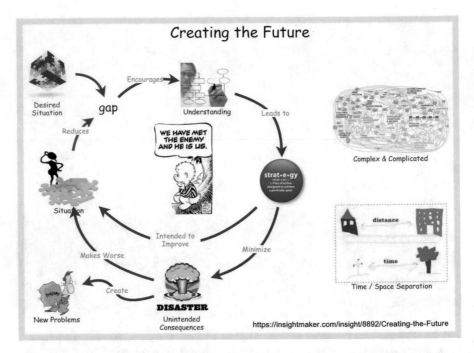

Fig. 2.4 The essence of systems thinking. Created by Gene Bellinger in Insightmaker, https://insightmaker.com/insight/8892/Creating-the-Future (Creative commons attribution licence)

(or a supra-system) and a supra-system constituted by a number of subsystems (defining the nested structure of systems).

Complex adaptive systems (CAS) are complex dynamic systems whose elements (agents) learn and adapt their behaviours to changing environments. In the complex adaptive systems literature the elements of the system are referred to as agents. Complex dynamic and complex adaptive system behaviour is influenced by the *system's history*, i.e. influences that have resulted in the current state of a system have ongoing effects on future states.

The make-up of the complex and complex adaptive systems presents certain problems in terms of being able to understand, describe, and analyse them. While simple and complicated systems lend themselves to cause-and-effect analysis, complex and complex adaptive systems require a mapping of relationships and drawing of inferences that may be theory based or drawn from multiple sources of knowledge. The Cynefin Framework [6] provides an excellent way to understand the different degrees of complexity in CAS and is discussed in detail in the next chapter.

Understanding the differences between types of systems is often the clearest way to differentiate the various types of systems. Table 2.1 summarises features of simple, complicated, and complex systems and the language used in the literature to describe them.

Table 2.1 Result of a long day at work

Types of Systems	Mechanical systems		Complex	
	Simple	Complicated	Complex (dynamic) systems	Complex adaptive systems
Structure of System	One-to-one relationships	One-to-many relationships	Many-to-many and system-to-system relationships (nested systems)	
Outcomes	Highly predictable	Mostly predictable	Alter with history and initial conditions / Unpredictable/emergent / Complex - Chaotic	
		Linear		
Outcome Patterns	A change in x results in a proportional change in y		A change in x results in a disproportional change in y	Attractor patterns that may be appear chaotic
Control of System	Engineered		Living systems follow the laws of nature	Social "laws". No controlling agent
				Purpose, goals and values define simple rules for interactions
Properties of System			Self-organisation results in emergent behaviour	
			Complexity of systems increases with the rise in number of agents	
Relationship to environment	Closed		Open âĂŞ loosely bounded	
Relationship of components/agents				
Behaviour of components/agents	Cause and effect repeatable, predictable	Cause and effect are separated over time and space	Cause and effect only coherent in retrospect and are not repeatable	No cause and effect relationships are perceivable (might or might not exist)
Analysis	Cause and effect analysis (reductionism)		Structure: mapping / Function: inference based on pattern recognition	Structure: mapping / Function: inference based on pattern recognition and/or prior knowledge
Testing	Lab	Lab/Discrete event and/or system dynamics modelling	Lab/field and/or system dynamics modelling	Agent-based modelling / Field trials
Generalizability	Yes	Yes	No	No

2.4   A Detailed Description of "Complex Adaptive Systems"

CAS are systems whose components/agents can change in their characteristics and behaviours over time as they are able to learn and adapt. Characteristics and behaviours of individual components/agents are often well understood; however, when components/agents interact in nonlinear ways and provide feedback to each other, the outcomes of the system's behaviour have a level of unpredictability. While the underlying "cause and effect relationships" resulting in the observed system's behaviour are understandable in retrospect, their behaviour cannot be precisely predicted looking forward [7].

Detailed definitions of the main CAS properties are listed in Table 2.2 and illustrated in relation to healthcare delivery and health policy.

The key concepts of a CAS [7, 36–49] are:

- *Agents* (or components) are connected within loosely defined or *fuzzy boundaries*; each CAS is simultaneously a subsystem of a larger system (or a supra-system) and is itself constituted by a number of subsystems (the nested structure of systems)
- *Agents* (e.g. humans) in a CAS can change in terms of their structural position in the system as in their relational behaviour
- The interactions between agents within a CAS define the systems *typically nonlinear dynamic*. Interactions are:

  - *Sensitive to initial condition*, i.e. bound by their historical and contextual conditions
  - *"Path dependent"*, i.e. prior decisions result in bifurcation (branching) of the systems behaviour
  - Are stable to many interventions, but change suddenly when reaching a *tipping point*
  - Result in *feedback loops*, i.e. an output becomes a new input, which modifies agents future behaviour (reinforcing or self-stabilising/balancing feedback)
  - *Emergent*, thus *self-organising*, as a result of the above

- For a social system to be a "goal-delivering CAS" its *purpose, goals, and values* need to be clearly defined a priori[4] [42, 49–54]
- Agreed *purpose, goals, and values statements* are the basis for defining the driver of the system; together they give rise to the "operational instructions" that coherently direct the interactions within a CAS. These are termed *"simple (or operating) rules"*, usually 3 but never more than 5, and must not be contradictory

---

[4]To avoid confusion: from a systems theoretical perspective (and design thinking approach) purpose, goals, and values are defined a priori, when exploring existing systems they can be deduced a posteriori. The analysis of systems will be explored in Part III.

Table 2.2 Key properties of complex adaptive systems (CAS)

Nonlinearity		
• Results not proportional to stimulus • Can lead to sudden massive and stochastic changes of the system • Sensitive to initial conditions • Accumulations, delays, and feedbacks	• Allergic responses and anaphylaxis • More intensive glucose control increase mortality [8] • Response to coumadin-therapy • Increasing the dose of chemotherapy does not improve therapeutic response or survival [9] • Chemotherapy initially not only reduces tumour size but also induces the promotion of secondary tumours [10]	• Large investment in health services has not been matched by a similar magnitude of improvement in inequity between social classes [11] • The introduction of electronic prescribing systems had mixed impacts on appropriateness and safety of prescribing and patient health outcomes [12, 13]
Open to environment		

• A system continuously interacts with its environment, e.g. exchanging material, energy, people, capital, and information
• Nonlinear responses to the external environment can lead to sudden massive and stochastic changes
 	
• Relies on four basic principles
  – Recursive feedback (positive and negative)
  – Balance of exploitation and exploration
  – Multiple interactions
	• Physiological function
	  – Immune system
	  – Respiratory tract
	  – Gastrointestinal tract
	  – Skin
	  – Semi-permeable membranes
	• Pathological function
	  – HIV/AIDS
	  – Asbestosis
	  – Food poisoning
	  – Burns
	• "Homeostasis" in health, e.g.
	  – Blood glucose levels
	  – Thyroxin levels
	  – Water balance and creatinine levels
	• And disease, e.g.
	  – Stable heart failure
	  – Intermittent claudication
	  – Hypogonadism
		• Strategies to train and maintain more health professionals need to account for competing individual, organisational and social factors in motivation, and other markets [14]
		• An epidemic like SARS arises from the global openness to fluidity, flows, mobility, and networks [15]
		• DRG (Diagnostic Related Group) payment mechanisms leads to
		  – Gaming
		  – Category creep
		  – Shift of emphasis [16]
		• The natural formation of viable high performing teams is based on multiple interactions and feedback [17]

(continued)

Table 2.2 (continued)

Self-organisation Emergence		

• Occurs when a number of simple entities (agents) operate in an environment, forming more complex behaviours as a collective
• Arises from intricate causal relations across different scales and feedback—interconnectivity
• The emergent behaviour or properties are not a property of any single such entity, nor can they easily be predicted or deduced from behaviour in the lower-level entities: they are irreducible
	• Appearance of superbugs in response to antibiotic therapies
	• Appearance of previously unknown infectious disease epidemics like SARS [18]
	• Emergence of drug side effects in particular individuals
	• Emergence of new patterns of morbidity, gene expression, as the population ages
	• Brain function from complex cellular self-organisation
		• Prevention paradox—inequities emerge when "innovative" health promotion guidelines are put into place without considering social and cultural assumptions between public health practitioners and target groups as is seen in
		  – Screening programmes
		  – Well baby checks
		  – Teenage pregnancy education
		  – Smoking cessation programmes [19]
		• The addition of nurse practitioners to primary care
		  – Did not alter costs or efficiencies
		  – Did address considerable other unmet needs [20]

Pattern of interaction		

• Different combinations of agents lead to the same outcome, or
• The same combination of agents leads to different outcomes
	• Sinus-rhythm heart-rate variability in patients with severe congestive heart failure [21]
	• Loss of beat-to-beat variability in autonomic neuropathy [22]
	• Cheyne–Stokes breathing [21]
	• Most patients with cancer display drastically different patterns of genetic aberrations [23]
	• Many biological factors (genetic and epigenetic variations, metabolic processes) and environmental influences can increase the probability of cancer formation, depending on the given circumstances [24]
		• Patterns of maternity provider interaction appropriate for the local context influence the emotional well-being of rural mothers [25]
		• International comparison shows that many diverse multifaceted health services lead to remarkably similar outcomes
		  – Smoking cessation successes [26]
		  – Obesity challenges exist across diverse cultures and levels of development despite evidence-based national dietary guidelines [27]

Adaptation and evolution		

• In the clinical context, numerous diseases develop over many years, during which time the "whole body system" has adapted to function in the altered environment
• Changes involve the whole system and are not restricted to a few clinically measurable factors
• Adaptation leads to a new homeostasis with new dynamic interactions [28]
	• Hypothyroidism
	• Coronary artery disease due to stable plaques
	• "Burnt-out" rheumatoid arthritis
	• Stable chronic obstructive airways disease
	• Coeliac disease
	• Cataract
	• Hearing impairment
		• Adjustments to the health care system due to challenges in
		  – Health care delivery
		  – Financing
		  – The rate of development of new health technologies
		  – Rising community expectations [29]
		• Stable ritual of clinical care delivery despite ongoing reforms, research, and interventions [30]
		• Healing tradition moves from mainstream health care to alternative health care [31]

Co-evolution		

• Each agent in the exchange is changed
• Parallel development of a subsystem with new characteristics and dynamics
	• The physician learns from the patient and the patient learns from the physician [32]
	• A person becomes blind AND develops superb hearing
	• Microorganisms succumb to antibiotic therapies AND some develop drug resistance
		• Local systems function well in response to local need in spite of or in parallel to top-down health initiatives
		  – User driven health care [33]
		  – Self-help groups [34]
		  – Health 2.0 [35]

The 2nd and 3rd columns provide examples that illustrate the effect of a property in the context of clinical care and health system reform

- "Simple rules" reflect the core values of a social systems. *Core values* are those that remain unchanged in a changing world.[5] If internalised and adhered to by all agents it results in the "smooth running" of the system (e.g. the flocking birds) [43, 47, 54, 55]
- "*Simple rules*" provide the necessary "safe space/freedom" to adapt an agent's behaviour under changing conditions. Adaptation is desirable; it fosters creativity and provides flexibility; it is the prerequisite for the emergence of the system and the achievement of its goals (learning) [43, 47, 54, 55]

In CAS "control" tends to be highly dispersed and decentralised [38]. CAS activity results in patterned outcomes, based on purpose, goals, and values within the constraints of the local context. These outcomes, while not necessarily intuitively obvious, are the result of the emergent and self-organising behaviour of the system. Local outcome patterns, while different, are "*mutually agreeable*".

Of note, system solutions—often termed innovations—are unique; they *cannot be transferred* from one place to another as the local conditions that resulted in the system's outcome will be different, the reason why even proven innovations fail when transferred into a different context [56].

2.5 Consequences of Complex Adaptive System Behaviour

Understanding the structure and dynamic behaviours of complex adaptive systems explains some of the seemingly perplexing observations:

- Nonlinearity means disproportional outcome responses to rising inputs, very small inputs may result in very large ("chaotic") responses and vice versa large inputs may result in no change whatsoever
- Nonlinear behaviour makes outcomes less predictable
- The "same" intervention in different location often results in a number of outcome patterns as the *initial conditions* vary somewhat between locations. *These patterns describe mutually agreeable outcomes*
- Feedback loops contribute to the robustness of a system
- Core values define a system's driver and "determine" the direction the system takes. Different core values within a system's subsystems can result in very different system behaviours which may or may not lead to conflict, e.g. the "*cure*-focus" of an oncologist may lead to desperate interventions whereas the "*care*-focus" of a palliative care physician may lead to ceasing treatments in favour of improving the patient's remaining quality of life

---

[5][What are core values? http://www.nps.gov/training/uc/whcv.htm, How Will Core Values be Used? http://www.nps.gov/training/uc/hwcvbu.htm]. Together they provide the foundation for solving emerging problems and conflict.

- In an integrated system, subsystems may have a set of unique purpose, goals, and values; however, in overall terms they need to align themselves with the main purpose, goals, and values of the system to contribute seamlessly to its overall function

References

1. Evens H (1972) Mathematical circles squared. Prindle, Weber and Schmidt, Boston
2. Cilliers P (2001) Boundaries, hierarchies and networks in complex systems. Int J Innov Manag 5(02):135–147
3. Box GEP, Draper NR (1987) Empirical model building and response surfaces. Wiley, New York
4. Mikulecky DC If the whole world is complex - why bother? http://www.people.vcu.edu/~mikuleck/alskuniv.htm
5. Stirzaker R, Biggs H, Roux D, Cilliers P (2010) Requisite simplicities to help negotiate complex problems. Ambio 39(8):600–607
6. Kurtz CF, Snowden DJ (2003) The new dynamics of strategy: sense-making in a complex and complicated world. IBM Syst J 42(3):462–483
7. Cilliers P (1998) Complexity and postmodernism. Understanding complex systems. Routledge, London
8. The Action to Control Cardiovascular Risk in Diabetes Study Group (2008) Effects of intensive glucose lowering in Type 2 diabetes. N Engl J Med 358(24):2545–2559
9. Leyvraz S, Pampallona S, Martinelli G, Ploner F, Perey L, Aversa S et al (2008) A threefold dose intensity treatment with ifosfamide, carboplatin, and etoposide for patients with small cell lung cancer: a randomized trial. J Natl Cancer Inst 100(8):533–541
10. Mittra I (2007) The disconnection between tumor response and survival. Nat Clin Pract Oncol 4(4):203
11. Blas E, Gilson L, Kelly MP, Labonté R, Lapitan J, Muntaner C et al (2008) Addressing social determinants of health inequities: what can the state and civil society do? Lancet 372(9650):1684–1689
12. Hider P (2002) Electronic prescribing: a critical appraisal of the literature. Department of Public Health and General Practice, Christchurch. Christchurch School of Medicine, Contract No.: 2
13. Ammenwerth E, Schnell-Inderst P, Machan C, Siebert U (2008) The effect of electronic prescribing on medication errors and adverse drug events: a systematic review. J Am Med Inform Assoc 15(5):585–600
14. Zurn P, Dolea C, Stilwell B (2005) Nurse retention and recruitment: developing a motivated workforce. Geneva
15. Ali S (2008) Infectious disease, global cities and complexity. Paper presented at the annual meeting of the American Sociological Association Annual Meeting, Sheraton Boston and the Boston Marriott Copley Place, Boston, MA, Jul 31, 2008 http://www.allacademic.com/meta/p_mla_apa_research_citation/2/3/7/3/0/p237304_index.html
16. Kuhn M, Siciliani L (2008) Upcoding and optimal auditing in health care (or The Economics of DRG Creep): SSRN, CEPR Discussion Paper No. DP6689
17. Grumbach K, Bodenheimer T (2004) Can health care teams improve primary care practice? JAMA291(10):1246–1251
18. Smith RD (2006) Responding to global infectious disease outbreaks: lessons from SARS on the role of risk perception, communication and management. Soc Sci Med 63(12):3113–3123

19. Frohlich KL, Potvin L (2008) Transcending the known in public health practice: the inequality paradox: the population approach and vulnerable populations. Am J Public Health 98(2):216–221

20. Laurant M, Reeves D, Hermens R, Braspenning J, Grol R, Sibbald B (2005) Substitution of doctors by nurses in primary care. Cochrane Database Syst Rev (2):CD001271

21. Goldberger A (1996) Non-linear dynamics for clinicians: chaos theory, fractals, and complexity at the bedside. Lancet 347:(9011) 1312–1314

22. Stella P, Ellis D, Maser RE, Orchard TJ (2000) Cardiovascular autonomic neuropathy (expiration and inspiration ratio) in type 1 diabetes. Incidence and predictors. J Diabet Complicat 14(1):1–6

23. Wood LD, Parsons DW, Jones S, Lin J, Sjoblom T, Leary RJ et al (2007) The genomic landscapes of human breast and colorectal cancers. Science 318(5853):1108–1113

24. Heng HHQ (2007) Cancer genome sequencing: the challenges ahead. Bioessays 29(8):783–794

25. Sutherns R (2004) Adding women's voices to the call for sustainable rural maternity care. Can J Rural Med 9(4):239–244

26. Treating tobacco use and dependence - a systems approach (2000) A guide for health care administrators, insurers, managed care organizations, and purchasers In: 2000 UPHS, editor. Washington, DC http://www.surgeongeneral.gov/tobacco/systems.htm.

27. Nishida C, Uauy R, Kumanyika S, Shetty P (2004) The joint WHO/FAO expert consultation on diet, nutrition and the prevention of chronic diseases: process, product and policy implications. Public Health Nutr (1A):245–250

28. Heng HHQ (2008) The conflict between complex systems and reductionism. JAMA 300(13):1580–1581

29. House of Representatives Standing Committee on Health and Ageing (2006) The blame game. Report on the inquiry into health funding. Commonwealth of Australia, Canberra, Nov 2006

30. Plamping D (1998) Looking forward: change and resistance to change in the NHS. Br Med J 317(7150):69–71

31. Snyderman R, Weil AT (2002) Integrative medicine: bringing medicine back to its roots. Arch Intern Med 162(4):395–397

32. Suchman AL (2006) A new theoretical foundation for relationship-centered care. Complex l. J Gen Intern Med 21(Suppl 1):S40–S4

33. Biswas R, Martin CM, Sturmberg JS, Mukherji KJ, Lee EWH, Umakanth S et al (2009) Social cognitive ontology and user driven health care. In: Hatzipanagos S, Warburton S (eds) Handbook of research on social software and developing community ontologies. IGI Global, London, pp 67–85

34. Martin CM, Peterson C, Robinson R, Sturmberg JP (2009) Care for chronic illness in Australian general practice - focus groups of chronic disease self-help groups over 10 years. Implications for chronic care systems reforms. Asia Pac Fam Med 8(1):1

35. Eysenbach G (2008) Medicine 2.0: social networking, collaboration, participation, apomediation, and openness. J Med Internet Res 10(3):e22. Available at: http://www.jmir.org/2008/3/e22/

36. Chen DT, Werhane PH, Mills AE (2007) Role of organization ethics in critical care medicine. Critical care medicine organizational and management ethics in the intensive care unit. Crit Care Med 35(2):S11–S17

37. Atun RA, Kyratsis I, Jelic G, Rados-Malicbegovic D, Gurol-Urganci I (2007) Diffusion of complex health innovations-implementation of primary health care reforms in Bosnia and Herzegovina. Health Policy Plan 22(1):28–39

38. Sturmberg JP, O'Halloran DM, Martin CM (2010) People at the centre of complex adaptive health systems reform. Med J Aust 193(8):474–478

39. Sturmberg JP, Martin CM (2010) The dynamics of health care reform - learning from a complex adaptive systems theoretical perspective. Nonlinear Dyn Psych Life Sci 14(4):525–540

40. Martin CM, Felix Bortolotti M, Strasser S (2010) W(h)ither complexity? The emperor's new toolkit? or Elucidating the evolution of health systems knowledge? J Eval Clin Pract 16(3):415–420
41. Paina L, Peters DH (2012) Understanding pathways for scaling up health services through the lens of complex adaptive systems. Health Policy Plan 27(5):365–373
42. Sturmberg JP, O'Halloran DM, Martin CM (2012) Understanding health system reform - a complex adaptive systems perspective. J Eval Clin Pract 8(1):202–208
43. Kottke TE. Simple Rules That Reduce Hospital Readmission. The Permanente Journal. 2013; 17(3):91–93
44. Marchal B, Van Belle S, De Brouwere V, Witter S (2013) Studying complex interventions: reflections from the FEMHealth project on evaluating fee exemption policies in West Africa and Morocco. BMC Health Serv Res 13(1):469
45. Swanson R, Atun R, Best A, Betigeri A, de Campos F, Chunharas S et al (2015) Strengthening health systems in low-income countries by enhancing organizational capacities and improving institutions. Glob Health 11(1):5
46. Shigayeva A, Coker RJ (2015) Communicable disease control programmes and health systems: an analytical approach to sustainability. Health Policy Plan 30(3):368–385
47. Plsek P (2001) Appendix B: redesigning health care with insights from the science of complex adaptive systems. In: Committee on quality of health care in America - Institute of Medicine, editor. Crossing the quality chasm: a new health system for the 21st century. National Academy Press, Washington DC, pp 309–322
48. Glouberman S, Zimmerman B (2002) Complicated and complex systems: what would successful reform of medicare look like? Ottawa: Discussion Paper No 8. Commission on the Future of Health Care in Canada, July 2002
49. Begun JW, Zimmerman B, Dooley K (2003) Health care organizations as complex adaptive systems. In: Mick SM, Wyttenbach M, (eds) Advances in health care organization theory. Jossey-Bass, San Francisco, pp 253–288
50. Gottlieb K (2013) The Nuka system of Care: improving health through ownership and relationships. Int J Circumpolar Health 72:doi:10.3402/ijch.v72i0.21118
51. Collins B (2015) Intentional whole health system redesign. Southcentral Foundation's 'Nuka' system of care. King's Fund, London
52. Kaplan RS, Porter ME (2011) How to solve the cost crisis in health care. Harv Bus Rev 89(9):47–64
53. Freedman LP, Schaaf M (2013) Act global, but think local: accountability at the frontlines. Reprod Health Matters 21(42):103–112
54. Bloom G, Wolcott S (2013) Building institutions for health and health systems in contexts of rapid change. Soc Sci Med 96:216–222
55. Gilson L, Elloker S, Olckers P, Lehmann U (2014) Advancing the application of systems thinking in health: South African examples of a leadership of sensemaking for primary health care. Health Res Policy Syst 12(1):30
56. Seelos C, Mair J (2012) Innovation is not the holy grail. Stanf Soc Innov Rev 10(4):44–49
57. Cilliers P (2013) Understanding complex systems. In: Sturmberg JP, Martin CM (eds) Handbook of systems and complexity in health. Springer, New York, pp 27–38

Addendum 1

The History of Complexity Sciences

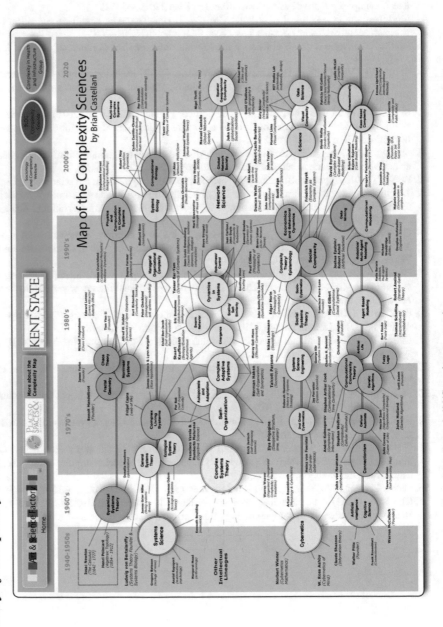

Addendum 2

The Philosophy of CAS - Paul Cilliers [57]

The notion "complexity" has up to now been used in a somewhat general way, as if we know what the word means. According to conventional academic practise it would now be appropriate to provide a definition of "complexity". I will nevertheless resist this convention. There is something inherently reductionist in the process of definition. This process tries to capture the precise meaning of a concept in terms of its essential properties. It would be self-defeating to start an investigation into the nature of complexity by using exactly those methods we are trying to criticise! On the other hand, we cannot leave the notion of "complexity" merely dangling in the air; we have to give it some content. This will be done by making a number of distinctions which will constrain the meaning of the notion[6] without pinning it down in a final way. The characterisation developed in this way is thus not final—in specific contexts there may be more characteristics one could add, and some of those presented here may not always be applicable—but it helps us to make substantial claims about the nature of complexity, claims that may shift our understanding in radical ways.

In the first place one should recognise that complexity is a characteristic of a system. Complex behaviour arises because of the interaction between the components of a system. One can, therefore, not focus on individual components, but on their relationships. The properties of the system emerge as a result of these interactions; they are not contained within individual components.

A second important issue is to recognise that a complex system generates new structure internally. It is not reliant on an external designer. This process is called self-organisation. In reaction to the conditions in the environment, the system has to adjust some of its internal structure. In order to survive, or even flourish, the tempo at which these changes take place is vital (see Cilliers, 2007 for detail in this regard). A comprehensive discussion of self-organisation is beyond the scope of this chapter (see Chap. 6 in Cilliers, 1998 for such a discussion), but some aspects of self-organisation will become clear as we proceed.

An important distinction can be made between "complex" and "complicated" systems. Certain systems may be quite intricate, say something like a jumbo jet. Nevertheless, one can take it apart and put it together again. Even if such a system cannot be understood by a single person, it is understandable in principle. Complex systems, on the other hand, come to be in the interaction of the components. If one takes it apart, the emergent properties are destroyed. If one wishes to study such systems, examples of which are the brain, living systems, social systems, ecological systems, and social-ecological systems, one has to investigate the system as such. It is exactly at this point that reductionist methods fail.

---

[6]The significance of "constraints" is discussed in the chapter.

One could argue, however, that emergence is a name for those properties we do not fully understand yet. Then complexity is merely a function of our present understanding of the system, not of the system itself. Thus one could distinguish between epistemological complexity—complexity as a function of our description of the system—and ontological complexity—complexity as an inherent character- istic of the system itself. Perhaps, the argument might go, all complexity is merely epistemological, that finally all complex systems are actually just complicated and that we will eventually be able to understand them perfectly.

If one follows an open research strategy—a strategy which is open to new insights as well as to its own limitations—one cannot dismiss the argument above in any final way. Nevertheless, until such time as the emergent properties of a system are fully understood, it is foolish to treat them as if we understand them already. Given the finitude of human understanding, some aspects of a complex system may always be beyond our grasp. This is no reason to give up on our efforts to understand as clearly as possible. It is the role of scientific enquiry to be as exact as possible. However, there are good reasons why we have to be extremely careful about the reach of the scientific claims we make. In order to examine these reasons in more detail, a more systematic discussion of the nature of complex systems is required. The following characteristics will help us to do this[7]:

1. Complex systems are open systems.
2. They operate under conditions not at equilibrium.
3. Complex systems consist of many components. The components themselves are often simple (or can be treated as such).
4. The output of components is a function of their inputs. At least some of these functions must be nonlinear.
5. The state of the system is determined by the values of the inputs and outputs.
6. Interactions are defined by actual input–output relationships and these are dynamic (the strength of the interactions changes over time).
7. Components, on average, interact with many others. There are often multiple routes possible between components, mediated in different ways.
8. Many sequences of interaction will provide feedback routes, whether long or short.
9. Complex systems display behaviour that results from the interaction between components and not from characteristics inherent to the components them- selves. This is sometimes called emergence.
10. Asymmetrical structure (temporal, spatial, and functional organisation) is developed, maintained, and adapted in complex systems through internal dynamic processes. Structure is maintained even though the components themselves are exchanged or renewed.

---

[7]These characteristics were formulated in collaboration with Fred Boogerd and Frank Bruggemans at the Department of Molecular Cell Physiology at the Free University, Amsterdam, based on the arguments in Cilliers (1998), and used in Cilliers (2005).

11. Complex systems display behaviour over a divergent range of timescales. This is necessary in order for the system to cope with its environment. It must adapt to changes in the environment quickly, but it can only sustain itself if at least part of the system changes at a slower rate than changes in the environment. This part can be seen as the "memory" of the system.
12. More than one legitimate description of a complex system is possible. Different descriptions will decompose the system in different ways and are not reducible to one another. Different descriptions may also have different degrees of complexity.

If one considers the implications of these characteristics carefully a number of insights and problems arise:

- The structure of a complex system enables it to behave in complex ways. If there is too little structure (i.e. many degrees of freedom), the system can behave more randomly, but not more functionally. The mere "capacity" of the system (i.e. the total amount of degrees of freedom available if the system was not structured in any way) does not serve as a meaningful indicator of the complexity of the system. Complex behaviour is possible when the behaviour of the system is constrained. On the other hand, a fully constrained system has no capacity for complex behaviour either. This claim is not quite the same as saying that complexity exists somewhere on the edge between order and chaos. A wide range of structured systems display complex behaviour
- Since different descriptions of a complex system decompose the system in different ways, the knowledge gained by any description is always relative to the perspective from which the description was made. This does not imply that any description is as good as any other. It is merely the result of the fact that only a limited number of characteristics of the system can be taken into account by any specific description. Although there is no a priori procedure for deciding which description is correct, some descriptions will deliver more interesting results than others
- In describing the macro-behaviour (or emergent behaviour) of the system, not all the micro-features can be taken into account. The description on the macro-level is thus a reduction of complexity, and cannot be an exact description of what the system actually does. Moreover, the emergent properties on the macro-level can influence the micro-activities, a phenomenon sometimes referred to as "top-down causation". Nevertheless, macro-behaviour is not the result of anything else but the micro-activities of the system, keeping in mind that these are not only influenced by their mutual interaction and by top-down effects, but also by the interaction of the system with its environment. When we do science, we usually work with descriptions which operate mainly on a macro-level. These descriptions will always be approximations of some kind

These insights have important implications for the knowledge-claims we make when dealing with complex systems. Since we do not have direct access to the complexity itself, our knowledge of such systems is in principle limited. The problematic status of our knowledge of complexity needs to be discussed in a little more detail. Before doing that, some attention will be paid to three problems: identifying the boundaries of complex systems, the role of hierarchical structure, and the difficulties involved in modelling complexity.

Addendum 3

Why Do We Need the Science of Complexity to Tackle the Most Difficult Questions? - David Krakauer

One quite useful distinction that one can make is between the merely complicated and the complex. So the universe is complicated in many parts; the sun is complicated, but in fact I can represent in a few pages of formula how the sun works. We understand plasma physics; we understand nuclear fusion; we understand star formation.

Now, take an object that's vastly smaller. A virus, Ebola virus. Got a few genes. What do we know about it? Nothing. So how can it be that an object that we'll never get anywhere close to, that's vast, that powers the Earth, that is responsible in some indirect way for the origin of life, is so well understood, but something tiny and inconsequential and relatively new, in terms of Earth years, is totally not understood? And it's because it's complex, not just complicated. And what does that mean?

So one way of thinking about complexity is adaptive, many body systems. The sun is not an adaptive system; the sun doesn't really learn. These do; these are learning systems. And we've never really successfully had a theory for many body learning systems. So just to make that a little clearer, the brain would be an example. There are many neurons interacting adaptively to form a representation, for example, of a visual scene; in economy, there are many individual agents deciding on the price of a good, and so forth; a political system voting for the next president. All of these systems have individual entities that are heterogeneous and acquire information according to a unique history about the world in which they live. That is not a world that Newton could deal with. There's a very famous quote where he says something like, I have been able to understand the motion of the planets, but I will never understand the madness of men. What Newton was saying is, I don't understand complexity.

So complexity science essentially is the attempt to come up with a mathematical theory of the everyday, of the experiential, of the touchable, of the things that we see, smell, and touch, and that's the goal. Over the last 10, 20 years, a series of mathematical frameworks—a little bit like the calculus or graph theory or combinatorics in mathematics that prove so important in physics—have been emerging for us to understand the complex system, network theory, agent-based modeling, scaling theory, the theory of neutral networks, non-equilibrium statistical mechanics, nonlinear dynamics. These are new, and relatively, I mean on the order of decades instead of centuries; and so we're at a very exciting time where I think we're starting to build up our inventory of ideas and principles and tools. We're starting to see common principles of organisation that span things that appear to be very different—the economy, the brain, and so on. So complexity science ultimately seeks unification—what are the common principles shared—but also provides us with tools for understanding adaptive, many body systems. And intelligence for me is in some sense, the prototypical example of an adaptive, many body system.

Ingenious: David Krakauer. The systems theorist explains what's wrong with standard models of intelligence. http://nautil.us/issue/23/dominoes/ingenious-david-krakauer

Chapter 3
Visualisation of Complex Adaptive Systems

Overview. In complex adaptive systems *function determines structure*. While interactions constantly change, these changes generally will maintain the system's overall function and structure.

In general terms, the interdependent nature between function and structure of complex adaptive systems can be best understood looking at visual representations. This book uses three images to illustrate different aspects of the system characteristics:

- A vortex is a helpful metaphorical representation of the dynamics that define the function and structure of a complex adaptive system.

  A vortex illustrates the key features of a complex adaptive system:

  - a complex adaptive system cannot emerge without a central focus (for a bathtub vortex to emerge one needs a plug hole)
  - the central focus provides the *bottom-up* energy for the function of the system
  - as the system evolves it builds different structures, i.e. subsystems, which have their own dynamic characteristics
  - while the system looks different at different organisational levels, its overall function is seamless and "controlled" by its central focus
  - disturbing the structure of a complex adaptive system will temporarily alter its dynamics and structure
  - only a change in the nature of the central focus will change the system permanently (or rather it allows its agents to reorganise themselves into a "new system")

- Drawing system maps and multiple cause diagrams are formal ways to describe the linkages between the agents of a system and their potential dynamic relationships
- The "Cynefin framework" helps to understand the different dynamic behaviours in a complex adaptive organisational system based on the strength of relationship between its agents

© Springer International Publishing AG 2018
J.P. Sturmberg, *Health System Redesign*, DOI 10.1007/978-3-319-64605-3_3

Points for Reflection

- When you think about a complex adaptive system, what kind of images does it provoke? You may want to draw a few before proceeding.

How can we come to grips with understanding the complexities arising from the interdependent nature of structure and function of complex adaptive systems? Three approaches are suggested:

- The vortex metaphor as a generic representation of the self-organising nature of CAS
- Drawing the structure of a system in a system map, and the interrelationships between the system's agents in influence, multiple cause, and sign graph diagrams
- The Cynefin framework as a representation of the nature and relationship of different dynamics in human systems

Each of these techniques provides some unique insights into the function of complex adaptive systems. None is inherently superior to another, and as will be illustrated in later sections of this book, each provides the basis for understanding a system or subsystem. Each visualisation allows for a different approach to wrestle with a "systemic" problems.

3.1 The Vortex Metaphor

As suggested by Capra [1] the theory of the structure and interrelationships of complex adaptive systems can be summarised by the (bathtub) vortex metaphor. The prerequisite for the formation of a vortex is its *central focus* (or driver) resulting in a bottom-up flow direction. A vortex is a structurally open system that is maintained by the constant flow of "matter" through it, and it maintains itself autonomously through self-organisation (Fig. 3.1).

While the "dynamics" along the vortex wall change, all of the dynamics depend on the presence of the central focus of the "plughole". Remove the central focus and the system will collapse. Temporary disturbance (or perturbation) of the vortex will change its shape and associated dynamics but ultimately the vortex will restore

Fig. 3.1 The vortex model as a metaphorical representation of complex adaptive systems. For a vortex to arise there has to be sufficient flow of energy from the bottom-up. Metaphorically again, a complex adaptive system emerges by the forces arising around its central point

itself to close of its original structure due to the *self-organising* properties exerted
by its central focus.

Within this metaphor one can conceptualise the different "physics/mathematical"
structures/dynamics along the vortex wall as representing different organisational
levels in social organisations. This acknowledges differences across the vertical
scale of organisation, but more importantly highlights the importance of the central
focus (purpose, goals, and values) as the core organising—bottom-up—force to
achieve fully integrated (seamless) system function.

3.2   System Structure and System Dynamics

A pragmatic approach to describe the structure and dynamic of a system is to draw
a *systems map*. It delineates the system of interest from related systems of a wider
supra-system. It also identifies the various agents of the system and allows the
grouping of related agents into subsystems.

Influence diagrams describe which agents are related to each other, and *multiple
cause diagrams* identify how a series of agents influence one another. *Sign graph
diagrams* document the direction of the relationships where (+) indicates that a
change in the agent at the beginning of an arrow causes a change in the same
direction in the agent at the tip of the arrow, and (−) a change in the opposite
direction (Fig. 3.2).

These diagrams are the basis for examining causal loops between a series of
agents which are responsible for the dynamic behaviour of the system or some
specific part [2]. A causal loop can be reinforcing (+) if the sum of all "+" and
"−" relationships between a series of agents is an even number and self-balancing
(−) if an uneven one (Fig. 3.3).

These tools form the basis for qualitative mapping as the basis for modelling
system dynamic behaviours and the evaluation of system change. This will be
discussed in greater detail in a later section.

3.3   Understanding Different Degrees of Complexity: The Cynefin Framework

Kurtz and Snowden [3] developed the Cynefin[1] framework to classify the dynamic
patterns in complex adaptive organisations according to the cause and effect
relationships between agents—they can be tightly coupled, more or less loosely
coupled or entirely decoupled (Fig. 3.4).

---

[1]Pronounced /ˈkʌnɪvɪn/; (English pronunciation spelling: kun-EV-in), a Welsh word meaning
"habitat" or "place of belonging".

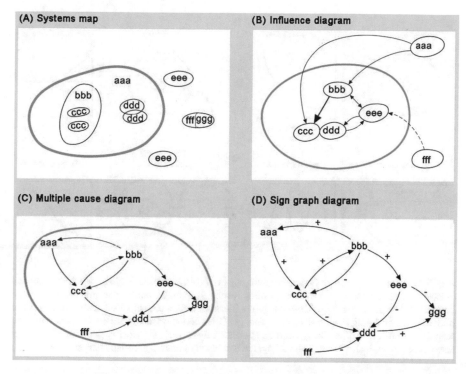

Fig. 3.2 Four different ways to map a system. Mapping systems and their dynamics: a *system map* (**a**) provides an overview of the system and its components; the *influence diagram* (**b**) conceptualises the main structural features and their relationships; the *multiple cause diagram* (**c**) analyses main relational causes within the system; and the *sign graph diagram* (**d**) provides the direction of influence amongst variables, "+" indicates an influence in the same direction, "−" an influence in the opposite direction

Tightly coupled cause and effect relationships produce highly predictable outcomes, the "obvious (formerly: simple) domain" where things are clearly *known*. Cause and effect relationships which include time delays result in outcomes *knowable* to experts and define the "complicated domain". The "complex domain" is defined by cause and effect relationships that can only be *understood in retrospect*, and situations that have no obvious signs of cause and relationship belong to the "chaotic domain".

Agents in human systems have unique identities and are able to change their behaviours in light of changing circumstances, individually and/or collectively, i.e. they have adaptive capacities. The Cynefin model provides a framework to broaden

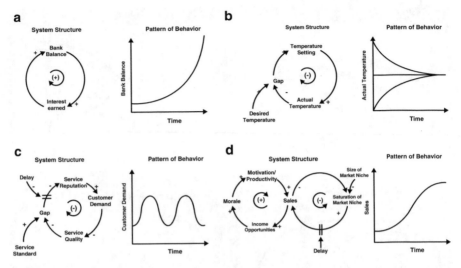

Fig. 3.3 Common system dynamic behaviours. (**a**) *Positive feedback loop*—positive feedback effects are called runaway loops or reinforcing feedback, a small change over time results in large changes; (**b**) *Negative feedback loop*—negative feedback effects are called self-balancing, they are both a source of stability and resistance to change. Often actions taken do not only show immediate results, …things take time. Delays make a system likely to *oscillate between two states* (**c**), and if delay is considered, changes can be anticipated and result in more controlled fashion of change (**d**)

our understanding about a problem by seeing various perspectives, all of which provide some insights but none of which exclusively describes the *whole in its entirety*.

The Cynefin framework has been developed as a tool to enhance:

• Communication
• Decision-making
• Policy making and item knowledge management

in complex social environments. In addition it allows a visual representation of the transitions between linear (greater concern with content) and nonlinear relationships (greater concern with context) between system components, and the related degree of certainty (that which can be taught) and uncertainty (that which needs to be learned) arising from their interactions. These movements will be explored in greater detail in Chap. 8.

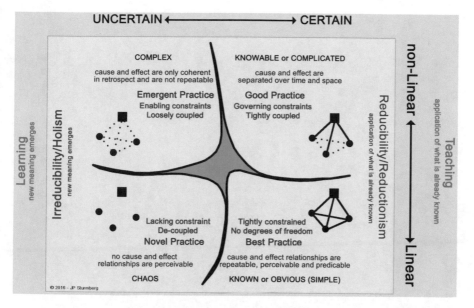

Fig. 3.4 The Cynefin framework as a tool to understand the different dynamics of relationships in complex adaptive organisations. The Cynefin framework provides a framework to link a number of commonly separate concepts into a coherent whole. (1) Things that are *known* and *certain* can be *taught*, things that are *complex* and *uncertain* have to be *learnt* and generate *new meaning*. (2) Things that are *known/knowable* can be *reduced* to their constituent parts, things that are *complex/chaotic* are *irreducible* from their parts. (3) Each quadrant describes particular *ways of knowing* and their associated *way of practice*

References

1. Capra F (1996) The web of life. HarperCollins Publishers, London
2. Sterman J (2000) Business dynamics. Systems thinking and modelling for a complex world. McGraw-Hill, Boston
3. Kurtz CF, Snowden DJ (2003) The new dynamics of strategy: sense-making in a complex and complicated world. IBM Syst J 42(3):462–483

Chapter 4
Defining Health

Overview. We all seem to know what health is, and we all seem to know how our health changes over time. It may thus sound counter-intuitive to even ask the question—what is *health*?

Many definitions of health have been proposed since the time of antiquity. None has been universally accepted, but all have one thing in common—all describe health as a *subjective experience*. A pragmatic definition of health defines health as the *personal state of feeling whole*.

What contributes to our health experience? The literature has identified four broad domains that contribute to our health:

- Our bodily experiences
- Our emotional experiences
- Our social experiences
- Our ability to make sense of our life experiences

When we feel healthy, these four domains are in a state of balance. We are at *ease* whereas disturbances in any domain results in the experience of *dis-ease*.

- The colloquial term "disease" refers to the presence of pathological changes that can be identified by health professionals. However, much of the experience of *dis-ease* is not associated with identifiable pathology, and even if pathology is identifiable, most people still experience "*good health*"
- Being able to *accept and adapt* to the inevitable onset of some form of disease across one's life is another defining characteristic of *health*
- Most of us are healthy—or at least healthy enough—most of the time to not perceive a need to seek care from a health professional
- It is now clear that, over a lifetime, *dis-ease* is a major contributor to the development of many common diseases and substantially effects our longevity
- Unsurprisingly, the question "*How do you rate your health on a scale of excellent - very good - good - fair - or poor*" is the single most predictive indicator of

© Springer International Publishing AG 2018
J.P. Sturmberg, *Health System Redesign*, DOI 10.1007/978-3-319-64605-3_4

- future health,
- the use of healthcare services, and
- mortality

- The ways how *the subjective experience of health and dis-ease* impacts on the development of disease have been untangled, but so far, these understandings have not been implemented in everyday clinical care

Understanding *health and dis-ease* as *personal experiences*, i.e. the focus on personal well-being, has important implications for the redesign of **health systems**.

- "Health systems" need to be distinguished from "healthcare systems". At present those responsible for the health system predominantly focus on the object of disease, hence a more accurate characterisation of the prevailing system would be "disease management" system
- Understanding the patient's *dis-ease*, regardless of its underlying cause, is essential to identify the most effective means to allow him to regain his state of *ease*. This is especially important when there is no disease associated with the experience of dis-ease; the medical literature somewhat disparagingly refer to these constellations as *somatisation*
- Given the epidemiology of health and disease, the health system needs to allocate a larger proportion of resources towards "health supporting services" and "community development"

Successful health system redesign would firmly focus on the interdependent environmental, personal, and biological factors that contribute to *health as a whole person experience*.

Points for Reflection

- How do you define *health*?
- Can you be healthy and be affected by a disease? How would you explain your answer?
- How do you know if you or one of your family members is healthy or not?
- What are factors in a person's life that contribute to or detract from their health?

We all seem to know what health is, and we all seem to know how our health changes over time. It may thus sound counter-intuitive to even ask the question— what is *health*?

Successfully engaging in healthcare reform or health system redesign requires an understanding of the *nature of health*. Health is a contentious notion, and so far no definition has been agreed upon [1–3].

It is important to distinguish *health systems* from *healthcare systems* (or health-care delivery systems). The latter are concerned with the necessary healthcare infrastructures and the provision of health professional services to people/patients. *Health systems* are more broadly concerned with all aspects of policies and societal activity that impacts on the health of people and communities.

For a health system as well as a healthcare system to achieve meaningful health outcomes requires a focus on health at a subjective level, i.e. health as a *complex adaptive "personal" state*.

Paradoxically many health reports measure the health of communities as the percentage of people with various diseases, a negative frame [4] that disregards the reality that most people are *healthy or at least healthy enough* most of the time.

And finally many health professionals are surprised that most of their patients would rate their health on a scale of *excellent - very good - good - fair or poor* as good or better, independent of age, gender, and the list of recorded conditions. The importance of one's *personal health experience* arises from its close correlation with future morbidity and mortality [5–7].

Understanding the *complex nature of health* is a key to transforming the health system to one that can achieve *health*. The emphasis is on the personal subjective nature of "*health, illness, and dis-ease*[1]" which needs to be distinguished from the biomedical/pathological definition of disease. These aspects are of great importance as there is widespread support for the notion that the "business of medicine" is the restoration of the "state of health" [3, 8–11], even though the activities in *healthcare services* often focus on "something else".

Unfortunately this chapter can only provide a brief overview of the many issues and more detail can be gained from the references provided.

4.1 Defining Health

Many definitions of health have been proposed since antiquity; all embrace its personal experiential nature (Table 4.1). Since the 1980s a number of authors proposed complexity-based conceptualisations of health [12–16] that reflect its personal adaptive nature [1, 3, 5, 6, 9, 12, 17–25].

---

[1]The spelling "dis-ease" is used to emphasise the original understanding of the term (Middle English disese, from Anglo-French desease, desaise, from *des-* dis- and *eise-* ease).

Table 4.1 The core notions of *health* [3]

Year	Concept/Model	Descriptions
	A multidimensional state of the whole person	Health as an application to human nature in all its parts, operations, levels, and dimensions—the physical, psychological, social, and spiritual. (Plato [26])
1911	A holistic ability to function well in the lifeworld	Health is a holistic ability to relate properly to and function well in the whole lifeworld in all its aspects, and disease a disturbance of this ability, on any of a variety of levels or in any of a variety of dimensions. (Husserl [22])
1946	Health as an ideal state	Health is a state of complete, physical, mental, and social well-being and not merely the absence of disease and infirmity. (WHO [27])
1951	Health involves effective compliance with expected or normal roles	Health in this sense becomes a prerequisite and a resource for maintenance of the social system. (Parson [28])
1960	Adaptation model	Health and happiness are the expressions of the manner in which the individual responds and adapts to the changes that he meets in everyday life. (Dubos [29])
1968	Existentialist model	Ultimate health is obtained through self-realisation. Man must search for meaning on his own grounds and live in accordance with his own values, skills, and free dispositions. (Maslow [30])
1972	A self-evaluative state	. . . a summary statement about the way in which numerous aspects of health, both subjective and objective, are combined within the perceptual framework of the individual respondent (Tissue [31])
1975	Role analysis of health and disease	Health is the capacity for human development and self-discovery and the transcendence of alienating social circumstances. (Kehlman [32])
1976	A positive state across the lifespan	Health is a positive state that dynamically spans across the stages of life—'The ability to adapt to changing environments, to growing up and to ageing, to healing when damaged, to suffering and to the peaceful expectation of death'. (Illich [21])

(continued)

Year	Concept	Definition
1979	Sense of coherence	The sense of coherence is a global orientation that expresses the extent to which one has a pervasive, enduring though dynamic feeling of confidence that one's internal and external environments are predictable. (Antonovsky [23])
1984	Sense of personal integrity/indigenous concept	Health is the outcome of a complex interplay between the individual, his territory of conception and his integrity: his body, his land, and his spirit. (Reid [33])
1986	Social medical explanation model	Health is equivalent to the state of the set of conditions which fulfill or enable a person to work to fulfill his or her realistic chosen and biological potentials. (Seedhouse [34])
1986	A resource for everyday life	Health is ...seen as a resource for everyday life, not the objective of living. Health is a positive concept emphasising social and personal resources, as well as physical capacities. (WHO Ottawa Charter for Health [35])
2006	Dignity, sharing in community, culture, and place of belonging	Health depends on many interconnected aspects of life: belonging to one's local environment/land, the sense of freedom, cultural and spiritual belonging, and the sense of dignity and security (Ingstad [24])
2007	Balance between body, mind, environment, and sense-making	Health is a dynamic balance within a complex adaptive somato-psycho-socio-semiotic framework (Sturmberg [36])

Notes. Since the above table had been compiled three noteworthy "complexity based notions" of health have been proposed.
In 2007 The Commission on Social Determinants of Health concluded that health is itself a property of other complex systems, from employment and work to transport and housing, that it relates to the social stages of industrialisation, urbanisation, and globalisation and, most importantly, that it relates to differential exposure to risks and differential coping capabilities, which are determined by the distribution of power, money, and resources in society [37].
In 2011 a working group proposed a dynamic concept of health for further elaboration: Health as the ability to adapt and to self-manage, in the face of social, physical, and emotional challenges [2].
In 2014 Bircher and Kuruvilla proposed a model of health (Meikirch Model) stating that: Health is a state of well-being emergent from conducive interactions between individuals' potentials, life's demands, and social and environmental determinants. The merits of this model have been debated extensively in the same publication [15].

4.1.1   Distinguishing Health from Disease

The terms "health" and "disease" imply distinct categorical states. However, as Pourbohloula and Kieny [38] emphasised: *Health* [and disease are] *not a standalone phenomenon with clear boundaries.*

Health as well as *illness* and *"dis-ease"* refer to subjective experiences and must be distinguished from the *object* "disease". It is the object of disease that preoccupies the minds of almost all actors in the health system. While having some agreed characteristics, the "object disease" is socially constructed and constantly re-constructed. For example, lowering "normal blood sugar" thresholds *labels* more people diabetic, and the creation of a new category between normal and abnormal blood sugar levels resulted in people being *labelled* pre-diabetic[2] [39–41].

These distinctions are slowly embraced on a broader base, e.g.

Australia's Health 2014 [42] takes this broad view of health and functioning, incorporating both physical and mental dimensions, and genetic, cultural, socioeconomic, and environmental determinants. It is based on the following concepts:

- health is an important part of well-being, of how people feel and function
- health contributes to social and economic well-being
- health is not simply the absence of disease or injury, and there are degrees of good health
- managing health includes being able to promote good health, identify and manage risks, and prevent disease
- disease processes can develop over many years before they show themselves through symptoms

4.2   The Complex Adaptive Nature of Health

The various notions of *health* have two features in common—*a balance between various aspects of a person's life experience*, and the need to *make sense of*, or *find meaning in* one's illness experience.

The experience of health, illness, and dis-ease has objective as well as subjective characteristics. Health, illness, and dis-ease are neither solely an individual construction nor solely a reflection of societal attributes.[3]

Health, illness, and dis-ease are dynamic states resulting from somatic, psychological, social, and cognitive (i.e. sense-making or semiotic) experiences. Health,

---

[2]Now renamed: impaired glucose regulation.

[3]A detailed discussion on the framework of self-perception of health has been provided by Marja Jylhä. She proposes a contextual framework of evaluation of self-rated health encompassing culturally and historically varying conceptions of "health"; resorting to reference groups, comparison with earlier health experiences, health expectations, positive or negative dispositions, and depression; and cultural conventions in expressing positive and negative opinions and in the use of a rating scale. [Jylhä. What is self-rated health and why does it predict mortality? Towards a unified conceptual model [6]].

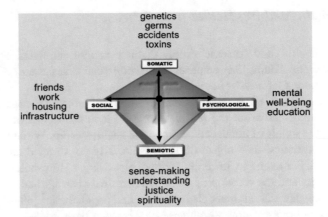

Fig. 4.1 The somato-psycho-socio-semiotic model of health

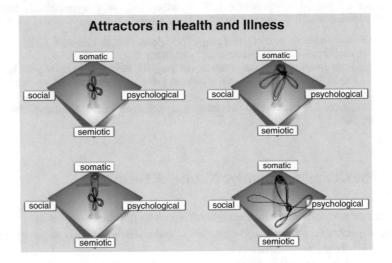

Fig. 4.2 How life experiences alter perception and disturb the balance of health

illness, and dis-ease are a holistic experiences that affect all parts of the person at a structural and functional level. Understanding health as a dynamic state better reflects the levelled reality of the human experience and is the foundation of the somato-psycho-socio-semiotic model of health (Fig. 4.1). Of note health can be experienced as much in the *absence* as in the *presence* of identifiable pathologies (the "object disease") [1, 3, 43].

Illness and dis-ease result from a disturbance of the somato-psycho-socio-semiotic balance. These disturbances can have many sources, Fig. 4.2 illustrates that many non-disease reasons result in much of the illness encountered in society. How can this be? The research field of psycho-neuro-immunology has untangled the physiological pathways between life events, coping, and physical malfunction.

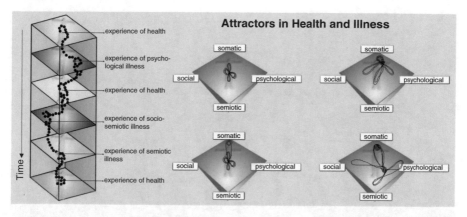

Fig. 4.3 The *system dynamics* of health. A person's health experience changes every day (*left panel*). When the basin of attraction remains around the centre, the person experiences health (*middle top*), an acute biomedical illness shifts the attractor temporarily to the somatic corner (*middle bottom*), a person with a usually stable chronic illness will have a stable state off the balance centre, typically towards the somatic corner, associated with occasional shifts when the consequences of the illness result in distressing limitations (*top right*), and a chaotic attractor with two predominant states—in the somatic and psycho-semiotic corners—in a person with "psychosomatic illness" (*bottom right*)

All illness alters perception and understanding and may result in the *experience of physical symptoms*. The experience of physical symptoms, independent of its cause, typically leads to contact with the healthcare system [44].

4.2.1 Disturbing the Balance of Health: The Patterns of Illness and Disease

The trajectory of changing from health to disease can be understood as shifting from a stable to more unstable state. Minor disturbances in any domain usually will not result in changes to one's health experience, however, greater disturbances over time can lead to the well-known patterns of acute illness, chronic illness, and somatisation (Fig. 4.3).

4.2.2 The Changing Relationships of Structure and Function in Health and Disease

Thus health has many contributing dimensions. For example, cells are well understood, and the detailed structure and function of organs (a collective of cells) is well understood by experts. However, the variability of organ function in health and

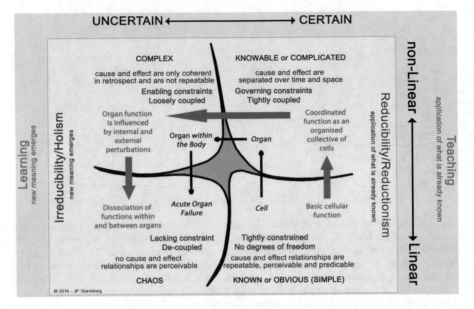

Fig. 4.4 The changing relationships of structure and function in health and disease

disease is much less clearly understood as many internal and external factors impact on the organised cellular function of the whole body. In acute disease there may be dissociation of function and structure within and between organs that baffles even the most experienced clinician (Fig. 4.4).

4.2.3   The Physiology of Health and Disease

Different research disciplines have contributed to the understanding of health and disease. Many emphasise the underlying *interconnected physiological network interactions* that maintain health or lead to disease. Of particular importance are those that regulate:

- Gene networks [45]
- The autonomic nervous system [46]
- The hypothalamic–pituitary–adrenal axis (HPA) [47, 48]
- The bioenergetics within the mitochondrion [49, 50]

Phenotypic disease, the individual uniqueness of a disease's characteristics and progression, results from intricate feedback interactions between the complex genomic, proteomic, metabolomic, neuroendocrine, immune, and bioenergetics networks. Furthermore networks are modulated by the complex dynamic environmental contexts of the patient (Fig. 4.5) [51, 52].

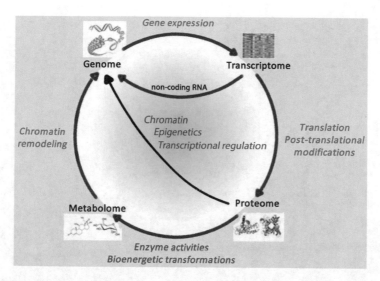

Fig. 4.5 Regulatory cycle linking the omics of life. The genome comprises the totality of genes within an organism, which constitute the blueprint for the transcriptome, whose translation leads to proteins that accomplish enzymatic functions including bioenergetics transformations that consume and produce metabolites constituting the metabolome. In turn, gene transcripts, proteins, and metabolites all impact expression of genetic elements via dynamic processes subject to regulation (originally published in Sturmberg, Bennett, Martin and Picard—The trajectory of Life [53])

Combining the experiential and the physiological perspectives on health and illness results in an image as represented in Fig. 4.6. Health and illness have many modifiable external factors impacting on the "in-born" physiological systems that maintain the homeokinetic stability required for health, and when overstretched lead to physiological breakdown associated with phenotypic diseases [53–55].

4.3 Measuring Health

It seems peculiar that most community health reports never actually report on health directly. Health is described in terms of life expectancy, leading causes of death, multiple causes of death (essentially chronic disease and/or generalized frailty), and risk of disease [42] (Fig. 4.7).

While figures are worth a thousand words, they also can mislead. The community prevalence of kidney disease, heart, stroke and vascular disease, and diabetes mellitus is about 15%. As the majority of all diseases are age related, the majority of patients affected by these conditions—predictably—are in the older age groups. Increasing age, however, is also the leading cause of mortality, putting the problems

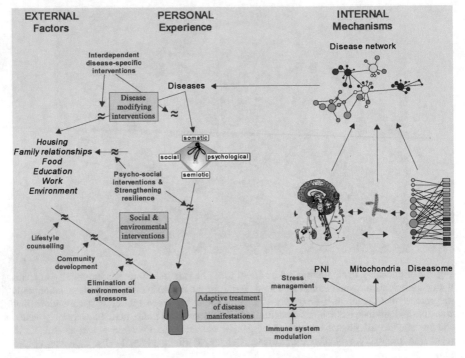

Fig. 4.6 Approaching the dynamics of "multimorbidity". Links between the external and internal factors that affect the person's experience of health. His health experiences positively and negatively modulate gene, bioenergetics and immune network functions which modulate disease network expression and result in the "phenotypic" manifestation of disease/s. Disease/s impact as much on self-rated health as on social status and engagement, closing the feedback loop of health, illness, and disease. Of note—there are numerous opportunities to strengthen a person's overall health in his physical and social environments other than disease-specific interventions. PNI: psychoneuroimmunology≈ indicates potential interventions that can restore homeokinetic network stability (originally published in: Sturmberg JP et al. "Multimorbidity" as the manifestation of network disturbances [54])

of kidney disease, heart disease, stroke and other vascular diseases, and diabetes mellitus in perspective.

4.3.1 Self-Rated Health

A more meaningful way of understanding the health of the community or specific population groups is looking at self-rated health. Self-rated health as a measure is closely related to future morbidity and mortality regardless of the presence or absence of identifiable pathologies (diseases) [5–7]. Independent of age, gender, and morbidity burden, people rating their health as good or better "do better"—

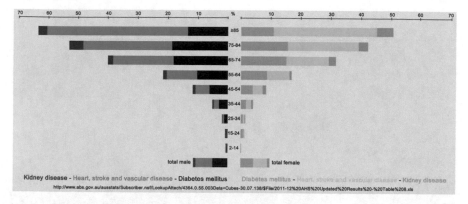

Fig. 4.7 Prevalence of kidney disease, heart, stroke and vascular disease, and diabetes mellitus in the Australian community. Note the large differences in age-related prevalence while only about 15% of the total community is affected. (Source: ABS 2011)

Fig. 4.8 may be surprising showing that more than 60% of those 85 and older still experience *good health*. This is important as emerging evidence indicates that better quality of life is associated with reduced health service use and cost [56].

The experience of health is affected by many factors; Figs. 4.9 and 4.10 show the differences in health experience by people from different socioeconomic backgrounds, their place of living (urban/rural), and the affects of disability.

4.4 Community Health and Health Service Utilisation

Studies consistently show that the majority of the community is healthy or at least "healthy enough" not to require health professional care—indeed, healthcare needs follow—as expected—a Pareto-distribution (power law probability distribution). Since the 1960s in any given month 80% of the community does not seek health care; of the 20% that seek health care 80% (or 16% of the total community) require primary care services to manage acute and chronic illnesses and to engage patients in health promotion and disease prevention activities. 80% of those requiring additional care (or 3.2% of the total community) require disease-specific secondary care; only the remaining 20% (or 0.8% of the community) require resource-intensive tertiary care [57–59] (Fig. 4.11, left).

Healthcare spending, however, is not following the distribution of health and disease. Even a casual look at Fig. 4.11 (right) shows that most of our healthcare efforts and resources go to the secondary and tertiary (hospital) sectors—consistent with the focus on the *object disease* of healthcare (delivery) systems. Little effort goes into maintaining and improving the social and environmental conditions that foster "good health" and prevent disease.

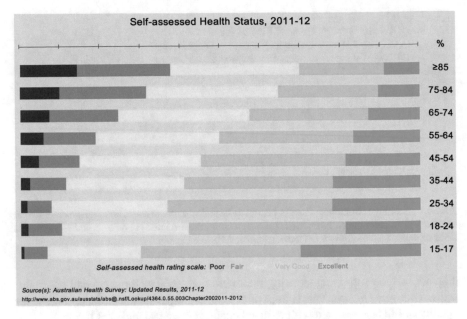

Fig. 4.8 Self-rated health of the Australian community. Ageing is associated with a decrease in health experience, nevertheless ≈ 2/3 of the oldest Australians still experience good or better health. (Source: ABS 2012)

Fig. 4.9 Excellent, very good, or good self-rated health according to different socioeconomic indicators in NSW, Australia. While 85.2%/82.7% of males/females in the highest socioeconomic quintile have excellent, very good, or good health, these numbers drop to 78.1%/75.9% of males/females in the lowest socioeconomic quintile (*left*). The differences for people living in urban and rural/remote locations are 82.2%/79.4% and 79.8%/78.7% for males/females (*right*). (Source: HealthStats NSW; http://www.healthstats.nsw.gov.au/Indicator/bod_self_age/ bod_self_age)

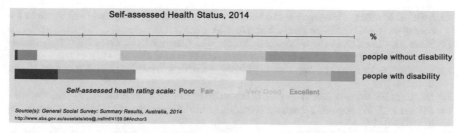

Fig. 4.10 The impact of disability on self-rated health. While about 8% of people without disability are in poor/fair health, this rises by more than four-fold to about 36% in those with disabilities. (Source: ABS 2014)

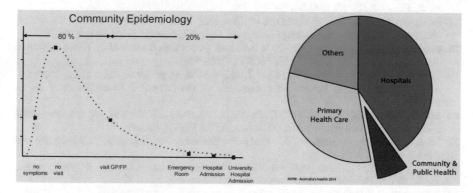

Fig. 4.11 Distribution of health service use in the community compared to the healthcare system's resource allocation. *Left*: Health service use hasn't altered over the past 50+ years [54–56]. Note: the long-tail in the distribution curve is characteristic of nonlinear distributions; *right*: only a "small" fraction of the total healthcare budget goes towards the *Community & Public Health* sector (adapted from AIHW [42])

References

1. Sturmberg JP (2009) The personal nature of health. J Eval Clin Pract 15(4):766–769
2. Huber M, Knottnerus JA, Green L, Horst Hvd, Jadad AR, Kromhout D et al (2011) How should we define health? Br Med J 343:d4163
3. Sturmberg JP (2013) Health: a personal complex-adaptive state. In: Sturmberg JP, Martin CM (eds) Handbook of systems and complexity in health. Springer, New York, pp 231–242
4. Lakoff G, Johnsen M (2003) Metaphors we live by. The University of Chicago Press, London
5. Idler EL, Benyamini Y (1997) Self-rated health and mortality: a review of twenty-seven community studies. J Health Soc Behav 38(1):21–37
6. Jylhä M (2009) What is self-rated health and why does it predict mortality? Towards a unified conceptual model. Soc Sci Med 69(3):307–316
7. Benyamini Y (2011) Why does self-rated health predict mortality? An update on current knowledge and a research agenda for psychologists. Psychol Health 26(11):1407–1413
8. Egnew TR (2005) The meaning of healing: transcending suffering. Ann Fam Med 3(3): 255–262
9. McWhinney IR (1989) An acquaintance with particulars. ...'. Fam Med 21(4):296–298

10. Mitchell D (2014) Philosophy at the bedside - phenomenology, complexity and virtue in the care of patients. J Eval Clin Pract 20(6):970–974
11. Scott JG, Cohen D, DiCicco-Bloom B, Miller WL, Stange KC, Crabtree BF (2008) Understanding healing relationships in primary care. Ann Fam Med 6(4):315–322
12. Uexküll Tv, Pauli HG (1986) The mind-body problem in medicine. Adv J Inst Adv Health 3(4):158–174
13. Macklem PT, Seely A (2010) Towards a definition of life. Perspect Biol Med 53(3):330–340
14. Bircher J (2005) Towards a dynamic definition of health and disease. Med Health Care Philos 8(3):335–341
15. Bircher H, Kuruvilla S (2014) Defining health by addressing individual, social, and environmental determinants: new opportunities for health care and public health. J Public Health Policy 35(3):363–386
16. Sturmberg JP (2014) Emergent properties define the subjective nature of health and dis-ease. J Public Health Policy 35(3):414–419
17. Pellegrino E, Thomasma D (1981) A philosophical basis of medical practice. Towards a philosophy and ethic of the healing professions. Oxford University Press, New York/Oxford
18. Picard M, Juster R, Sabiston C (2013) Is the whole greater than the sum of the parts? Self-rated health and transdisciplinarity. Health Aff 5(12A):24–30
19. Vogt H, Ulvestad E, Eriksen TE, Getz L (2014) Getting personal: can systems medicine integrate scientific and humanistic conceptions of the patient? J Eval Clin Pract 20(6): 942–952
20. WHO - Western Pacific Region (2007) People at the centre of health care. Harmonizing mind and body, people and systems. WHO Western Pacific Region, Geneva
21. Illich I (1976) Limits to medicine. Medical nemesis: the expropriation of health. Marion Boyars Book, London
22. Husserl E (2006) The basic problems of phenomenology: from the lectures. Winter Semester, 1910–1911. Springer, Dordrecht
23. Antonovsky A (1979) Health, stress and coping. Jossey-Bass, San Francisco
24. Ingstad B, Fugelli P (2006) "Our health was better in the time of Queen Elizabeth": the importance of land to the health perception of the Botswana San. In: Hitchcock RK, Ikeya K, Lee RB, Biesele M (eds) Updating the San: image and reality of an African people in the 21st century (Senri Ethnological Studies No 70). Senri; National Museum of Ethnology, Osaka
25. Engel GL (1977) The need for a new medical model: a challenge for biomedicine. Science 196(4286): 129–136
26. Moes M (2001) Plato's conception of the relationship between moral philosophy and medicine. Perspect Biol Med 44(3):353–367
27. WHO (1978) Declaration of Alma-Ata. International conference on primary health care, Alma-Ata, USSR, 6–12 Sept 1978. World Health Organisation, Geneva
28. Parsons T (1951) The social system. Free Press, Glencoe
29. Dubos R (1960) The mirage of health. Allen and Unwin, London
30. Maslow HA (1968) Toward a psychology of being. Van Nostrand Reinhold Company, New York
31. Tissue T (1972) Another look at self-rated health among the elderly. J Gerontol 27(1):91–94
32. Kehlman S (1975) The social nature of the definition problem in health. Int J Health Serv 5(4):625–642
33. Reid J (1984) Body, land and spirit. Queensland University Press, St Lucia
34. Seedhouse D (1986) Health: the foundations for achievement. Wiley, New York
35. WHO (1986) Ottawa charter for health promotion. First international conference on health promotion. Ottawa, 21 Nov 1986: WHO/HPR/HEP/95.1. Available at: http://www.who.int/hpr/NPH/docs/ottawa_charter_hp.pdf
36. Sturmberg JP (2007) The foundations of primary care. Daring to be different. Radcliffe Medical Press/Oxford San Francisco

37. WHO Commission on Social Determinants of Health (2007) Globalization, global governance and the social determinants of health: a review of the linkages and agenda for action. www.who.int/social_determinants/resources/gkn_lee_al.pdf

38. Pourbohloul B, Kieny M-P (2011) Complex systems analysis: towards holistic approaches to health systems planning and policy. World Health Organ Bull World Health Organ 89(4):242

39. Rosenberg CE (1989) Disease in history: frames and framers. Milbank Q 67(Suppl1):1–15

40. Rosenberg CE (2003) What is disease? In memory of Owsei Temkin. Bull Hist Med 77(3): 491–505

41. Sturmberg JP, Martin CM (2016) Diagnosis - the limiting focus of taxonomy. J Eval Clin Pract 22(1):103–111

42. Australian Institute of Health and Welfare (2014) Australia's welfare 2014. Australian Institute of Health and Welfare, Canberra. Contract No.: Cat. no. AUS 178. Available at: http://www.aihw.gov.au/australias-health/2014/

43. Pârvan A (2016) Monistic dualism and the body electric: sn ontology of disease, patient and clinician for person-centred healthcare. J Eval Clin Pract 22(4):530–538

44. Dantzer R (2001) Cytokine-induced sickness behavior: where do we stand? Brain Behav Immun 15(1):7–24

45. Goh K-I, Cusick ME, Valle D, Childs B, Vidal M, Barabási A-L (2007) The human disease network. Proc Natl Acad Sci 104(21):8685–8690

46. Tracey KJ (2007) Physiology and immunology of the cholinergic antiinflammatory pathway. J Clin Invest 117(2):289–296

47. Glaser R, Kiecolt-Glaser JK (2005) Stress-induced immune dysfunction: implications for health. Nat Rev Immunol 5(3):243–251

48. Cole SW (2013) Social regulation of human gene expression: mechanisms and implications for public health. Am J Public Health 103(S1):S84–S92

49. Picard M, Juster RP, McEwen BS (2014) Mitochondrial allostatic load puts the 'gluc' back in glucocorticoids. Nat Rev Endocrinol 10(5):303–310

50. Wallace DC (2013) A mitochondrial bioenergetic etiology of disease. J Clin Investig 123(4):1405–1412

51. Loscalzo J, Kohane I, Barabási A-L (2007) Human disease classification in the postgenomic era: a complex systems approach to human pathobiology. Mol Syst Biol 3(1):124

52. Barabási A-L (2007) Network medicine - from obesity to the "Diseasome". N Engl J Med 357(4): 404–407

53. Sturmberg JP, Bennett JM, Picard M, Seely AJE (2015) The trajectory of life. Decreasing physiological network complexity through changing fractal patterns. Front Physiol 6:169

54. Sturmberg JP, Bennett JM, Martin CM, Picard M (2017) "Multimorbidity" as the manifestation of network disturbances. Implications for whole person care. J Eval Clin Pract 23(1):199–208

55. Sturmberg JP, Botelho RJ, Kissling B (2016) Integrated multimorbidity management in primary care: why, what, how, and how to? J Comorbidity 6(2):114–119

56. Hutchinson AF, Graco M, Rasekaba TM, Parikh S, Berlowitz DJ, Lim WK (2015) Relationship between health-related quality of life, comorbidities and acute health care utilisation, in adults with chronic conditions. Health Qual Life Outcomes 13:69

57. White K, Williams F, Greenberg B (1961) The ecology of medical care. N Engl J Med 265(18):885–892

58. Green L, Fryer G, Yawn B, Lanier D, Dovey S (2001) The ecology of medical care revisited. N Engl J Med 344(26):2021–2025

59. Johansen ME, Kircher SM, Huerta TR (2016) Reexamining the ecology of medical care. N Engl J Med 374(5):495–496

Part II

A "Best Adapted" Health System: Meeting the Challenges

> *Modern medicine is a negation of health. It isn't organized to serve human health, but only itself, as an institution. It makes more people sick than it heals.*
>
> Ivan Illich (1826–2002)
> American sociologist

A "Best Adapted" Health System

Part I of this book described the foundational elements that underpin the formation of a *complex adaptive* health system:

- Key aspects from systems and complexity sciences:

  - *Nonlinear behaviour*:
    disproportional response between inputs and outputs
    makes outcomes less predictable
    leads to *self-similar outcome patterns*, each of which is the "best adapted" outcome under a particular set of circumstances
  - *Feedback loops* contribute to the nonlinear behaviour of systems and:
    result in learning
    enable adaptation
    achieve robustness
  - Complex adaptive organisations (or social systems) arise around *shared (or core) values* which "determine" the direction the organisation will follow
  - In a seamlessly integrated complex adaptive organisation *purpose, goals, and values align* within and across all subsystems and organisational levels

- Visualisation techniques help to understand a *"system as a whole"*:

  - A *vortex* is a generic representation of a complex adaptive system and illustrates the self-organising nature of such a system around its focal point
  - *System maps, influence, multiple cause, and sign-graph diagrams* highlight the structural and dynamic interrelationships between the system's agents
  - The Cynefin framework clarifies the nature and relationship of different dynamics in organisational systems

- Health is a personal complex adaptive state:

  - Health is *experiential*
  - The experience of health is *adaptive* in light of changing internal and external circumstances
  - *Most* people are healthy *most of the time*
  - *Good health experience* (as in self-rated health) is highly predictive of future morbidity, mortality, and health service use

Part II of this book outlines how these foundational elements can be applied to the redesign of a *complex adaptive health system*.

"Health systems" need to be distinguished from *"healthcare systems"*—simply, the focus of the system must shift from *disease* to **health**, and from *disease management* to **health creation**!

Redesign of a *health system* in the first instance then is a shift in *mindset or focus*. A changed focus on the *experience of health* and its *contributing factors* will allow the emergence of a "best adapted" health system based on the reconfiguration of the relationships of its agents and their way of interacting.

Three examples from very different contexts illustrate the emergence of "best adapted" health systems. Each emerged based on its unique focus on *the needs of the people they care for*. Explicitly and/or implicitly each system defined its set of *purpose, goals, and values* statements (reflecting the mindset shift) which gave rise to the definition of its set of *"simple (operational) rules"* (reflecting the way of interacting).

Complex adaptive organisations require a leadership approach that is *committed to uphold* its values and *maintain* its members' focus on common purpose and common goals.

Leaders of complex adaptive organisation engage with their members to solve common problems—rather than to prescribe solutions. This style of leadership *"shows the way"*, it gives *"direction without directives"*. Leaders lead by *moral authority* rather than *institutional power*.

An important part of leading in complex adaptive organisations is the inevitable need to manage limitations arising from system constraints. The three examples show how leaders have approached system constraints in ways outlined by Goldratt [1]. They:

- Identified the system's constraints
- Decided how to exploit the system's constraints
- Subordinated everything else to the above decision
- Elevated the system's constraints
- If in the previous steps a constraint had been broken, they went back to step one, and did not allow inertia to cause another system constraint

References

1. Goldratt EM (1990) What is this thing called THEORY OF CONSTRAINTS and how should it be implemented? Great Barrington, MA, The Northern River Press

Chapter 5
A Complex Adaptive Health System Redesign Based on "First Principles"

Overview. Redesign of a *complex adaptive health system* needs to be based on "first principles"—a focus on *health, equity, and sustainability*. A *complex adaptive health system* will:

- Have the *person and his health experience* as its central focus—this will achieve **person-centredness**
- Provide all those services required to achieve the *person's desired health experiences*—this will achieve **equity**
- Put *equal emphasis* on treating the person's *dis-ease* and his *diseases* as well as the *context* in which his *dis-ease* and his *diseases* occur—this will achieve **sustainability**

A *complex adaptive health system* is the umbrella system that contains the many diverse subsystems, subsubsytems, and so forth of a health system. The health system maintaining the focus on the core principles, as outlined above, allows the emergence of a seamlessly integrated health system, both within and across its multiple organisational levels.

Importantly, the **healthcare system** is **only ONE of many subsystems** of a *complex adaptive health system*. It is that part of the *health system* that delivers a wide range of *health professional*—colloquially known as medical—*care*. Primary care, secondary care, and tertiary care are some of the subsystems of the *healthcare system*. Each of these subsystems has a particular focus and role in the care of a person/patient.

Health systems are *organisational systems*. The design of a complex adaptive organisation needs to embrace three key principles:

- The definition of its *purpose* and *goals*
- The definition of its *value* and "*simple (operating) rules*"
- The alignment of its subsystems with the system's *overarching* purpose, goals, and values framework

© Springer International Publishing AG 2018
J.P. Sturmberg, *Health System Redesign*, DOI 10.1007/978-3-319-64605-3_5

In a *complex adaptive health system*:

- Purpose, goals, values, and "simple (operating) rules" are *explicit and known to everyone* involved in the system—this will achieve **person-centredness and sustainability**
- Leaders help their staff to be creative in finding *local solutions for local problems*. They ensure that these solutions are *compatible* with the organisation's overarching purpose, goals, and values—this will achieve **sustainability, equity, and sustainability**
- Health professionals focus on the *needs* (needs have to be separated from demands) of their patients and work in partnership with others to ensure those needs are met—this will achieve **person-centredness, equity, and sustainability**

Points for Reflection

- What would a *complex adapted health system* look like?
- What would be the design principles for such a system?
- How could such a *complex adapted health system* be implemented?
- What kind of changes may help to achieve the goal through incremental steps?

> *"But man is so addicted to systems and to abstract conclusions that he is prepared deliberately to distort the truth, to close his eyes and ears, but justify his logic at all cost."*
>
> Fyodor Dostoevsky (1821–1881)
> Russian novelist, short story writer, essayist, journalist and philosopher

Healthcare systems around the world are not working. The state of healthcare systems can be paraphrased in Walter Cronkite's words as: (insert your country) *health system is neither healthy, caring, nor a system.*[1] This characterisation should not be a surprise as healthcare systems act in isolation as institutions concerned with managing diseases.[2]

While the healthcare system is a unique system in its own right, it also is part of larger system—the health system which in turn is embedded in the whole of government system—and itself consists of multiple subsystems, e.g. public health system, hospital system, mental health system, or primary care system.

5.1   If *Healthcare Systems* Are Not Working … What Is a New Vision for a *Health System*?

An alternative view holds that we need to design *health systems*. A *health system* focuses on all aspects that affect human health—education, work, food supply, social and environmental infrastructures as well as the delivery of illness and disease specific healthcare services.

Health systems are *complex adaptive social systems*. They have:

- A large and diverse number of *agents*: health ministers, health bureaucracy, health financing organisations, hospitals and community offices, the various health professionals, health user groups and individuals (note: agents in systems terms can be people, organisations, institutions, etc.)
- Uncountable *interactions* amongst its agents: through their ongoing interactions agents "*learn*" and adapt, constantly reshaping the system within the limits of the system's constraints

---

[1] Walter Cronkite (1916–2009), American journalist and broadcaster.

[2] The frustration with the healthcare system has let Andrew Weil (American physician, proponent of holistic health and integrative medicine) to state: *I have argued for years that we do not have a health care system in America. We have a disease-management system—one that depends on routinely expensive drugs and surgeries that treat health conditions after they manifest rather than giving our citizens simple diet, lifestyle and therapeutic tools to keep them healthy.*

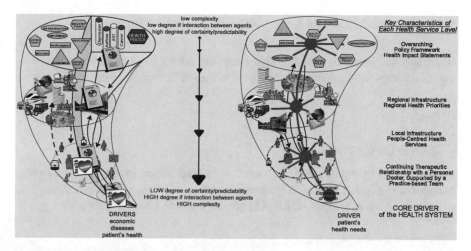

Fig. 5.1 The vortex model of the Australian "health system"—the current healthcare system compared to an alternatively designed complex adaptive health system. The *left side* of figure shows the *fragmentation within and between the various organisational levels* in the Australian *healthcare system* resulting from differences in drivers of subsystem units like: focus on person's health experience at the primary care level, disease focus in hospitals, focus on public health priorities at the community services level, and a focus on global disease and health budgets at the policy level. The vortex representation on the right shows a *seamlessly integrated complex adaptive health system* that *assumes as its overarching system driver* the "person's health needs". As an overarching driver, levels across as and within the health system would all align their activities towards achieving the system's "*common goal*", but would do so autonomously in their own ways (i.e. subsystems determine their own drivers within the overarching system drivers). Also note that the *complexity* and *degrees of certainty* are *inversely related* across the organizational scale (for a detailed discussion on the scale/complexity relationship see: Bar-Yam Y. Dynamics of Complex Systems. Reading, Massachusetts: Addison-Wesley; 1997. http://www.necsi.org/publications/dcs/

Complex adaptive social organisations function based on three key organisational principles:

- Their defined *purpose and goals*
- Their defined *value and "simple (or operating) rules"*
- The alignment of their organisation's subsystems

Based on these principles Sturmberg, O'Halloran, and Martin analysed the Australian health system through a complex adaptive system lens [1, 2]. The result is represented through the *health vortex* (Fig. 5.1, left) which shows that Australia has—at best—a "disease-management system". At the policy level "health departments" are organised around disease silos that exert their influence on the state/regional/local level to implement (mostly) hospital-based disease care. However, at the primary care level health professionals are largely confronted with patients' *dis-ease* whose management does not readily fit into the "disease policy frame". The right-hand side of Fig. 5.1 illustrates an alternative vision of a *health system* organised around people's health and health needs, which at times will require the expertise inherent in the *healthcare system*.

5.2 Organisations as Complex Adaptive Systems

Organisational research has identified some key principles that underpin the function of a complex adaptive organisation, namely the definition of its:

- Purpose
- Goals
- Values
- "Simple (or operational) rules"

These need to be explicit and they need to be understood and accepted by every member of the health system to achieve a seamlessly integrated health service. This requires leadership, a topic explored in greater detail in Chap. 7 and 8.

5.2.1 Purpose and Goals

The *purpose and goals* of a *"complex adaptive person-centred, equitable, and sustainable health system"* would be to provide patients with all of the services required to meet their health needs to achieve their desired health experiences.[3]

As health care is a dyadic endeavour, purpose and goals need to be considered from the person/patient and the provider perspective.

- The emphasis is on *"health experience"* as defined by individuals in their own way. Health experiences can be good or poor regardless of the presence or absence of specific diseases.

  It is remarkable how often there is a lack of concordance between the patient's subjective and the health professionals' objective view about "the health of this person". Any mismatch ought to be avoided as it can lead to under-servicing, over-servicing, or the provision of undesirable services
- For health system leaders the emphasis is on *maintaining the focus* of all agents on the *purpose* of their work. This requires them to provide the necessary creative space and support to solve problems, and to ensure that the required resources are available.

  Seamlessly integrated health systems require leaders to work within and across the various levels of a health system's organisation to facilitate cooperation and to remove barriers to enable the achievement and maintenance of individual and community health.

  Effective leaders, rather than seeing their role as "fixing problems", *"facilitate the necessary adaptive work that frontline workers have to do"* in pursuit of the organisation's desired goals and outcomes [3]

---

[3]The importance of *health experience* on morbidity and mortality has been demonstrated by self-rated health researchers like Idler & Benyamini and Jylhä (see Chap. 4). Self-rated health must be distinguished from patient satisfaction, an entirely unrelated concept.

5.2.2   Values

An organisation's values act as its "moral anchor and compass". Of particular importance to an organisation are its *core values*,[4] those that *stay unchanged in a changing environment.*

For the health system value should be defined from the *perspective of the people using the health system*, a proposition that is gaining increasing acceptance [4]. Various organisations have embraced the broad notion of *"meeting the needs of the patient"* as the core value for their health system, like:

- *"The needs of the patient come first"* (Mayo Clinic [4])
- *"respect for the patient's values, preferences, and expressed needs; coordinated and integrated care; clear, high-quality information and education for the patient and family; physical comfort, including pain management; emotional support and alleviation of fear and anxiety; involvement of family members and friends, as appropriate; continuity, including through care-site transitions; and access to care"* (Gerteis et al. [5])
- *"patient values guide all clinical decisions"* (Institute of Medicine [6])
- *"A Native Community that enjoys physical, mental, emotional and spiritual wellness"* (NUKA-system of Care [7])
- *"What matters to you? as well as What is the matter?"* (Barry and Edgman-Levitan [8]).

For a health system to truly function as a seamlessly integrated organisation its members have to *"internalise their health system's core values"* and enact them at every point along the way [9, 10].

However, as the health system in pluralistic societies entails many different organisations with their own agendas, it is unsurprising to find that values for health and healthcare systems are defined in a variety of ways, not all of which are congruent with the notions of a *person-centred, equitable, and sustainable health system.*

The more important point here is simply that considering *values* is now an issue open for discourse. For example, the New England Journal of Medicine has just started a new series on promoting health system redesign based on values.[5]

A more provocative approach by Keckly suggests the need to change *from an assembly line* approach to healthcare to one where *healthcare became a system that*

---

[4][What are core values? http://www.nps.gov/training/uc/whcv.htm, How will core values be used? http://www.nps.gov/training/uc/hwcvbu.htm.]. Together they provide the foundation for solving emerging problems and conflict.

[5]Care Redesign: Creating the Future of Health Care Delivery. They explicitly state: *What does the transition "from volume to value" mean for health care and the organisation that deliver it? The redesign of care around value—meeting patient's needs and doing so as efficiently as possible—has begun in earnest in the U.S. and around the world.* www.catalyst.nejm.org/events/care-redesign-creating-the-future-of-health-care-delivery-2015.

delivers high value to patients.[6] He suggests that adding the *needs and preferences* of patients in the context of their *psycho-social-demographic* characteristics to the usual frame of *signs, symptoms, risk factors, and co-morbidities* would move us quickly towards a value-delivering health system [11].

The addenda to this chapter provide an overview of *value perspectives* amongst different stakeholders.

The term *value* is used with two connotations in mind–a *quality* like a "good consultation" or a "bad treatment outcome", and in the sense of *worth* like a "cost-effective treatment" or a "good investment". While not mutually exclusive for a health system to function in a seamlessly integrated fashion, we, i.e. **society at large** as well as individual **service organisations** must agree on an overarching value statement for health care. We need to be clear which values we want to pursue.

Here is an overview of different perspectives which are quoted in detail in the addenda:

- A philosophical perspective about the value of medicine by the medical philosophers Edmund Pellegrino and David Thomasma [Addendum 1]
- A multi-stakeholder perspectives about the value of health care from a "health industry" workshop conducted by the Institute of Medicine [Addendum 2]
- A performance and accountability perspective offered by Michael Porter and Elizabeth Teisberg that defines value as outcome relative to costs [Addendum 3]
- Two industry perspectives [Addendum 4]

  - Metronic sees value as much as the benefit arising from their therapeutic devices as economic benefits from more efficient care delivery and system waste
  - The pharmaceutical industry sees value largely from a profit perspective, using marketing and discount offers (especially in the USA) to increase market share for each of their products

5.2.3   "Simple (or Operating) Rules"

The importance of purpose, goals, and values (as determinants of a system's driver) are now widely acknowledged in the management world [12–15].

"*Simple rules*" are operating principles; they provide "guidance" for decision-making to all agents regardless of their place and role in the health system. Developing *simple rules* is a *deliberative process* that takes into account core values and available knowledge as well as an understanding of the principles of system dynamic behaviours.

Suggested "*simple rules*" or "how to rules" for a "*complex adaptive, equitable and sustainable health system*" might be:

- Develop ongoing trustful patient relationships
- Understand the patient's experiences, needs, and preferences

---

[6]Arguing the economic perspective, he states: *Arguably, they are the industry's most important constituent.*

- Enhance peoples' capabilities to manage their own health
- Explore with patients and their families the impact of treatments on their future health
- Engage with the community to build a local health promoting environment

The spirit of these suggested *"simple rules"* is reflected in the NUKA-system's set of *"simple rules"*—*"S-C-F: shared responsibility, commitment to quality and family wellness"*. How these *"simple rules"* affect the leadership and health service delivery will be explored in Chaps. 7 and 8 [6].

5.3   Disambiguation: Patient Needs Versus Patient Wants

A frequent gut reaction to the notion of "meeting patients' needs" is: patients want everything, and that is simply not affordable. While the latter point is self-evident, one has to distinguish between "needs" and "wants".

Needs have biological origins (regulated and controlled through HPA-axis regulation [16]) and secure survival; they entail the need for food, clothing, shelter, and care. These biological needs are independent of socio-cultural needs which are defined by society's accepted amounts and types of necessities required to satisfy the "collectively defined" needs [17, 18].

Wants go beyond needs, wants define residual desires that remain after needs have been met [17]. However, it can at times be difficult to clearly distinguish between a *true need* and an *aspirational want*. These ambiguities can only be resolved through a broad public discourse [18]. It is noteworthy that increasingly residual desires are *defined by law, convention, fashion, and advertising* rather than the requirements for **health, morality, and livelihood** [17].

The gap between needs and wants defines the realm of *scarcity*. In policy terms *scarcity is relative* and determines public policy formulation, i.e. devising solutions that balance wants against society's available resources, a point all too familiar in the healthcare sector [17].

People's needs are as much *biologically determined* [15] as *socially constructed* [17, 18]. Doyal and Gough [18] argue that *health* rather than *survival*—both physical and mental—are the most basic human needs. To achieve physical health a person will always require a minimum amount of nutrition and fluid intake, varying amounts of sleep, exercise, and shelter. The achievement of mental health requires an empirical minimum of human contact, emotional support, opportunity for emotional expression and privacy.

Thus *"health care needs"* arise from the person's perception of needing help in light of changes in his health experience, be they physical, social, emotional, or cognitive/sense-making in nature [19, 20]. This view is supported by Doyal and Gough [18] who emphasise that *"people* [do] *have strong feelings about what they need and these feelings do vary enormously between cultures and over time."*

Needs must be distinguished from *demands*—defined as unquestionable expectation. Interpreting needs as demands usually reflects a lack of understanding the reasons behind the need or may allude to a lack of resources to meet people's "true needs".[7]

5.4   The Emergence of a Complex Adaptive, Equitable, and Sustainable Health System

Potentially the most important insight from understanding health systems as "complex adaptive organisations" is the need to clearly define the *organisation's driver*. The driver of the system is a reflection of the organisation's purpose, goals, and values statements. It is the organisation's driver that "determines" (the term is used in a literal sense) the configuration of its agents and their interactions (behaviours).

As a health system is a nested system, to function seamlessly across the various system domains, its subsystems all need to adhere to its overall driver. This does not detract from the fact that subsystems may need their own specific drivers, however, when a subsystem pursues entirely different aims it emerges as one of the "causative factor" (the term is used in a literal sense) for system dysfunction (Fig. 5.1, left panel).

Based on the outlined principles of the organisation and function of complex adaptive systems, how might a *complex adaptive, person-centred, equitable, and sustainable health system* emerge? It:

* Needs to put the person at its centre
* Requires leadership that aligns policies and activities around people's needs at and across all levels of organisation
* Gives local health services permission to self-organise in such a way that achieves the goal of meeting the needs of their people

To that end visualisations, like suggested in Fig. 5.1 on the right, are helpful means to appreciate the structural and functional—nested—relationship of the different agents at the various organisational levels within a health system.

A *complex adaptive health system* is one that is *best adapted* to the needs of people in a local setting and "determines" (in an emergent fashion) how to best organise the delivery of health services at the primary care level. Primary care practice, however, is embedded in the larger network of its health and social infrastructure—other primary care practices, secondary care practices, community

---

[7]Responding to people's needs may go beyond that of direct medical care. Berry and Seltman describe how a needs-focused complex adaptive health system (Mayo Clinic) responded to the need of a woman dying from cancer—to see her daughter getting married before passing on. In response the clinic staff *adapted their priorities* and within hours organised her daughter's wedding ceremony in the hospital atrium (Berry L, Seltman K. Management Lessons from Mayo Clinic: Inside One of the World's Most Admired Service Organizations [8, p. 57]).

care facilities, hospitals, social services, etc. The capacity as well as the capabilities of community health services in turn are constrained by local social, economic, educational, living, environmental etc. characteristics (often simply referred to as the social determinants of health). Both factors are constraints that limit a health service's ability to achieve "predetermined" outcomes.[8]

Within the nested structure of systems, local communities are embedded in local regions, which in turn are embedded in local/state healthcare systems, and state healthcare systems in turn are part of the national health service framework. This embeddedness of a system within systems results in multidirectional interactions. While the structure and function of a *patient-centred, equitable and sustainable* health system principally arises from the local level, the local level health system configuration is influenced by the inputs of regional, state, and national levels. Equally, local level health system outcomes influence regional, state, and national system functions.

References

1. Sturmberg JP, O'Halloran DM, Martin CM (2010) People at the centre of complex adaptive health systems reform. Med J Aust 193(8):474–478
2. Sturmberg JP, O'Halloran DM, Martin CM (2013) Health care reform - the need for a complex adaptive systems approach. In: Sturmberg JP, Martin CM (eds) Handbook of systems and complexity in health. Springer, New York, pp 827–853
3. Heifetz R (1994) Leadership without easy answers. Harvard University Press, Cambridge, MA
4. Mayo Clinic (2007) Our shared commitment - Mayo Clinic 2007 annual report
5. Gerteis M, Edgman-Levitan S, Daley J, Delbanco T (1993) Through the patient's eyes. Jossey-Bass, San Francisco
6. Institute of Medicine (2001) Crossing the quality chasm: a new health system for the 21st century. www.iom.edu/file.asp?id=27184
7. Gottlieb K (2013) The Nuka system of care: improving health through ownership and relationships. Int J Circumpolar Health 72. doi:10.3402/ijch.v72i0.21118
8. Barry MJ, Edgman-Levitan S (2012) Shared decision making - the pinnacle of patient-centered care. N Engl J Med 366(9):780–781
9. Sturmberg JP, O'Halloran DM, Martin CM (2013) Health care reform - the need for a complex adaptive systems approach. In: Sturmberg JP, Martin CM (eds) Handbook of systems and complexity in health. Springer, New York, pp 827–853
10. Cloninger CR, Salvador-Carulla L, Kirmayer LJ, Schwartz MA, Appleyard J, Goodwin N et al (2014) A time for action on health inequities: foundations of the 2014 Geneva declaration on person- and people-centered integrated health care for all. Int J Person Centered Med 4(2):69–89
11. Keckly P (2015) The healthcare blog [Internet]. Available from: http://thehealthcareblog.com/blog/2015/12/03/the-meaning-of-value-in-health-care/
12. Dolan SL, García S, Diegoli S, Auerbach A (2000) Organisational values as "attractors of chaos": an emerging cultural change to manage organisational complexity. Department of Economics and Business, Universitat Pompeu Fabra

---

[8]The argument here is the policy making perspective, *predetermined* outcomes may or may not be the ones that patients, families, and communities *need*.

13. Rouse WB (2008) Health care as a complex adaptive system: implications for design and management. The Bridge 38(1):17–25
14. Ham C, Dixon A, Brooke B (2012) Transforming the delivery of health and social care. The case for fundamental change. King's Fund, London
15. Seelos C, Mair J (2012) Innovation is not the holy grail. Stanf. Soc Innov Rev 10(4):44–49
16. Pecoraro N, Dallman MF, Warne JP, Ginsberg AB, Laugero KD, la Fleur SE et al (2006) From Malthus to motive: how the HPA axis engineers the phenotype, yoking needs to wants. Prog Neurobiol 79(5–6):247–340
17. Raiklin E, Uyar B (1996) On the relativity of the concepts of needs, wants, scarcity and opportunity cost. Int J Soc Econ 23(7):49–56
18. Doyal L, Gough I (1984) A theory of human needs. Crit Soc Policy 4(10):6–38
19. Sturmberg JP (2009) The personal nature of health. J Eval Clin Pract 15(4):766–769
20. Sturmberg JP (2013) Health: a personal complex-adaptive state. In: Sturmberg JP, Martin CM (eds) Handbook of systems and complexity in health. Springer, New York, pp 231–242
21. Pellegrino E, Thomasma D (1981) A philosophical basis of medical practice. Towards a philosophy and ethic of the healing professions. Oxford University Press, New York/Oxford
22. Young PL, Olsen LA, McGinnis JM (2010) Value in health care: accounting for cost, quality, safety, outcomes, and innovation. Institute of Medicine. Washington DC, National Academies Press
23. Porter ME, Teisberg EO (2006) Redefining health care: creating value-based competition on results. Harvard Business School Press, Boston
24. Medtronic. Value and innovation: today's definitions are not tomorrow's reality. http://blog.han.nl/gwem/files/2015/11/Medtronic-2011.-Today%E2%80%99s-Definitions-Are-Not-Tomorrow%E2%80%99s-Reality.pdf
25. Leemore SD, Christopher JO, Schmitt MA (2016) Undermining value-based purchasing - lessons from the pharmaceutical industry. N Engl J Med 375(21):2013–2015

Addendum 1

Medicine and Philosophy - Edmund Pellegrino and David Thomasma [21]

When medicine and philosophy converge, they can greatly advance man's search for a unified image of himself and the world; when they diverge, that image becomes fragmented, puzzling, and even absurd. ...The philosophical threat to medicine today is not excessive and unrestrained system building but an excessive faith in reductionistic and positivistic modes of thought and explanation.

...

Philosophy of Medicine - Discipline or Philosophical Mélange?

...Medicine does, in fact, derive much of its method, logic, and theory from the physical and biological sciences, so it is to a certain extent a branch of those sciences. But medicine is also a *praxis* in the Aristotelian sense—knowledge applied for human ends and purposes. In this sense, medicine can be classed among the technologies. But medicine also sets out to modify the behaviour of individuals and societies, and thus has roots in the behavioural sciences. Finally, medicine operates through a personal, and therefore an ethical, relationship intended to "help" the person to "better" health. It is a value-laden activity, with roots in ethics and the humanities.

...

Medicine, even as science, must encompass the special complexities of *man as subject* interacting with *man as object* of science. Physiology, unlike the clinical science of medicine, studies physical processes while ignoring the lived reality of the experimental subject—his or her self-perceived history, uniqueness, and individuality. Thus even when it functions as clinical science, medicine must correlate the explanatory modes of the physical sciences with those of the social and behavioural.

But neither the basic sciences nor the clinical sciences can be properly considered as medicine until they are used in a particular clinical context, in a particular individual, and for a particular purpose to effect the attainment of health. The purpose of medicine *qua* medicine, then, transcends that of medical science per se— which is primarily to know. Medical science, basic or clinical, becomes medicine only when it is used to promote health and healing—that is, only when it is an intervention in an individual human life to alter the human condition. Medicine, thus construed, has a telos which distinguishes it from its component sciences, whose telosis to understand physical processes in as general a way as possible, and certainly not to particularise that knowledge in an individual human life. For medicine *qua* medicine cannot deal with general scientific laws as such, but must locate them in a time, place, and person. ...

Medicine is, in short, a practical theory of human reality. It is a moral activity, since it operates through a personal interrelationship in which physician and patient are co-participants in defining the goal and achieving it—cure of illness or promotion of health. ...It is the unravelling of that nexus for this patient, here and now, that constitutes medicine. The resultant synthesis is more than the sum total of the component sciences—physical, social, and moral—which contribute to that unraveling.

... The patient presents himself in a state of wounded humanity. He has lost some of his freedom since he must come to the physician; he must give consent when he is in pain and discomfort, and he does so in the presence of an information gap which can never be closed fully. Medical science, therefore, becomes medicine only when it is modulated and constrained in unique ways by the humanity of physician and patient. Its telos takes it out of the realm of *theoria* and puts it into the realm of *praxis*.

It is the totality of this unique combination which constitutes the clinical moment and the clinical encounter, without which authentic medicine does not exist. ...

Finally, we must add the social dimensions of medicine *qua* medicine—the applications of medical knowledge on an aggregate of humans rather than an individual. This "social encounter" is a parallel of the clinical encounter with an individual patient. Without taking the time to carry out a parallel analysis, it is clear that scientific knowledge can also be used to improve the health of the community. Here medicine is concerned with values, choices, and priorities which relate to the "good" of society. Such issues as the distribution of health services, the purposes for which medicine is used, for whom, who decides, and upon what principles, would constitute the elements of a social philosophy of medicine. ...

Up to this point, we have tried to distinguish among three levels of meaning of the term "medicine": (a) the basic sciences component, which seeks to understand physical processes in a living being, healthy or ill; (b) the clinical sciences component, which seeks to understand physical processes in a perceiving subject in whom mind and body are united; and (c) medicine per se, or medical *praxis*, in which the clinical and basic sciences are particularised in the clinical moment or encounter, with all the complexities outlined above. In medicine *qua* medicine, the sciences are not only means of understanding but also means to intervention in the lives of persons or societies. ...

Medicine clearly is a domain of activity which is distinctive and distinguishable as science, art, and *praxis*. It comprises a set of legitimate philosophical issues and questions which derive from the unique nature of the clinical encounter. **It is precisely the clinical encounter that constitutes the singular ordering concept which distinguishes medicine from the sciences and which is the ground for the logic, the epistemology, and the metaphysics of medical practice** [emphasis added].

...

Some Urgent Philosophical Issues Arising in Medicine

... There is a growing need to weave together the numerous separate strands of information about human existence.

... Intimately related to the philosophical conception of man are the definitions of health and disease, of cure, and of disability. The definitions of health and disease, of cure, and of disability. The presuppositions physicians hold about these conceptions shape medical theory and practice. ...

The process of modernisation is associated with bureaucratisation and technology, which have become values in themselves. They are prime shapers of the cognitive style of our culture and of modern medicine. They are part of what Foucault calls our *epistemé*—the aggregate history of a human endeavour which enables it to occupy a specific space in a given culture.[58] Has the *epistemé* of medicine arising from its own bureaucratisation already determined what society seeks from medicine, and created a self-reinforcing cycle carrying man ever further from what is distinctly human? Will this distorted view contribute further to man's philosophical infirmity?

58. Foucault, *The Birth of the Clinic: An Archaeology of Medical Perception* (New York: Random House, 1973).

Excerpts from pp 9–38

Addendum 2

Common Themes - Institute of Medicine [22]

During the workshop discussions, a number of converging issues emerged. These common themes explored the exigency and facets of the value proposition in health care, the diversity of perspectives on value, and the possibility of implementation and change. Themes touching on the need to improve value and the elements that have to be addressed in achieving this goal included the following:

- **Urgency:** *The urgency to achieve greater value from health care is clear and compelling.* The persistent growth in healthcare costs at a rate greater than inflation is squeezing out employer healthcare coverage, adding to the uninsured, and doubling out-of-pocket payments—all without producing commensurate health improvements. We have heard that perhaps one-third to one-half of health expenditures are unnecessary for targeted health outcomes. The long-term consequences for federal budget obligations driven by the growth in Medicare costs have been described as nearly unfathomable, amounting to an estimated $34 trillion in unfunded obligations, about two-thirds of the total of $53 trillion as yet unfunded for all mandatory federal entitlements (including Social Security and other civilian and military benefits)
- **Perceptions:** *Value means different things to different stakeholders, so clarity of concepts is key.* We have heard that for patients, perceived value in health care is often described in terms of the quality of their relationship with their physician. It has been highlighted that value improvement means helping them better meet their personal goals or living lives that are as normal as possible. It does *not* necessarily mean more services or more expensive services, since it was stated patients are more likely driven by sensitivity to the value of time and ensuring that out-of-pocket payments are targeted to their goals. Provider representatives suggest that value improvement means developing diagnostic and treatment tools and approaches that offer them increased confidence in the effectiveness of the services they offer. Employers discuss value improvement in terms of keeping workers and their families healthier and more productive at lower costs. Health insurers assert that value improvement means emphasising interventions that are crisply and coherently defined and supported by a high level of evidence as to effectiveness and efficiency. Representatives from health product innovators and manufacturers have spoken of value improvement as products that are better for the individual patient, are more profitable, and contribute to product differentiation and innovation
- **Elements:** *Identifying value in health care is more than simply the right care for the right price as it requires determination of the additional elements of the applicability and circumstances of the benefits considered.* We have heard that value in any endeavour is a reflection of what we gain relative to what we put in, and in health care, what is gained from any given diagnostic or treatment

intervention will vary by individual. Participants believe that value determination begins with learning the benefits—what works best, for whom, and under what circumstances—as applied to individuals because value is not inherent to any service but rather specific to the individual. Value determination also means determining the right price, and we heard that, from the demand side, the right price is a function of perspective—societal, payer, and patient. From the supply side, the right price is a function of the cost of production, the cost of delivery, and the incentive to innovation

- **Basics:** *Improving value requires reliable information, sound decision principles, and appropriate incentives.* Since the starting point for determining value is reliable information, workshop discussants underscored the importance of appropriate investment in the infrastructure and processes for initial determination and continuous improvement of insights on the safety, efficacy, effectiveness, and comparative effectiveness of interventions. Action to improve value, then, also requires the fashioning and use of sound decision principles tailored to the circumstances and adequate incentives to promote the desired outcome

- **Decisions:** *Sound decision principles centre on the patient, evidence, context, transparency, and learning.* Currently, decision rules seem to many stakeholders to be vague and poorly tailored to the evidence. Workshop participants contended that the starting point for tailoring decisions to circumstances is with information on costs, outcomes, and strength of the information. They also discussed assessing value at the societal level using best available information and analytics to generate broad perspective and guidance for decision-making on availability, use, and pricing. Yet we also heard that value assessment at the individual patient level takes account of context and patient preferences, conditioned on openness of information exchange and formal learning from choices made under uncertainty. We also heard that an informed patient perspective that trumps a societal value determination can still be consistent with sound decision principles

- **Information:** *Information reliability derives from its sources, methods, transparency, interpretation, and clarity.* We have heard about the importance of openness on the nature, strengths, and limitations of the evidence and the processes of analysis and interpretation—and of tailoring decision principles according to the features in that respect. Because the quality of evidence varies, as do the methods used to evaluate it, transparency as to source and process, care as to interpretation, and clarity in communication are paramount

- **Incentives:** *Appropriate incentives direct attention and rewards to outcomes, quality, and cost.* Often noted in the workshop discussions was that the rewards and incentives prevalent in the American healthcare system are poorly aligned—and even oppositional—to effectiveness and efficiency, encouraging care that is procedure- and specialty-intensive and discouraging primary care and prevention. We heard that if emphases are placed on individual services that are often high cost and inadequately justified, rather than on outcomes, quality, and efficiency, the attainment of system-wide value is virtually precluded

- **Limits:** *The ability to attain system value is likely inversely related to the level of system fragmentation.* Transforming health care to a more direct focus on value is frequently noted as an effort that requires broad organisational, financial, and cultural changes—changes ultimately not attainable with the level of fragmentation that currently characterises decision-making in the US healthcare system. We have heard that obtaining the value needed will continue to be elusive until better means are available to draw broadly on information as to services' efficiency and effectiveness, to set priorities and streamline approaches to filling the evidence gaps, to ensure consistency in the ways evidence is interpreted and applied, and to marshal incentives to improve the delivery of high-value services while discouraging those of limited value

- **Communication:** *System-level value improvement requires more seamless communication among components.* Related to system fragmentation, among the primary barriers to achieving better value are the communication gaps noted among virtually all parties involved. Patients and providers do not communicate well with each other about diagnosis and treatment options or cost implications, in part because in complex administrative and rapidly changing knowledge environments, the necessary information is not readily available to either party. Communication, voice or electronic, is often virtually absent between and among multiple providers and provider systems for a single patient, increasing the prospect of service gaps, duplications, confusion, and harm, according to discussants. Further, communication between scientific and professional organisations producing and evaluating evidence is often limited, resulting in inefficiencies, missed opportunities, and contradictions in the production of guidance. Accordingly, communication between the many groups involved in developing evidence and the practitioners applying it is often unstructured and may be conflicting

The diversity of stakeholder perspectives on value was highlighted from multiple vantage points.

- **Providers:** *Provider-level value improvement efforts depend on culture and rewards focused on outcomes.* Workshop presentations identified several examples of some encouraging results from various programs in terms of progress to improve provider sensitivity to, and focus on, value from health care. These range from improving the analytic tools to evaluate the effectiveness and efficiency of individual providers, institutions, and interventions, to incentive programs such as pay-for-performance, the patient-centred medical home, and employer-based programs for wellness, disease prevention, and disease management. We heard, for example, that certain provider organisations, in effect, specialise in the care of the poorest and sickest patients and can provide services that in fact have better outcomes and lower costs because they are geared to focus on interprovider communication, continuity of care, and links with social welfare organisations. However, they have also negotiated the necessary flexibility with payers. We heard that the clearest barriers to provider-level value improvement appear to lie in the lack of economic incentives for a focus on outcomes (both an analytic and a structural issue) and also in cultural and structural disincentives to tend to the critical interfaces of the care process—the quality of the links in the chain of care elements

- **Patients:** *Patient-level value improvement stems from quality, communication, information, and transparency.* It was noted that patients most often think of value in terms of their relationship with their provider—generally a physician—but ultimately the practical results of that relationship, in terms of costs and outcomes, hinge on the success of programs that improve practical, ongoing, and seamless access to information on best practices and costs and of payment structures that reward accordingly. Workshop discussants offered insights into the use of various financial approaches to sensitise and orient patient decisions on healthcare prices—individual diagnostics and treatments, providers, or health plans—according to the evidence of the value delivered. Successful broad-based application of such approaches will likely hinge on system-wide transformation in the availability of the information necessary and transparency as to its use
- **Manufacturers:** *Manufacturer-level regulatory and purchasing incentives can be better oriented to value added.* Health product manufacturers and innovators naturally focus on their profitability—returning value to shareholders—but we are reminded that product demand is embedded in the ability to demonstrate advantage with respect to patient value—better outcomes with greater efficiency. Hence, manufacturers expressed an interest in exploring regulatory and payment approaches that enhance performance on outcomes related to product use

Pierre L. Young, Leigh Anne Olsen, and J. Michael McGinnis. Value in health care: accounting for cost, quality, safety, outcomes, and innovation, pp 3–7

Addendum 3

What Is Value in Health Care? - Michael Porter [23]

In any field, improving performance and accountability depends on having a shared goal that unites the interests and activities of all stakeholders. In health care, however, stakeholders have myriad, often conflicting goals, including access to services, profitability, high quality, cost containment, safety, convenience, patient-centredness, and satisfaction. Lack of clarity about goals has led to divergent approaches, gaming of the system, and slow progress in performance improvement.

Achieving high value for patients must become the overarching goal of health care delivery, with value defined as the health outcomes achieved per dollar spent.[1] This goal is what matters for patients and unites the interests of all actors in the system. If value improves, patients, payers, providers, and suppliers can all benefit while the economic sustainability of the health care system increases.

Value—neither an abstract ideal nor a code word for cost reduction—should define the framework for performance improvement in health care. Rigorous, disciplined measurement and improvement of value is the best way to drive system progress. Yet value in health care remains largely unmeasured and misunderstood.

Value should always be defined around the customer, and in a well-functioning health care system, the creation of value for patients should determine the rewards for all other actors in the system. Since value depends on results, not inputs, value in health care is measured by the outcomes achieved, not the volume of services delivered, and shifting focus from volume to value is a central challenge. Nor is value measured by the process of care used; process measurement and improvement are important tactics but are no substitutes for measuring outcomes and costs.

Since value is defined as outcomes relative to costs, it encompasses efficiency. Cost reduction without regard to the outcomes achieved is dangerous and self-defeating, leading to false "savings" and potentially limiting effective care.

1. Porter ME, Teisberg EO. Redefining health care: creating value-based competition on results. Boston: Harvard Business School Press, 2006.

Addendum 4

Industry Approaches to Value

Metronic [24]

The good news is that the construct of value in healthcare is widely recognised. The US government has already approved reforms that focus on paying for better patient outcomes, not just for the number of services, products, and tests provided. But improving patient outcomes after diagnosis isn't enough. We need to increase value in the healthcare system throughout the continuum of care.

At Medtronic, when we recognised this fact several years ago, we introduced a concept we call economic value and incorporated it as a cornerstone of our business strategy. In short, we saw a shift in what our customers expect from us. They don't just need clinical value from our therapy innovations, they need economic value as well. The product or service we deliver must also provide an economic benefit such as making care delivery more efficient, minimising system waste, or expanding patient access to therapies.

As a leading medical technology company, we accepted this broader perspective of value. We shifted our business to address this challenge, and we haven't looked back. Since embracing economic value, we identified an opportunity to increase value not only with our devices, but also through our clinical expertise and therapeutic knowledge. That's one of the reasons we created the Medtronic Integrated Health Solutions^SM business—a new offering that moves beyond devices to focus on system-level services and solutions. Today, Medtronic Integrated Health Solutions is helping hospitals, public and private payers, and health systems align value within the care continuum by delivering more efficient and improved care to patients.

Pharmaceutical Industry [25]

Value-based plan design—a term that describes payers' efforts to align consumer cost sharing with the value generated by a service or drug—may sound like a new development in health care, but it's old news for prescription drugs. For years, insurers and pharmacy benefits managers have steered consumers towards generic and other high-value drugs by categorising drugs into "tiers" and requiring lower copayments for preferred drugs. ... Tiering not only encourages consumers to use high-value drugs, it also gives insurers leverage during price negotiations with manufacturers.

Under tiering, insurers offer manufacturers favourable tier placement in exchange for better discounts. ... Insurers can also negotiate lower prices for drugs that have therapeutic substitutes or questionable benefits by threatening to exclude them from their formularies entirely. . . .

In recent years, drug manufacturers have counterattacked by offering "copayment coupons."[2] These coupons or discount cards—distributed by physicians' offices, through the mail, and online—enable the manufacturer to pay some or all of a consumer's copayment for a prescription. By severing the link between cost sharing and the value generated by a drug, copayment coupons can undo the beneficial effects of tiering. With such coupons, consumers' cost sharing may actually be lower for higher-tier brand-name drugs than for lower-tier therapeutic substitutes or generic bioequivalents. Since insurers typically cover about 80% of the total price of a prescription, however, the combined amount that the insurer and the consumer spend for higher-tier drugs remains substantially greater. If coupons shift spending towards these higher-priced drugs, the net effect will be higher pharmaceutical spending and, ultimately, higher health insurance premiums.

Not only do copayment coupons have the potential to pull consumers away from high-value drugs, they also greatly reduce the incentive for drug manufacturers to offer price concessions in exchange for preferred tier placement. In fact, the opposite strategy becomes profitable: charge insurers the highest price possible while remaining on the formulary, and then use a copayment coupon to promote use. The only recourse insurers have is to exclude a drug from their formulary entirely, and that may be much worse for patients than placing it in a high tier.

2. Ross JS, Kesselheim AS. Prescription drug coupons - no such thing as a free lunch. N Engl J Med 2013; 369: 1188–9.

Chapter 6
A Complex Adaptive Health System Redesign from an Organisational Perspective

Overview. The organisational literature considers an organisation's function and structure at four different scales. The organisation of a *health system* involves at:

- The *macro* level policy and governance issues
- The *meso* level the organisation and coordination of regional health, community, social and infrastructure services
- The *micro* level the provision of local/individual care delivery in the local community
- The *nano* level issues of personal health, functional independence, and the self-management of one's well-being and diseases

As outlined in the previous chapter a *seamlessly integrated complex adaptive* organisation needs to *maintain its overarching focus* on its purpose, goals, values, and "simple (operating) rules".

From a complex adaptive systems perspective, a *seamlessly integrated complex adaptive, equitable, and sustainable health system* needs to:

- Develop its own *value based* systems, and translate them in its "organisational structures and interactions" (in the form of "*simple rules*")
- Recognise that within a health system there are simple, complicated, and complex domains each necessitating different organisational and management approaches
- Have leaders that "*direct without directives*" and foster *co-operation* between all staff
- Have leaders that embrace the emergent nature of health systems and healthcare systems in their *unique local contexts*
- Accept that health system outcomes will *inevitably vary* depending on the conditions of the *local environment*

These principles ***do not*** prevent subsystems to adopt their own set of purpose, goals, values, and "simple (operating) rules", however, these need to be consistent with those of the "*health system as a whole*".

© Springer International Publishing AG 2018
J.P. Sturmberg, *Health System Redesign*, DOI 10.1007/978-3-319-64605-3_6

Points for Reflection

Thinking of your own organisation:

- What are the various levels in your organisation?
- What are the activities occurring at each of these levels?
- How are these activities interacting across the whole of the organisation?
- Who is in control at each level?
- Who is in control of the whole organisation?
- How does control affect the overall function of the organisation?

Organisational theory views organisations as multi-levelled with macro, meso, micro, and nano level structures and functions (the roles and responsibilities at each organisational level are detailed in Addendum 1). In the context of the health systems we typically think of:

- The *macro level* as dealing with policy and governance issues
- The *meso level* managing regional health, community, social and infrastructure services
- The *micro level* providing local/individual care delivery in the local community
- The *nano level* describing personal/organismic health and disease characteristics/functions [1]

This conceptualisation of the health system as a multi-level organisation with multiple subsystems is consistent with the complexity notion of *nested systems*. Each organisational level and each subsystem will have their own unique structures and activities with well-defined roles and sets of well-defined rules which may appear to work effectively when viewed in isolation. However, it is critically important for the "system as a whole" to interact in such a way that it can achieve the seamless delivery of its desired goals.

6.1 Agents at Different Levels of the System

Critical analysis demonstrates that there are a wide range of agents with diverse interests in the health system (Addendum 2 lists some for the Australian health system according to system levels). Most notably many agents/subsystems have a limited and self-serving focus. This in most obvious at the macro-level; a health minister has to mediate justifiable health delivery demands against resource concerns. Lobbyists, representing industry interests, citizens lobby groups, or other non-government organisations, argue for those decisions that are most advantages to their constituents, regardless of the consequences of those decision on the "system as a whole".

6.2 Links Across Organisational/System Levels Are Not Necessarily Always Aligned

There are understandable constraints on agents at any organisational/system level to take a "whole of systems" perspective, i.e. one that works coherently to achieve the organisation's/system's common purpose and goals in accordance with its values.

- Organisational levels/subsystems may adopt purpose goals and values out of alignment, or even divorced from those of the "system as a whole". Systems without an identifiable unifying driver make the system more like a "conglomeration of discrete units". Thus even if agents act in accordance with the rules of their own subsystem, they may not contribute to the overarching goal-orientation of the "system as a whole"

- Due to an organisational system's highly distributed nature, it may not be immediately clear what course of action at an organisational/subsystem level will be most promising to lead to the desired outcomes and what effects it may have on any other part of the system or for the "system as a whole"

6.2.1   The Example of "Food Regulation"

Macro-level agents like a minister and his bureaucrats rarely take a "whole of systems" perspective when faced with a specific issue. Consider the regulation of the food industry; what are the consequences of food regulation over a 10–20 year time frame considering a product's salt and sugar content, or the amount and type of advertising targeting children (schematically Fig. 6.1)?

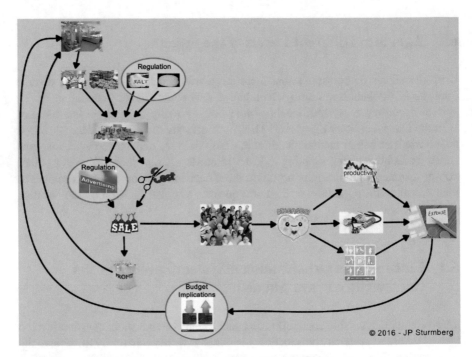

Fig. 6.1 Influence diagram of food regulation. Influence diagrams can serve as the basis for a model to simulate the impact of food regulation on the Governments "budget balance" and changes on the income of the food industry as well as the health and social resource use of the community

The example of food regulation alludes to "whole of system" dynamics i.e. changes to food regulation (a macro-level activity) will interfere with the status quo of food industry economics (meso level) (people employed, cost of inputs, profit margins, taxes paid), the cost of foods available to consumers, but also the potential cost savings to the health system due to better health of individuals and the community. The latter though will have economic implications to private sector health service providers. The potential need for fewer health services affects health professionals' earning capacity, potentially resulting in an increase in the cost of services to health system users. At the nano level, community education about healthier food choices might lead to a greater demand for healthier food, thus providing additional incentives for food producers to change their production processes and product ranges. People might have to rebalance their budgets; some higher spending on food may be offset against less spending on health services. In addition, changes in food choices at the nano level may require adaptation in taste and the acquisition of additional cooking skills (Fig. 6.2).

However current "whole of government" perspectives are generally limited on "short term budgetary impacts" and historically is associated with the need for increased spending in the future. A system focused on the long-term *health* of the community could easily evaluate the short and long-term implications from food regulation on the economics, healthcare costs, and health outcomes using readily available modelling tools (for details, see Chap. 11).

6.3   Aligning the Agendas of Agents Across All Organisational Levels

An organisation that wants to achieve a *person-centred, equitable, and sustainable complex adaptive health system* needs to clearly define its *purpose, goals,* and *core values*, and use these to align all of the systems activities within and across all organisational/subsystem levels to deliver such care (Addendum 3). In a *person-centred, equitable, and sustainable complex adaptive health system* the key responsibilities of agents—based on the *purpose, goals, values,* and *"simple rules"* as outlined in the previous chapter—would ensure that:

- Leaders support all staff across all levels of the organisation to collaboratively make the necessary changes required to achieve agreed goals
- Communities determine the priorities for health promoting physical and social infrastructures development
- All health service providers deliver health, illness, and disease care that meets people's psychosocial needs and personal aspirations
- People acquire personal health care skills that promote their health and prevent premature disease development

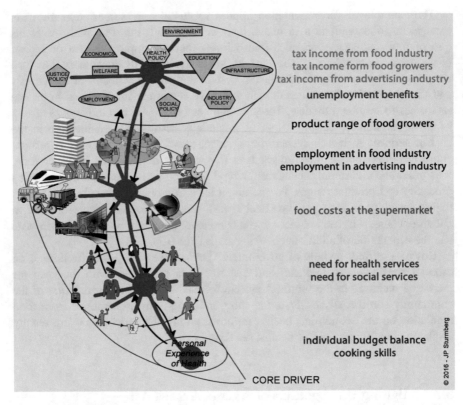

tax income from food industry
tax income form food growers
tax income from advertising industry
unemployment benefits

product range of food growers

employment in food industry
employment in advertising industry

food costs at the supermarket

need for health services
need for social services

individual budget balance
cooking skills

CORE DRIVER

© 2016 - JP Sturmberg

Fig. 6.2 Impact of tightening food regulation on the "whole person-centred health system". Note the diverse impacts of food regulation on different agents in different layers. Everyone has to adapt to achieve the *common goals* reflecting *common values*

6.4   Complex Adaptive Organisations

There is a large health service/policy literature that has examined health system organisations from a complexity perspective. The key findings include:

- The importance of organisations to develop their own *value-based* systems [2–12] and to translate them in their "organisational structures and interactions" (in the form of "*simple rules*") [5, 8, 13–18] to achieve a seamlessly integrated stable and resilient health system
- Recognition that within health (delivery) systems there are simple, complicated, and complex domains each necessitating different organisational and managerial approaches [9, 19]
- Leadership in complex adaptive organisations leads by providing "*direction without directives*" [3, 8, 20–23], and fosters co-operation between all agents [10, 11, 21, 24–26]

- Leadership in complex adaptive organisations embraces the *emergent nature* of a health service/system as the system's behaviour arises from the *nonlinear* processes *unique to the local context*
- Leadership in complex adaptive organisations accepts that complex adaptive dynamics in complex adaptive organisations are inevitably *not precisely predictable* BUT deliver *"mutually agreeable outcomes"* arising from *local constraints* [10, 11, 26–28]
- Leadership in complex adaptive organisations appreciates that every organisations is *bounded historically* by the prevailing socio-cultural norms which "direct" their future developments (*"path dependence"*) [8, 15, 16, 22, 23, 29]

The next chapter will provide examples that illustrate the creation and operation of *"best adapting"* complex adaptive health systems.

References

1. Martin CM, Sturmberg JP (2006) Rethinking general practice - Part II: strategies for the future. Patient-centred, socially and economically responsible primary care and the leadership challenges. Asia Pac Fam Med 5(5). www.apfmj-archive.com/afm5_2/afm48.pdf
2. Lindstrom R (2003) Evidence-based decision-making in healthcare: exploring the issues though the lens of complex, adaptive systems theory. Healthc Pap 3(3):29–35
3. Chen DT, Werhane PH, Mills AE (2007) Role of organization ethics in critical care medicine. Critical care medicine organizational and management ethics in the intensive care unit. Crit Care Med 35(2):S11–S17
4. WHO - Western Pacific Region (2007) People at the centre of health care. Harmonizing mind and body, people and systems. WHO Western Pacific Region, Geneva
5. Rouse WB (2008) Health care as a complex adaptive system: implications for design and management. The Bridge 38(1):17–25
6. Kaplan RS, Porter ME (2011) How to solve the cost crisis in health care. Harv Bus Rev 89(9):47–64
7. Sturmberg JP, O'Halloran DM, Martin CM (2012) Understanding health system reform - a complex adaptive systems perspective. J Eval Clin Pract 18(1):202–208
8. Freedman LP, Schaaf M (2013) Act global, but think local: accountability at the frontlines. Reprod Health Matters 21(42):103–112
9. Kottke TE (2013) Simple rules that reduce hospital readmission. Perm J 17(3):91–93
10. Gottlieb K (2013) The Nuka system of care: improving health through ownership and relationships. Int J Circumpolar Health 72. doi:10.3402/ijch.v72i0.21118
11. Martin D, Pollack K, Woollard RF (2014) What would an Ian McWhinney health care system look like? Can Fam Phys 60(1):17–19
12. Cloninger CR, Salvador-Carulla L, Kirmayer LJ, Schwartz MA, Appleyard J, Goodwin N et al (2014) A time for action on health inequities: foundations of the 2014 Geneva declaration on person- and people-centered integrated health care for all. Int J Person Centered Med 4(2): 69–89
13. Glouberman S, Zimmerman B (2002) Complicated and complex systems: what would successful reform of medicare look like? Discussion Paper No 8. Commission on the Future of Health Care in Canada, Ottawa, July 2002
14. Sturmberg JP, O'Halloran DM, Martin CM (2010) People at the centre of complex adaptive health systems reform. Med J Aust 193(8):474–478
15. Sturmberg JP, Martin CM (2010) The dynamics of health care reform - learning from a complex adaptive systems theoretical perspective. Nonlinear Dynamics Psychol Life Sci 14(4):525–540

16. Saxton JF, Johns MME (2010) Barriers to change in engineering the system of health care delivery. Engineering the system of healthcare delivery. Stud Health Technol Inform 153:437–463
17. Bloom G, Wolcott S (2013) Building institutions for health and health systems in contexts of rapid change. Soc Sci Med 96:216–222
18. Marchal B, Van Belle S, De Brouwere V, Witter S (2013) Studying complex interventions: reflections from the FEMHealth project on evaluating fee exemption policies in West Africa and Morocco. BMC Health Serv Res 13(1):469
19. Martin CM, Felix Bortolotti M, Strasser S (2010) W(h)ither complexity? The emperor's new toolkit? or Elucidating the evolution of health systems knowledge? J Eval Clin Pract 16(3):415–420
20. Plsek P (2001) Appendix B: redesigning health care with insights from the science of complex adaptive systems. In: Committee on quality of health care in America - Institute of medicine, editor. Crossing the quality chasm: a new health system for the 21st century. National Academy Press, Washington DC, pp 309–322
21. Tsasis P, Evans JM, Owen S (2012) Reframing the challenges to integrated care: a complex-adaptive systems perspective. Int J Integr Care 12:e190
22. Gilson L, Elloker S, Olckers P, Lehmann U (2014) Advancing the application of systems thinking in health: South African examples of a leadership of sensemaking for primary health care. Health Res Policy Syst12(1):30
23. Swanson R, Atun R, Best A, Betigeri A, de Campos F, Chunharas S et al (2015) Strengthening health systems in low-income countries by enhancing organizational capacities and improving institutions. Glob Health 11(1):5
24. van der Vlegel-Brouwer W (2013) Integrated healthcare for chronically ill. Reflections on the gap between science and practice and how to bridge the gap. Int J Integr Care 13:e019
25. Varghese J, Kutty V, Paina L, Adam T (2014) Advancing the application of systems thinking in health: understanding the growing complexity governing immunization services in Kerala, India. Health Res Policy Syst 12(1):47
26. Prashanth N, Marchal B, Devadasan N, Kegels G, Criel B (2014) Advancing the application of systems thinking in health: a realist evaluation of a capacity building programme for district managers in Tumkur, India. Health Res Policy Syst 12(1):42
27. Paina L, Peters DH (2012) Understanding pathways for scaling up health services through the lens of complex adaptive systems. Health Policy Plan 27(5):365–373
28. Borgermans L, De Maeseneer J, Wollersheim H, Vrijhoef B, Devroey D. A Theoretical Lens for Revealing the Complexity of Chronic Care. Perspect Biol Med. 2013;56(2):289–299
29. Ho S, Sandy L (2014) Getting value from health spending: going beyond payment reform. J Gen Intern Med. 29(5):796–797

Addendum 1

The Roles and Responsibilities of Agents at Each System Level

Macro or Policy-Level Policy and financial frameworks need to address population needs as well as the needs of vulnerable groups. The principle of optimal health for all citizens is central to policy innovations in any model of primary health care. Currently prescriptive, "top down", hierarchical, and linear policy approaches predominate. In "bottom up" approaches, general practice may advocate for patients and lobby for strategies that provide considered multimodal frameworks in which all stakeholders work together to develop locally appropriate solutions.

Meso or Organizational and Local-Level Addressing health needs and health related determinants at a regional/local level requires coordinated responses from both health providers and administrators. In order to facilitate the evolution of new, locally relevant service models, it is important to allow key stakeholders to operate in an open rather than heavily prescriptive planning environment. For example, the general practitioner/family physician, thus has a developing organizational and knowledge brokerage role in interdisciplinary and intersectoral care, and in the uptake of new technologies, while at the same time maintaining the core principles of personalized care delivery. This requires the translation of research knowledge, ensuring patients' equity and access to timely health care, and the sharing and coordinating of health care between the wide range of health care and non-health agencies.

Micro or Individual-Level Patients and their communities are the centre point around which care is provided and organized. The effectiveness of the roles and responsibilities of general practice rests in the consultation and the personalized interaction of the doctor/provider with an individual. The consultation is the basic "production unit" in medicine—here decisions about resource consumption are negotiated between the doctor and the patient. Yet roles and responsibilities in this area are evolving with care delegation, new patient expectations, electronic information systems, and internet medicine. Crucially there is an increasing advocacy and leadership role to keep the patient (not a disease, a cost, or a multidisciplinary team) central to the health system and to ensure their core care remains continuous, coordinated, relationship-based, and located in primary health care.

Nano or Organismic-Level The level of health—subjective as well as objective—reflects the entire impact of the forces influencing human health. Health perception, that is, the subjective experience of health or disease, is the result of the person's interdependence (a term coined by Ban-Yar) with his/her environment. In other words, a patient's experience of healthcare is an outcome reflecting the effectiveness of consultations—nature and nurture, and the workings of the health system at large. However, in the end it is the organism and its embodied experiences of mind, body, and emotion that we label "health". This is where health care is directed and has its raison d'être. The judgement of primary health care success is ultimately located at this level. Increasingly this is where the role and responsibility of general practice lies.

Martin CM, Sturmberg JP. Rethinking General Practice—Part II: Strategies for the Future. Patient-Centred, Socially and Economically Responsible Primary Care and the Leadership Challenges [1].

Addendum 2

The Divergent Interests of Agents in the Health System

Level	Agents of influence	Agents' interests

Macro	• Government policymakers
	
	  – Health
	  – Social services
	  – Social infrastructure
	  – Economics and finance
	  – others—education, work employment, housing, etc.
		• Resource allocation
		
		  – Determined by perceived priorities
		  – Has financial control over health
		  – Currently "Balanced Budgets"

	• Private enterprise
	
	  – Pharmaceutical industry
	  – Device makers
	  – Medical associations
	  – Health insurance industry
		• Market share and profits
		
		  – Getting new drugs developed and
		  – accepted on formularies
		  – Financial interest of members
		  – Growing membership and market share from public health system

	• Citizen lobby groups
	
	  – Health consumer forum
	  – Disease-specific support groups
		• Getting greater resources for their specific interests

	• Non-government Organisations – Research councils	• Getting greater resources for their specific interests organisations

Meso	• Local community infrastructure/ environment
	
	  – Work
	  – Education
	  – Housing
	  – Roads
	  – Social infrastructure
	  – Open spaces
	  – Others
		• Dependent on cooperation with other interests
		• Resource constraints
		• Focused on specific tasks
		• Shifting priorities with shifting government agendas

(continued)

Level	Agents of influence	Agents' interests

	• Public hospital care
	
	  – Hospital departments
	  – Community outreach services
		• Resource constraints
		
		  – Compartmentalised according to
		  – organ-system or technology
		  – Unstable workforce
		  – Staffing shortages
		  – High level of bureaucracy
		  – Performance based on throughput and reported safety

	• Private hospital care	• Return on investments
		
		  – Customer focus: doctors and specialists
		  – Performance based on maximizing revenue per patient day

Micro	• Health service delivery
	• Primary care
	
	  – GP-practice team, incl. reception staff, nurses, psychologists, indigenous health workers, others
	
	• Pathology/Radiology
	• Partialist (Specialist)
	• Community
	
	  – Community nursing
	  – Physiotherapy
	  – Psychology
	  – Other allied health professionals
	  – Family, friends, and social networks
		• Private enterprise concerns
		
		  – FFS-system of remuneration
		  – Competition between practices
		  – Resourcing according to income generation potential
		  – Over-servicing incentive
		  – Time = money, referral an easy option
		  – Fragmentatory care
		  – Limited liaison with other health professional providers
		  – Limited evaluation of health outcomes
		  – Financial constraints
		  – Limited knowledge about patient care and support
		  – Difficulties accessing community support services

Nano	• The person	• Concerned about their health experience, does it limit desired levels of activity • Safety of self-management • Financial constraints • Difficulties accessing community support services

Addendum 3

The Focus and Actions of Agents in a Person-Centred, Equitable, and Sustainable Complex Adaptive Health System

Level	Agents of influence	Agents' focus based on the health system's purpose, *goals, values, and "simple rules"*

Macro	• Government policymakers
	
	  – Health
	  – Social services
	  – Social infrastructure
	  – Economics and finance
	  – others—education, work and employment, housing, etc.
		• Leadership
		
		  – Promote values of the system
		  – Facilitate the necessary adaptive work that needs to be done
		  – Ensure they have the resource required
		  – Collaborate across other portfolios

	• Private enterprise
	
	  – Pharmaceutical industry
	  – Device makers
	  – Medical associations
	  – Health insurance industry	

	• Citizen lobby groups
	
	  – Health consumer forum
	  – Disease-specific support groups	

Meso	• Local community infrastructure/environment	• Community engagement
		• Think about long-term changes (10-year time frame)
		
		  – Work
		  – Education
		  – Housing
		  – Roads
		  – Social infrastructure
		  – Open spaces
		
		• Willing to understand multiple, perspectives work with complexity in all its challenging messiness, and recognise the importance of both local detail and the over-arching big picture. It's no small task in this age of the quick fix and the sound bite.

	• Hospital level care	

(continued)

Level	Agents of influence	Agents' focus based on the health system's purpose, *goals, values, and "simple rules"*

micro	• Health service delivery
	• Primary care
	
	  – GP-practice team, incl. reception staff, nurses, psychologists, indigenous health workers, others
	
	• Pathology/Radiology
	• Partialist (Specialist)
	• Community
	
	  – Community nursing
	  – Physiotherapy
	  – Psychology
	  – Other allied health professionals
	
	• Family, friends, and social networks
		• Person/patient-centredness
		• Simultaneous focus on the physical, social, emotional, and cognitive/ sense-making domains of the illness
		• Joint decision-making taking into account
		
		  – Personal choices
		  – Acceptance of uncertainty and risk
		  – Impact of environmental factors on health and well-being
		
		• Engagement with community advocacy and development
		• Focus on strengthening linkage with
		
		  – Family
		  – Friends
		  – Difficulties accessing community support services

Nano	• The person	• Focus on strengthening
		
		  – Self-care
		  – Stress management
		  – Healthy food, exercise, medication adherence
		  – Engagement with family and social networks
		
		• Focus on prevention in light of
		
		  – Family history (genetics)
		  – Significant life events (epigenetics)
		  – Harmful environmental exposures—air and other environmental pollutants, poor housing, work place hazards

Chapter 7
A Complex Adaptive Health System: Real-World Examples

Overview. *Person-centred, equitable, and sustainable complex adaptive health systems* are not a pipe dream. This chapter describes three examples of *complex adaptive health systems* which evolved in a unique way arising from a particular challenge. Remarkably, each of these complex adaptive health systems emerged in a different way:

- *Spontaneously*, like the primary care system in the slums of Nairobi, that emerged from the charitable work of caring for people dying from HIV/AIDS
- *Connecting* diverse existing services, as was the approach of the Brazilian government to the threat of HIV/AIDS resulting in the collapse of the Brazilian health services and/or state
- Through *community consultation* amongst the Alaska Native and American Indian people who defined the core characteristics of a health system that met their health and cultural needs (the NUKA system of primary health care)

The one thing that these examples have in common is the development of a set of *purpose, goals and values* which provided the basis to *guide/drive* the actions and interactions required to achieve a *person-centred, equitable and sustainable complex adaptive health systems*.

- **The Eastern Deanery AIDS Relief Program (EDARP)**
  EDARP is an example of the *apparent spontaneous emergence* of a health system in the slums of Nairobi. "Caring for people dying from HIV/AIDS" was a missionary programme that started with a handful of nurses and community health workers[1] (CHW). After gaining trust in the programme community members approached the programme outlining their need for additional services. The programme quickly responded and expanded to manage tuberculosis, a common co-occurring disease with HIV/AIDS. The success of controlling HIV/AIDS and tuberculosis was the result of cooperation with some small support from

---

[1]CHW are essentially lay volunteers living and working within their own community.

© Springer International Publishing AG 2018
J.P. Sturmberg, *Health System Redesign*, DOI 10.1007/978-3-319-64605-3_7

the health department in Nairobi. Managing these two diseases was the catalyst to widen the services to include the prevention and spread of HIV/AIDS from mothers to babies, and social and educational support programmes for children and adolescents orphaned by the death of their parents from HIV/AIDS or tuberculosis.

- **HIV/AIDS in Brazil: A Whole of Government Response**

  The Brazilian government, faced with a HIV/AIDS pandemic, accepted as a starting point that there would be no "easy answers" to solve the problem. They realised that they needed a different mindset to prevent the collapse of society. Asking *how* (triggering creative responses) rather than *what/why* questions (triggering responses of justification) identified the need to employ many different strategies. It also identified that many diverse groups had also identified the risk that HIV/AIDS posed to society who independently provided services. Surprisingly though these groups were unaware of each other's efforts. The government recognised that linking and supporting these groups with their unique understandings of the epidemic in their local environment would be the key to averting a HIV/AIDS crisis. Brazil's approach linked the efforts across and between all levels of health system organisation and succeeded in preventing an impending crisis.

- **The NUKA Primary Care System**

  In 1998 the Washington controlled, failing native health service, was handed over to the local Native Community who became the owners, operators, and users of the service. Health system redesign started with an extensive consultation process that identified the community's expectations—a *shared relationship* with their primary care provider, *being treated with* courtesy, respect, and cultural understanding, and having *access to care* when needed. Ongoing evaluation and feedback allow the system to quickly adapt to changing needs and demands.

  The NUKA System is seen as a model for the redesign of primary care by many organisations from around the world.

Points for Reflection

Thinking about a *person-centred, equitable, and sustainable complex adaptive health systems*:

- How would you define that for your environment?
- What would you propose to be its key features?
- How would you approach such a redesign effort?
- What might be some of the hurdles to achieve your vision?

Having thought about the three cases presented in this chapter:

- What do you regard as the key features for their success?
- Thinking about the features that underpinned the success of these examples, how would you alter your approach to redesign in your organisation?

"You can't do fine things without having seen fine examples"
William Morris Hunt (1824–1879) - American artist

If the previous two chapters appear to be too theoretical, here are "three fine examples" that illustrate the design of *person-centred, equitable, and sustainable complex adaptive health systems*:

- The *de-novo* "bottom-up" primary/community health system that emerged in response to people's clearly articulated needs in an underprivileged community in Kenya
- The *reconfiguration* of health and community services in response to the HIV/AIDS crisis threatening the entire health system in Brazil
- The community consultation-based redesign of a health system following the transfer of the health service from central government to indigenous community control in Alaska

These services succeeded as they established relationships and alliances based upon statements of *common purpose, goals, and values* which guided the development of "*simple (or operational) rules*". The adherence to these principles by all system agents at all organisational levels provided the frame for agents to reconfigure their relationships and adjust their interactions. Feedback ensured the *emergence* of new and novel solutions to challenges and developing problems.

These complex adaptive approaches to manage systemic problems stand in stark contrast to prevailing linear and top-down hierarchical approaches and the desire to find and implement "of the shelf solutions".

The examples are structured to illustrate the utility of the system tools and frameworks discussed in Part I of this book:

- A brief description of the local context
- A health vortex representation of the system that highlights the cross organisational dynamics
- The vision statement that formed the basis for the development of the system's driver
- A Cynefin map that shows the various change dynamics

7.1   The De-Novo Emergence of a Community Health Service in the Slums of Nairobi

This case study illustrates the emergence of a "bottom-up" community health system in the Nairobi Eastland's area with a population of at least 2.16 million people and an estimated adult HIV prevalence of 5.2%.

The Eastern Deanery AIDS Relief Program (EDARP—http://www.edarp.org/index.php) initially solely aimed to relieve the suffering of dying AIDS patients. The programme rapidly realised that to be successful in the long term in treating and preventing the spread of HIV/AIDS and improving the general health of the community it would be necessary to engage with the whole community. It became apparent that Community Health Workers (CHW) play a pivotal role in achieving these goals [1, 2]. CHWs were recruited from the community, trained in the community and as trusted community members worked within their own community.

The collaborative approach between EDARP, CHWs, and community members constantly identified new needs and new approaches to meet these needs. A *community driven* community health service has emerged that constantly adapts to changing medical, personal, and social community needs. The key milestones in the development of this service are (Fig. 7.1):

- 1993—focus on dying AIDS patients
- 1995—focus on the spread of untreated TB-infections as a co-morbidity in HIV/AIDS patients. A partnership with the Centre for Disease Control Kenya (CDC) achieved the implementation of HIV/TB screening and treatment programmes
- 1996—focus on developing a local TB-testing facility as travel to the main hospital was unaffordable. In collaboration with the main TB-laboratory a young school leaver with good science marks was trained as a TB-technician. As patients could not travel between the health centres EDARP bought a bike and engaged a community member as a courier to deliver sputum samples to the lab and return results to the health centres
- 2001—additional focus on medication adherence for HIV and TB patients. Treatment adherence was increased by also providing urgently needed nutritional support, donated by a local miller
- 2004—focus on HIV prevention. In collaboration with the Centre for Disease Control Kenya (CDC) a highly active anti-retroviral therapy (HAART) programme was implemented. The team had a specific programme focus on pregnant women and their newborns to prevent Mother-to-Child transmission
- 2014—focus on the social consequences of HIV. The rising number of orphaned and abandoned children/adolescents necessitated the development of integrated clinics and family support services to deal with the emotional and social consequences of HIV/AIDS [3]

7.1.1   EDARP's Organisational Foundations

To offer sustainable affordable quality healthcare for all, EDARP Services aim at providing affordable quality health care. In this regard EDARP always endeavours to be an organisation that will promote the following:

1. Compassion
2. Professionalism
3. Patient Focus

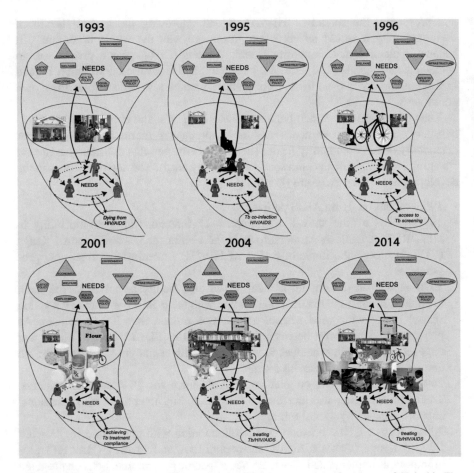

Fig. 7.1 The developmental milestones of the EDARP project in the slums of Nairobi. The programme quickly grew from initially only caring for dying HIV/AIDS patients (1993) to dealing with the concomitant infection of TB as a threat to the whole community (1995). Local recruitment and training established a functional TB testing service accessible across the large community (1996) and the treatment outcomes for both TB and HIV were enhanced by offering desperately needed nutritional support donated by a philanthropic miller (2001). Collaboration with the Centre for Disease Control (CDC) Kenya resulted in initiation of highly active anti-retroviral treatment (HAART) in the community with a special focus on mothers and their newborns (2004 onwards). Since 2014 additional programmes now focus on the emotional and social needs of orphaned/abandoned children/adolescents due to HIV/AIDS (originally published in Sturmberg and Njoroge. People-centred health systems, a bottom-up approach: Where theory meets empery [3])

4. Quality
5. Integrity
6. Leadership and development
7. Teamwork

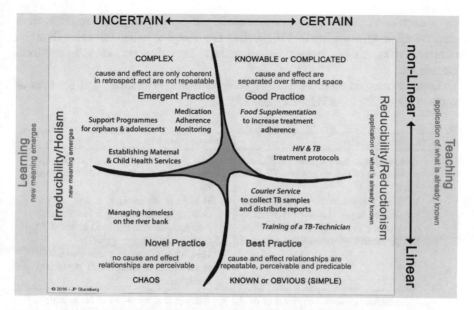

Fig. 7.2 Cynefin map of EDARP's approaches. **Best practice approaches** for training and logistics. **Good practice approaches** for disease management. **Emergent practice approaches** for improving treatment adherence and new service development. **Novel practice approaches** for reaching the "hard to reach"

7.1.2 Each Problem has a Different Degree of Complexity: Matching Challenges and Solutions

EDARP used strategies covering all domains in the Cynefin framework. Responses to various challenges mandated either the adoption of well-proven and predictable or experimentation with emergent and novel strategies. As Fig. 7.2 illustrates managing the main diseases in the community was straightforward; however, engaging with the multiple consequences of TB and HIV/AIDS required the courage of trying context-driven but unproven approaches and a willingness to adapt these in light of their—desired as well as undesired—achievements.

7.2 Avoiding a HIV/AIDS Pandemic in Brazil

In the late 1990s the Brazilian government recognised that the emerging HIV/AIDS epidemic would cause a major crisis for the country. Is this threat a "complicated problem" or a "complex problem"? Rather than asking *what-questions* (What do we do? What will it cost?—triggering responses of justification) assuming a "complicated problem" for which there are simple answers, they asked *how-questions* (How can we achieve...? How can we reduce costs?—triggering responses resulting from creative thinking) realising that HIV/AIDS is a complex issue with many different contributing factors and many different contexts depending on individual and local circumstances.

Glouberman and Zimmerman [4] contrasted these questions and answers as follows (examples from Tables 11 and 12).

Complicated problem	Complex problem
• What will drug costs be for our infected population? or Whom can we afford to treat? • With our limited resources, should we focus more on prevention or treatment? or What are the resources for an effective prevention treatment?	• How can we reduce costs so that we can provide treatment for all who need it? • If food is an issue, how can we use existing charities to provide food so that patients can get food at the right time for their drug regime? • How can we achieve our prevention goals while treating all of those currently infected?
• Meaningful solutions require sophisticated, integrated national health care systems • We cannot provide treatment to all when the costs are so high. Choices must be made	• We will find ways to use the resources we have to respond to the problem • We will find a way to provide treatment to all who need it by dramatically reducing costs

While both perspectives are based on a coherent set of assumptions about reality and change they inevitably also assume a particular approach to problem solving:

- The *complicated approach* suggests external managers—or mechanics—are need to fix the system and/or its parts
- The *complex approach* suggests that solutions (and new problems) have the potential to emerge from within, and that the external roles of leadership become more facilitative than mechanical

7.2.1   The Brazilian Government's Organisational Foundations

The Brazilian Government's response to the HIV crisis demonstrates how a broad and integrated policy response can provide the necessary framework for the emergence of interconnected service delivery systems. Here leadership is deliberately dispersed across the continuum between macro to nano level organisational structures. Accepting that HIV is a complex problem asking the "creative question" *how?* to solve the problem resulted in a list of very diverse answers:

- Promotion of "treatment as prevention"
- Use of humour to promote condom use
- Free anti-retroviral medications

- Teaching proper medication use (drawings to overcome communication difficulties in communities with high illiteracy rates)
- Local drug manufacturing (against WTO and pharmaceutical industry threats)
- Linking to NGO food programmes for the most disadvantaged
- Linking existing informal service networks (over 600 NGOs and local level care organisations)

All answers ultimately contributed to the engagement of everyone necessary to achieve the final outcome of controlling the disease in affected people and preventing its spread through the community at large (Fig. 7.3).

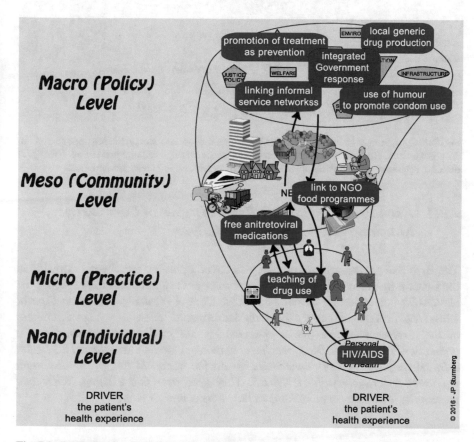

Fig. 7.3 HIV/AIDS is a "whole of system problem". HIV/AIDS as a "whole of system problem" requires solutions that fit the characteristics of each organisational scale. All solutions emerged from the "unifying focus" on treating ALL affected people and preventing spread to the rest of the community

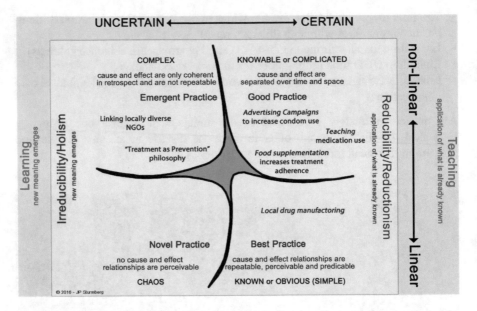

Fig. 7.4 Cynefin map of the Brazilian government's approaches. **Best practice approaches** for drug production. **Good practice approaches** for disease management and prevention. **Emergent practice approaches** for linking diverse organisations and shifting population mindsets

7.2.2   Each Problem Has a Different Degree of Complexity: Matching Challenges and Solutions

The Brazilian government used strategies covering all but the chaotic domains in the Cynefin framework (Fig. 7.4). The dynamics of the approaches have stopped the HIV/AIDS epidemic; the Center of Disease Control (*Center for Disease Control Daily News*, 2000) summarised this remarkable result: "*There were huge differences in the services available across the country and to different segments of the population. Their HIV/AIDS efforts have, to quite an extent, strengthened the health infrastructure, or web of connections, to do the treatment and prevention work necessary to grapple with HIV/AIDS. They used over 600 existing NGOs and community level care organszations to reach the country's poor*".

7.3   The NUKA-System of Primary Care

Southcentral Foundation (https://www.southcentralfoundation.com/nuka/) is an Alaska Native-owned and operated nonprofit health care organisation serving nearly 65,000 Alaska Native and American Indian people living in Anchorage, Matanuska-Susitna Valley, and 55 rural villages in the Anchorage Service Unit.

Historically the Indian Health Service was centrally controlled from Washington with no local input. Unsurprisingly staff morale was poor as they felt dis-empowered, access to primary care was poor, and service providers had a low regard for people's cultural needs—the net outcome of the service was reflected in poor health statistics of Native peoples.

In 1998 the health service was handed over to the local community. Service redesign started with extensive surveys about people's *values, priorities, and needs*—they wanted:

- A relationship with their primary care provider
- Being treated with courtesy, respect, and cultural understanding
- Having access to care when needed

7.3.1   NUKA's Organisational Foundations

Having clearly identified the health service users' values, priorities, and needs translated to a vision statement of:

- *A Native Community that enjoys physical, mental, emotional and spiritual wellness*

and a mission statement that emphasised "working together" as a core principle

- *Working together with the Native Community to achieve wellness through health and related services*

Vision and mission determined the services "*simple (or operating) rules*"

- *Shared responsibility*
- *Commitment to quality*
- *Family wellness*

7.3.2   The NUKA Health System

The NUKA System is a fully integrated service including primary, secondary, and tertiary care (Fig. 7.5). It embraces the patient-centred medical home strategies (https://pcmh.ahrq.gov/), providing multidisciplinary teams that integrate health care and social services through primary care centres and community outreach. Traditional Alaska Native healing is offered alongside other health services including dental, mother and child programmes and elder programmes. The health system also drives awareness, prevention, and support initiatives such as domestic violence programmes, abuse and neglect support, smoking cessation, weight loss

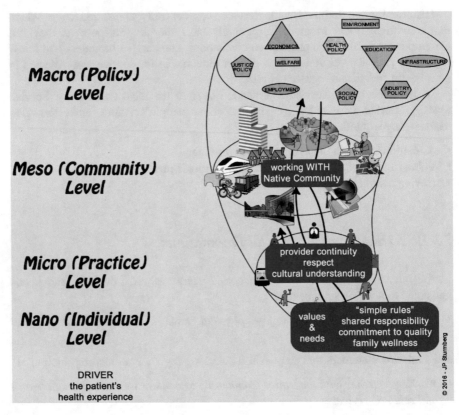

Fig. 7.5 The development of the NUKA health service. The development of the NUKA health service is strongly based on its values and needs statements which guide all activities within the health service. *Health* results as much from individual service provision as community engagement and support

and nutrition support, and cancer prevention/support across the population through education, training, and community engagement.

The NUKA leadership team is constantly improving its services by:

- listening to people's feedback and understanding their needs **AND**
- explaining the changes being made in response to their feedback **AND**
- then communicating the organisation's successes in delivering what the community asked of it [5, 6][2]

---

[2]A smaller scale example of redesigning health services in light of patients and their family's needs has just been described in an article of the NEJM Catalyst initiative—Warner JJ. How Our Community Designed a Better Hospital [7].

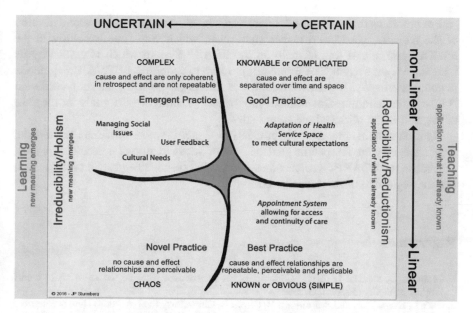

Fig. 7.6 Cynefin map of the NUKA system's approaches. **Best practice approaches** for administrative streamlining. **Good practice approaches** for *culturally appropriate* disease management. **Emergent practice approaches** for engaging in community development and ongoing service redesign

7.3.3   Each Problem Has a Different Degree of Complexity: Matching Challenges and Solutions

The NUKA system's approaches lead to service redesign that covered all but the chaotic domains in the Cynefin framework and reflects the emphasis on relationships, working with people and their social and environmental contexts (Fig. 7.6). The health service continues to develop collaborations with other local, regional, and national partners as gaps in services are identified. The change in outcomes includes markedly improved access to primary care services, improved performance of health services, high user satisfaction, a 36% reduction in hospital days, a 42% reduction in urgent and emergency care services, and a 58% reduction in visits to specialist clinics [5, 8].

7.4   What These Cases Have in Common

These three case studies highlight the importance of adhering to a set of pre-defined *purpose, goals, and values* statements that *guide/drive* the actions of the system's agents.

For problems that affect the "system as a whole", change requires a re-definition of the *purpose, goals, and values* statements, which was done explicitly in the NUKA-System, and less formally in the EDARP-System which is guided by its Christian values system. The Brazilian approach to curtailing a HIV/AIDS epidemic in contrast is *explicitly goal driven* and was able to galvanise agents across different "Government and non-Government subsystems" to embrace the goals for the sake of the well-being of the whole community.

As each system emerged over time its *purpose and values* remained unchanged, what changed were its specific goals in light of newly identified needs. This is most obvious in the EDARP-System and resulted in the sustainable growth of the system and the expansion of services offered.

References

1. Lehmann U, Sanders D (2007) Community health workers: what do we know about them? World Health Organisation, Geneva
2. Chen L, Evans T, Anand S, Boufford JI, Brown H, Chowdhury M et al (2004) Human resources for health: overcoming the crisis. The Lancet 364(9449):1984–1990
3. Sturmberg JP, Njoroge A (2017) People-centered health systems, a bottom-up approach. J Eval Clin Pract 23(2):467–473
4. Glouberman S, Zimmerman B (2002) Complicated and complex systems: what would successful reform of medicare look like? Discussion Paper No 8. Commission on the Future of Health Care in Canada, Ottawa
5. Gottlieb K (2013) The Nuka System of Care: improving health through ownership and relationships. Int J Circumpolar Health 72. doi:10.3402/ijch.v72i0.21118
6. Collins B (2015) Intentional whole health system redesign. Southcentral Foundation's 'Nuka' system of care. King's Fund, London
7. Warner JJ How our community designed a better hospital. www.catalyst.nejm.org/how-our-community-designed-a-better-hospital/
8. Kings Fund (2015) The Kings fund - ideas that change health care - Nuka system of care Alaska. Available from: www.kingsfund.org.uk/publications/population-health-systems/nuka-system-care-alaska

Chapter 8
Leadership: Working Together Effectively and Efficiently to Achieve a Common Purpose

Overview. As Heifetz and colleagues put it: "*People have long confused the notion of leadership with authority, power and influence. We find it extremely useful to see leadership as a practice, an activity that some people do some of the time*". In their words, true leadership entails that "*leaders facilitate the necessary adaptive work that needs to be done by the people connected to the problem*".

The role of leaders and their leadership is to solve the *complex* problems facing their organisation. Such *complex* problems are often referred to as *wicked*; they span disciplines and organisations, and create constant tension amongst stakeholders and their objectives. Rittel characterised complex/wicked problems as exhibiting the following characteristics:

- Many wicked problems are only be fully understood after we have found a solution for the problem
- Wicked problems rarely can be truly solved, one is forced to live with the outcome one has achieved when one's resources run out
- Solutions to wicked problems are neither right nor wrong, the judgement of a solution depends on a stakeholder's inherent values and goals
- Every wicked problem is unique and novel, it will never again be experienced in this particular way
- Every solution to a wicked problem is a "one shot operation", you cannot solve a wicked problem without trying a solution, but every solution has potentially unintended consequences giving rise to new wicked problems
- Wicked problems have no alternative solutions, an applied solution is the one out of many possible ones chosen and implemented based on its stakeholders' judgement

The nature of today's problems has created a *VUCA world*, a world of **V**olatility, **U**ncertainty, **C**omplexity and **A**mbiguity.

How do we best manage the *wicked problems* of our *VUCA world*? The most crucial step in managing these type of problems is to *recognise* and *accept* that the prevailing linear approaches to solve *wicked problems* in a *VUCA world* are

© Springer International Publishing AG 2018
J.P. Sturmberg, *Health System Redesign*, DOI 10.1007/978-3-319-64605-3_8

themselves a hindrance to solving wicked problems. Wicked problems cannot be solved by a single person, they require a collaborative approach. *VUCA problems* require *VUCA approaches*, approaches of **V**ision, **U**nderstanding, **C**larity and **A**gility.

Learning, the *creation* and *transfer of knowledge*, is the only way to manage wicked problems. As Alvin Toffler put it: *"The illiterate of the 21st century will not be those who cannot read & write, but those who cannot learn, unlearn and relearn."* We are all leaders some of time, hence, we all have to learn that:

- We cannot command but have to seek the knowledge of our collaborators
- We always know more than we can say, and we always can say more than we can write. Written knowledge is reflective knowledge, valuable but not pragmatic in circumstances where decisions have to be made
- Knowledge is deeply contextual; we only readily retrieve our most important knowledge when demanded by circumstances

Leaders thus have to *learn* to lead and *unlearn* to prescribe solutions. Ron Heifetz described leadership as: *leaders facilitate the necessary adaptive work that needs to be done by the people connected to the problem.* Adaptive leaders *allow others to grow*, they:

- Give permission to experiment
- View failure as an opportunity for individuals and the organisation to learn
- Learn about the multiple realities that people experience in various parts of the organisation

Leading an organisation and facilitating its members' adaptive work requires an understanding of the "organisation as a whole", in particular that:

- An organisation is composed of many interdependent parts that *all work towards a common goal*
- The 80/20 rule applies, not all system/organisational components are equally capable or equally crucial to achieve its *common goals*
- An organisation's constraints limit its ability to achieve its common goals. Leaders need to focus their organisation's resources on those constraints as the most affective means towards achieving its *common goals*

Organisations with adaptive leadership:

- Create trust amongst all members
- Facilitate personal and organisational sense-making
- Maintain a focus on the organisation's purpose, goals and values
- Have a deeper understanding of the *organisation as a whole*, have a focus on understanding problems within their context, and appreciate the importance of the organisation's culture

Points for Reflection

- What is leadership?
- What are different approaches to leadership?
- Is there a difference between leaders and managers? If so, what are the differences?
- How can leaders "direct without directions"?
- How do adaptive leaders solve conflict in their organisation?
- Who is in control at each level?
- Who is in control of the *organisation as a whole*?
- How does control affect the overall function of the organisation?

"Ultimately, leadership is not about glorious crowning acts. It's about keeping your team focused on a goal and motivated to do their best to achieve it, especially when the stakes are high and the consequences really matter. It is about laying the groundwork for others' success, and then standing back and letting them shine"

Chris Hadfield (born 1959) - Canadian astronaut

"I suppose leadership at one time meant muscles; but today it means getting along with people"

Mahatma Gandhi (1869–1948) - Indian leader

"Management is doing things right, leadership is doing the right things"

Peter Drucker (1909–2005) - American management consultant and philosopher

These three quotes characterise the nature of leadership—leading as the *"improvisational dynamic process of moving forward"* around a common cause [1–7]. Thus, the main task of leading is to focus people's mindset on the organisation's common cause and goals. This ensures that people work together to solve the organisation's problems effectively and efficiently; after all, together we can achieve more than we can as individuals.

8.1   Understanding Our Complex Adaptive World

The twentieth century has seen an unprecedented growth in social interactions and knowledge exchange. While these developments have achieved tremendous growth in societal and economic developments, they also have uncovered the nature of the complex social networks that allowed the emergence of this complex adaptive world. This world can be described by the acronym *VUCA* [8], and its challenges as *wicked problems* [9].

8.1.1   VUCA

During the 1990s it became more obvious that we live in a challenging and unpredictable world. The US military [8] first attempted to better understand and navigate the challenges in unpredictable environments. These environments are defined by characteristics summarised by the acronym *VUCA*:

Volatility—the dynamics of change; volatility arises from the ever changing nature and rate of change

Uncertainty—the lack of predictability; current situation and future outcomes are unclear

Complexity—results from the multiplicity of interdependent key decision factors; complex situations have no cause-and-effect relationships to explain them

Ambiguity—the haziness of reality; ambiguity reflects the lack of clarity about the meaning of a current event, often resulting from cause-and-effect confusion

8.1.2   Wicked Problems

Problems in a complex adaptive world are mostly ill-defined and have been characterised by Rittel [9] as *wicked problems.*[1] Its key characteristics are:

- *You don't understand the problem until you have developed a solution*
  "One cannot understand the problem without knowing about its context; one cannot meaningfully search for information without the orientation of a solution concept; one cannot first understand, then solve." [10]
- *Wicked problems have no stopping rule*
  The problem-solving process ends when you run out of resources, such as time, money, or energy, not when some optimal or "final and correct" solution emerges.
- *Solutions to wicked problems are not right or wrong*
  Solutions are assessed in a social context in which *"many parties are equally equipped, interested, and/or entitled to judge* [them]," [10] and these judgements are likely to vary widely and depend on the stakeholder's independent values and goals.
- *Every wicked problem is essentially unique and novel*
  There are so many factors and conditions, all embedded in a dynamic social context, that no two wicked problems are alike, and the solutions to them will always be custom designed and fitted.
- *Every solution to a wicked problem is a "one-shot operation"*
  You can't learn about the problem without trying solutions, but every solution you try is expensive and has lasting unintended consequences which are likely to spawn new wicked problems.
- *Wicked problems have no given alternative solutions*
  There may be no solutions, or there may be a host of potential solutions that are devised, and another host that are never even thought of. Thus, it is a matter of creativity to devise potential solutions, and a matter of judgement to determine which are valid and which should be pursued and implemented.

---

[1]The term was first introduced by Horst Rittel in a seminar at the University of California Architecture Department in 1967.

8.2   Shifting Mindsets to Cope in a Complex Adaptive World

One needs to distinguish between leaders (the person and his/her attributes) and leadership (the activities undertaken by a leader). Heifetz and colleagues describe the difference this way: *"People have long confused the notion of leadership with authority, power and influence. We find it extremely useful to see leadership as a practice, an activity that some people do some of the time"* [11].

It is unavoidable that people in any organisation are constantly confronted with emerging problems. The old way of looking for an "of-the-shelf solution" [6] rarely works (and often fail spectacularly despite huge amounts of effort and cost). Emerging problems arise in a local context and require local solutions. Those affected by the problem need the organisation's support to find the best possible solutions in the context of their local constraints.

Solutions arise in your mind. Finding novel solutions requires imagination. Design thinking [12, 13] taps into people's imaginative space—new solutions emerge within a framework of "what ought to be done" and "what can be done given our constraints".

The challenge for leaders is to understand the prevailing mindsets in their organisation. Is this mindset conducive to solving the problems the organisation faces? If not, how can we help our members to explore and change their mindsets?

Leaders are confronted with at least three significant challenges in influencing the thinking of individuals:

- Reductionism and its consequences (see extended quote by Mark Beresford on the lessons from medical reductionism in Addendum 1)

   For the past 300 years our thinking is firmly entrenched in Descartes doctrines. He proposed that the only sound thinking practice when confronted with a problem was to isolate the constituent parts of a phenomenon from each other and their environment. The process of reduction, simplification, and clarification is based on a disjunctive logic of "either/or".

   This pattern of thinking has become firmly entrenched in Western society—it embraces reductive thinking (applied and promoted by the "evidence-based medicine movement"). Reductive thinking disregards ambiguity, ignores inter-dependence, and rejects outright any observable paradoxes [14].

   Reductionist thinking fostered the growth of hierarchical organisational bureaucracies. Managers were given tools to isolate and categorise tasks and decisions, in their mind organisations deal with:

   - separable and thus independent units
   - cause-and-effect have linear relationships
   - relationships are reversible
   - the behaviour of the organisation is knowable
   - an organisation's future is predictable

- Creating complexity mindsets (see extended quote on the frames and habits of mind for complexity thinkers by Kevin Rogers et al. in Addendum 2)

Rogers et al. [14] outlined how to create complexity mindsets for a VUCA world [8]. The missing element is guidance on how to apply this complexity mindset to solving challenging problems. One proposal suggests to see VUCA also as an acronym to approach the wicked problems [15]:

Volatility becomes **Vision**
jointly working together to create a shared future; requires clear communication and assurance that all stakeholders understand the intended outcomes

Uncertainty becomes **Understanding**
requires all to take a break, look, and listen, it is the prerequisite for building trust; requires flexibility

Complexity becomes **Clarity**
facilitates sense-making when people see a confusing (chaotic) picture; requires collaboration and an acceptance that solutions are always only temporary

Ambiguity becomes **Agility**
success arises from collaborative (network) rather than rigid hierarchical approaches; requires listening and acceptance of diverse solutions

- Facilitating the necessary adaptive work that needs to be done (see extended quote on the characteristics of adaptive work in clinical care by Ron Heifetz in Addendum 3)

The role of leaders and their leadership is to solve often rather *complex problems*. Complex problems span disciplines and elegant "single discipline" "reductionist solutions" no longer provide solutions.

As the plate poignantly illustrates, the main leadership task in an uncertain world is that of making sense of the problem in this context at this point in time.

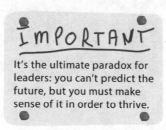

It's the ultimate paradox for leaders: you can't predict the future, but you must make sense of it in order to thrive.

Making sense of a problem and finding the best possible solution requires leaders who, in Ron Heifetz's words [1], "*facilitate the necessary adaptive work that needs to be done by the people connected to the problem*".

Leaders are challenged by the complexities of their organisations (Fig. 8.1). These complexities can be explored in terms of *how we think* and *how we act*. Most importantly leaders need to appreciate that most of the knowledge about the organisations resides with their frontline workers and their supervisors. Engaging every member of the organisation will create a *learning organisation* capable of solving its challenges in a complex world.

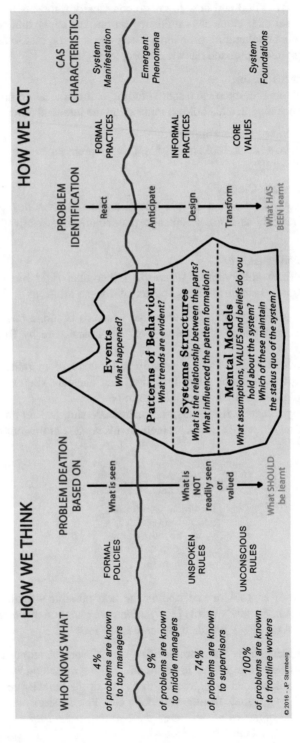

Fig. 8.1 The iceberg metaphor of knowledge in an organisation. Top level managers don't know the majority of problems encountered by the members of the organisations. Their responses typically are reactive rather than explorative

8.3 Learning and Adapting in a Complex Adaptive World

Reiterating Heifetz and colleagues' point: *"People have long confused the notion of leadership with authority, power and influence. We find it extremely useful to see leadership as a practice, an activity that some people do some of the time"* [11].

True leadership, Ron Heifetz [1] concluded, means *"leaders facilitat*[ing] *the necessary adaptive work that needs to be done by the people connected to the problem"*.

For leaders to succeed in our *VUCA world* they have to focus their leadership on the facilitation of organisational learning. Collaborative learning ensures that one finds the most adaptive responses to the many challenges in our environment.

8.3.1 Learning: The Generation and Transfer of Knowledge

Succeeding in an ever changing world demands constant learning. As Alvin Toffler[2] put it: *"The illiterate of the 21st century will not be those who cannot read & write, but those who cannot learn, unlearn and relearn."*

Learning is a complex dynamic process. It entails the generation as well as the transfer of knowledge. Knowledge itself has to be de-constructed. In short:

- One has to distinguish "knowing what"—naming facts and relationships—from "knowing how"—explaining procedures [16]
- One also has to distinguish *explicit* knowledge which can be codified and easily communicated, from *tacit* knowledge [16] which cannot be codified and therefore cannot be easily passed on to others

  Polanyi [16] described *tacit knowledge* as "personal knowing"—in part arising from one's wealth of experience, in another arising from one's cognitive mindset of beliefs, perceptions, ideals, values, emotions, and mental models.

Knowledge transfer has its own dynamics which have been described by Snowden:

1. *Knowledge can only be volunteered; it cannot be conscripted for the very simple reason that I can never truly know if someone is using his or her knowledge. I can know they have complied with a process or a quality standard. But, we have trained managers to manage conscripts not volunteers.*
2. *We can always know more than we can tell, and we will always tell more than we can write down. The nature of knowledge is such that we always know, or are capable of knowing more than we have the physical time or the conceptual ability to say. I can speak in five minutes what it will otherwise take me two weeks to get round to spend a couple of hours writing it down. The process of writing*

---

[2]American writer and futurist (1928–2016).

something down is reflective knowledge; it involves both adding and taking away from the actual experience or original thought. Reflective knowledge has high value, but is time consuming and involves loss of control over its subsequent use.

3. *We only know what we know when we need to know it, human knowledge is deeply contextual, it is triggered by circumstance. In understanding what people know we have to recreate the context of their knowing if we to ask a meaningful question or enable knowledge use. To ask someone what he or she knows is to ask a meaningless question in a meaningless context, but such approaches are at the heart of mainstream consultancy method [23].*

The most important facets of knowledge generation and knowledge transfer, i.e. learning, are summarised in Table 8.1. It highlights how we learn and it emphasises why we may encounter difficulties in learning and adapting for rapidly changing environments.

8.3.2   Understanding Change and Change Management in Organisations: The Cynefin Change Management Framework

Organisations are complex adaptive social systems. Like all systems, they consist of many subsystems each having a particular focus and a specific role in the overall system. Each part of the system involves a number of people with different attitudes, skills, goals and so forth to contribute to the overall function of the organisation.

Organisational research identified that not all problems faced by an organisation are equally difficult, some can be solved straight away on the spot, others take some research to solve, and some appear insurmountable.

As described in Chap. 3, Kurtz and Snowden [24] developed the Cynefin[3] framework to classify the dynamic patterns of interaction in complex adaptive organisations. The Cynefin framework visualises the nature (matter and context) of the different problems according to their level of comprehensibility. It allows all members of an organisation to see which approach to problem solving is most appropriate, and who in the organisation is best able to deal with a particular issue (Fig. 8.2).

Accordingly [23]:

- Problems of the "obvious domain" are solved by *best practice* approaches
- Problems of the "complicated domain" can be solved by *expert practice*
- Problems of the "complex domain" demand *emergent practice*
- Problems of the "chaotic domain" require *novel practice* approaches

---

[3]Pronounced /'kʌnɪvɪn/; (English pronunciation spelling: kun-EV-in) a Welsh word meaning "habitat" or "place of belonging".

Table 8.1 Four learning frameworks that help to shift world views (for details see Rogers [14])

Learning framework	Key concepts	Implementation
Explicit/Tacit Knowledge Framework (Polanyi [17])	• Explicit knowledge can be transferred • Tacit knowledge is personal and difficult to transmit	• Transfer of tacit knowledge is about negotiating meaning between individuals/stakeholders
Unlearning Selective Exposure (Cohen and Levinthal [18]; Miller and Morris [19])	• Learning patterns are strongly influenced by prior knowledge (learning)	• Narrowly focused knowledge experts exhibit difficulties to see what else has emerged in other fields and • have to actively unlearn before being able to learn something new
Conscious/competence learning matrix (Howell [20])	Four stages of learning • *Unconscious incompetence*—They don't know that they don't know! • *Conscious incompetence*—They know they don't know! • *Conscious competence*—They know they know! • *Unconscious competence*—They don't know they know!	• The reflective learner—people *consciously challenge their assumed knowledge* with the view of finding gaps in their knowledge that need to be filled (the proposed fifth stage of learning)
Learning loops model (Argyris and Schön [21]; Raelin [22])	• *Single-loop learning*—practical knowing • *Double-loop learning*—propositional knowing • *Triple-loop learning*—dialectical knowing	• Actions are based on *general rules of thumb*—arise from reductionism[a] • Actions are based on acknowledging *context sensitivity* of knowledge—reflects pseudo-complexity • Actions are based on reflection of *underlying assumptions*—lived complexity

[a]Morin linked the three types of learning loops to reductionism, pseudo-complexity, and lived complexity [Morin, E. 2008. *On complexity* [33]]

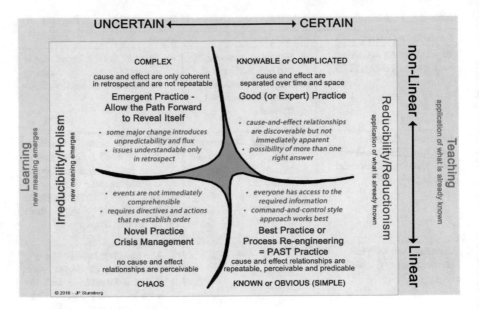

Fig. 8.2 Approaching problems according to their "place of belonging"

The Cynefin framework provides leaders with a tool to more successfully manage the multiple dynamics within an organisation [24]. As is well known, most problems arise from "being stuck" with "familiar/proven ways" of handling everyday problems. This familiarity of "doing things" prevents many to see arising problems, which, when finally seen, are often of a catastrophic nature.

Pre-empting the emergence of catastrophic problems demands the skilful management of organisational dynamics. While breaking undesirable structures and practices creates uncertainty and anxiety, it nevertheless is a prerequisite to allow the emergence of new and better adapted ones in a changing environment. Figures 8.3 and 8.4 summarise the sources contributing to the dynamics of change in organisations and alludes to possible management strategies.

8.3.3   Managing System Constraints

Goldratt [25] emphasised that *every system is built for a purpose*. It is of utmost importance to recognise that *any action* taken by *any one* in *any part* of the system/organisation must be judged on *its impact on the system's global goal*.

Constraints in a system are all things—physical resources as much as the level of staff and their skill sets as well as internal policies—that *limit the system from achieving its global goals*.

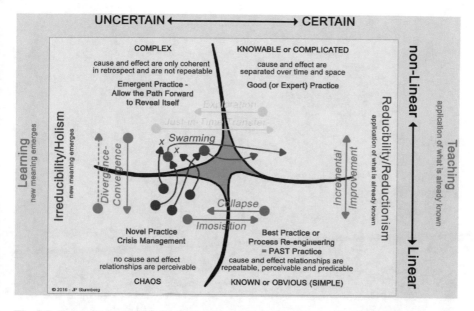

Fig. 8.3 Dynamics in the Cynefin framework (adopted from Kurtz and Snowden [24]). **Moving between spaces**. Movement from known and chaos—*asymmetric collapse* (usually a disaster), and chaos to known—*imposition* (forcing order). Repeated movement at the known-knowable boundary—*incremental improvement* (promotes technological advancement). Movement between the knowable and complex—*exploration* (generation of new ideas), and complex to knowable—just-in-time transfer (passing new knowledge when required). Movement from the chaotic to the complex to the knowable—*swarming* (can be emergent and selective; the most productive way to restore new order). Repeated movement at the chaotic-complex boundary—*divergence-convergence* (disruption in the innovation space)

How then can one manage system constraints? Goldratt described a five step process (for an extended quote on system constraints by Goldratt see Addendum 4):

- **Identify the system's constraints**—when identified they need to be prioritised in terms of their impact on the system's global goal as they are the factors that limit the whole system
- **Decide how to exploit the system's constraints**—allow the non-constraints to supply everything the constraints require
- **Subordinate everything else to the above decision**—whatever the constraint, there must be ways to limit its impact
- **Elevate the system's constraints**—if we maintain the focus on a constraint for long enough it will break and no longer limit the function of the system, however, new constraints will emerge
- **If in the previous steps a constraint has been broken, go back to step one, but do not allow inertia to cause a system constraint**

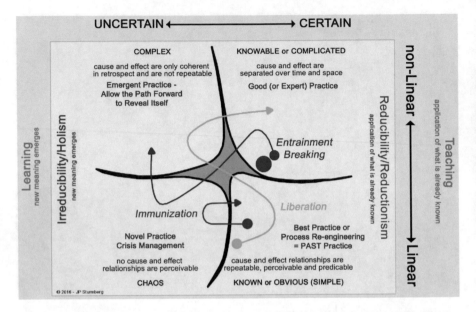

Fig. 8.4 Dynamics in the Cynefin framework (adopted from Kurtz and Snowden [24]). **Visiting the chaotic space to break up rigid structures**. Periodic movement from the knowable to the chaotic to the complex—*entrainment breaking* (disrupting entrained thinking of experts). Periodic movement from the known to the complex to the knowable—*liberation* (engaging both internal and external contacts to allow new patterns to emerge). Temporary movement from the known to the chaotic—*immunisation* (stir up things enough to cause reflection without destabilisation)

Leaders must be aware that managing constraints involves psychological work (as Heifetz also emphasised)—eliminating system constraints entails change, and change threatens the *emotional security* of the status quo.

8.4   Leading: The *Improvisational Dynamic Process of Moving Forward*

There is an important distinction between leadership (the activities undertaken by a leader) and leaders (the person and his/her attributes). As Heifetz and colleagues pointed out: "*People have long confused the notion of leadership with authority, power and influence.*" [11].

The emphasis of leadership is shifting towards the process of leading,[4] where leading is the "*improvisational dynamic process of moving forward*" around a common cause [1–3, 5–7].

---

[4]The emphasis here is on the verb—the process of leading, not the noun—leadership as a quality of competence.

Table 8.2 The difference between leaders and managers

Leaders ...	Managers ...
Create a vision	Create goals
Are change agents	Maintain the status quo
Are unique	Copy
Take risks	Control risk
Are in it for the long haul	Think short-term
Grow personally	Rely on existing, proven skills
Build relationships	Build systems and processes
Coach	Direct
Create fans	Have employees

Compiled from: William Arruda. Nine differences between being a leader and a manager https://www.forbes.com/sites/williamarruda/2016/11/15/9-differences-between-being-a-leader-and-a-manager/#1e1997fe4609

8.4.1   Leading an Organisation

A prerequisite for leading an organisation and facilitating its members' adaptive work is an understanding of the "organisation as a whole", in particular that:

- The organisation is composed of many interdependent parts that *all work towards a common goal*
- The 80/20 rule applies, not all system/organisational components are equally capable or equally crucial to achieve its common goals
- The organisation's constraints limit its ability to achieve its common goals thus focussing the organisation's resources on constraints will be the biggest step towards achieving its common goals

8.4.2   Leaders Lead, Managers Manage

While the terms leadership and management are frequently used interchangeably, there are important distinctions between the two. Leadership deals with people, managers deal with "things"; the differences are summarised in Table 8.2.

8.4.3   Leading a Complex Adaptive Organisation

Not all complex dynamic systems have equal capacity to adapt and evolve. Highly ordered systems—like very bureaucratic organisations—are too rigid and resistant to adaptive change. Highly chaotic systems—organisations without a defined purpose—have too few stable components to cope with even small additional disruptions and tend to fail, as they have too few stable components to buffer them, and small forces tend to result in system disruption [26].

Complex adaptive systems—organisations with a well-defined purpose, goals, and values—sit in between these two extremes. It is the *common cause of an organisation* that defines its identity and *must reside in the heads and hearts of its members. Thus, in the absence of an externalised bureaucratic structure, it becomes more important to have an internalised cognitive structure of what the organisation stands for and where it intends to go—in short, a clear sense of the organisation's identity. A sense of identity serves as a rudder for navigating difficult waters* [27].

Leading an adaptive organisation means *engaging people in solving problems.*[5] Leaders understand that they cannot prescribe solutions as each problem is unique, and that the attempt to transfer a solution from one context to another is usually unsuccessful. Such attempts stifle progress as they fail to promote the accumulation and sharing of knowledge [6].

Successful leaders of adaptive organisations provide permission to experiment and they view failures as an opportunity for individuals and the organisation as a whole to learn [5, 6, 26]. Their engagement in the problem-solving process will elicit the multiple realities experienced by people in various positions, a prerequisite to facilitate an understanding of people's various positions (sense-making). In such an open-minded environment people will approach the necessary work to find the best possible solution for each challenge [1, 5–7, 28].

---

[5]In a recent blog post *Wisdom and Wei* emphasised five key features that support teams in successfully solving their problems:

1. **Psychological safety:** Can team members take risks by sharing ideas and suggestions without feeling insecure or embarrassed? Do team members feel supported, or do they feel as if other team members try to undermine them deliberately? (for more detail see: Amy Edmondson. *Psychological safety and learning behaviour in a work team.* Administrative Science Quarterly 1999;44(2):350–383)
2. **Dependability:** Can each team member count on the others to perform their job tasks effectively? When team members ask one another for something to be done, will it be? Can they depend on fellow teammates when they need help?
3. **Structure and clarity:** Are roles, responsibilities, and individual accountability on the team clear?
4. **Meaning of work:** Is the team working towards a goal that is personally important for each member? Does work give team members a sense of personal and professional fulfillment?
5. **Impact of work:** Does the team fundamentally believe that the work they're doing matters? Do they feel their work matters for a higher-order goal?

http://catalyst.nejm.org/psychological-safety-great-teams/?utm_campaign=
Connect+Weekly&utm_source=hs_email&utm_medium=email&utm_content=
36496976&_hsenc=p2ANqtz--eeQgbmqpLIQPE_OySPUfa6_\penalty-
\@MBvLkSywiWU2Z3tIP3j6HCZFMOApROrD1fZRbnWlqRXTRrpy\penalty-
\@M_wbt3GMQiS774f8DXeEQA&_hsmi=36496976.

8.5   Leaders of Adaptive Organisations

Leaders in a complex adaptive organisation are more like dandelions than banyans. Like a dandelion they nurture their surroundings to make it resilient and adaptive to challenges.

As Vivek Bapat put it: *"Just as the dandelion helps other plants to flourish, leaders must focus not on expanding their own empires (in banyan-like fashion) but on allowing others to thrive"* [29] (Fig. 8.5).

This brief overview emphasises four key aspects about the nature of leadership in complex adaptive organisations—*adaptive* leadership:

- *Creates trust*—does every person understand the common frame of reference for decision-making. Leaders ensure that this common frame is adhered to when facing significant challenges
- *Facilitates sense-making*—how do those affected understand the problem and how do they see the solution, thus breaking down "traditional" power relationships
- *Maintains a focus on the organisation's purpose, goals, and values*[6]—which of the possible envisaged solutions best align with these
- *Understands the "system as a whole", focuses on understanding problems within the local context and appreciates the importance of local culture*—what is the unique context of the problem and how will this context shape the "most adapted" solution for the "organisation as a whole". Large "whole system" problems often have multiple, mutually agreeable, solutions (there is no place for one-size fits all solution thinking)

Leadership in complex adaptive organisations clearly is much more demanding and slower but more effective in *solving problems for good* so that one can move on into new territory rather than having to revisit the same issues again and again over time. As Yogi Berra said: *"If you don't know where you're going, when you get there you'll be lost."*

Nonaka provided a thoughtful *comparison between three different leadership approaches* that have been summarised in Table 8.3—each has a context-dependent place in managing an organisation.

---

[6]"Actors act intelligently when they show an understanding of the relationship between I and their context" (Hosking D and Fineman S. Organizing processes [34].) and "Intelligent social action can come into play when the context is perceived to be such that existing rules and procedures are not working; the intelligent social action is to ignore the existing context and work to create a new one in which values will be more relevant and meaningful" (Hosking D (1988) Organizing, leadership and skilful process [34], as cited in Fulop [Fulop L and Mark A. Relational leadership, decision-making and the messiness of context in healthcare [28]].)

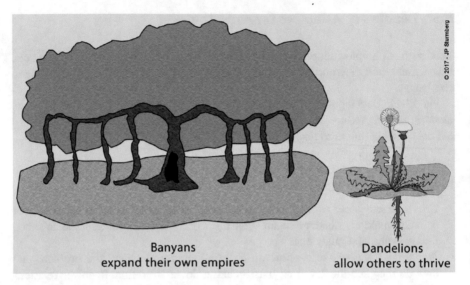

Banyans
expand their own empires

Dandelions
allow others to thrive

Fig. 8.5 Why the Lowly Dandelion Is a Better Metaphor for Leaders than the Mighty Banyan
"There are good reasons the metaphor is so popular. Like the banyan, many well-regarded leaders get their start by capitalising on a nascent opportunity. Similar to the branches and roots of the banyan, they flourish by surrounding themselves with like-spirited colleagues, bonding around the core. They successfully expand their span of control outward from the centre, gathering more influence over time.

However, the same attributes that spawn initial success also expose some intrinsic flaws. As the banyan's roots grow out from the centre, into what resembles a formidable trunk, it completely surrounds and suffocates the original host tree, leaving a hollow core at the centre. Correspondingly, leaders who grow their influence like the great banyan can unwittingly smother the initial spark of innovation and disruptive thinking at the core of an organisation's ethos - that magic that made it successful in the first place.

In stark contrast to the banyan is a small weed that lives an unremarkable, fleeting life - the dandelion.

But ...could the small, frail dandelion ...offer a better metaphor for modern day leadership? Dandelions fall under a class known as beneficial weeds, which help the plants around them. Dandelions do this by sending taproots deep into the ground. These taproots pull nutrients up to the surface, improving the quality of the soil and feeding shallow-rooted plants nearby. Dandelions also attract insects that enable pollination, like bees, which help other flowering plants. Plants that might not otherwise have a chance to germinate or survive get a shot at life because of the nutrients and insects that dandelions send their way. Yes, dandelions are prolific and fight for territory, but they don't grow large and they fade quickly after blooming, giving other species a chance to thrive. They may not be the showiest plants, but they leave the environment a better place." Vivek Bapat [29]

Table 8.3 Comparison of management approaches [30, 31]

	Top-down	Complex adaptive (middle-up and down)	Bottom-up
Agent of knowledge	Top management	Self-organising teams lead by middle managers	"Entrepreneurial/charismatic" individual within a group
Type of knowledge	Explicit	Tacit/explicit	Tacit
	Documented	Shared in diverse forms	Wisdom of the crowds, promulgated by individual/s
Management process	Leaders as commanders	Leaders as catalysts	Leaders as sponsors
Style …	Hands off	Hands on and off	Hands on
Context …	Within headquarters	Among designated people within a group	Volunteers within a group
Emphasis on …	Information processing	Creating organisational knowledge	Creating personal information
Fosters …	Hierarchical subservience	Emergence	Self-organisation/Emergence
Order …	Avoid chaos at all costs	Purposefully create/amplify chaos to generate new perspectives	Chaos is assumed and "order of some kind" will emerge
Synergies …	Focus on money	Focus on knowledge	Focus on people
Problems …	Analysis paralysis	Exhaustion	Inductive ambiguity
	High dependency on top management	Lack of overall control of the organisation	Time consuming, difficult to coordinate individuals

References

1. Heifetz R (1994) Leadership without easy answers. Harvard University Press, Cambridge, MA
2. Mintzberg H (1998) Cover leadership: notes on managing professionals. Knowledge workers respond to inspiration not supervision. Harv Bus Rev 76(6):140–147
3. Pye A (2005) Leadership and organizing: sensemaking in action. Leadership 1(1):31–49
4. Cheverton J (2007) Holding our own: value and performance in nonprofit organisations. Aust J Soc Issues 42(3):427–436
5. Ham C, Dixon A, Brooke B (2012) Transforming the delivery of health and social care. The case for fundamental change. King's Fund, London
6. Seelos C, Mair J (2012) Innovation is not the holy grail. Stanf Soc Innov Rev 10(4):44–49
7. Lindberg C, Schneider M (2013) Combating infections at maine medical center: insights into complexity-informed leadership from positive deviance. Leadership 9(2):229–253
8. Stiehm JH (2002) The U.S. army war college: military education in a democracy. Temple University Press, Philadelphia
9. Conklin E, Weil W (2005) Wicked problems: naming the pain in organizations. www.touchstone.com/tr/wp/wicked.html. Accessed 20 Sept 2005
10. Rittel HWJ, Webber MM (1973) Dilemmas in a general theory of planning policy sciences. Pol Sci 4(2):155–169
11. Heifetz R, Grashow A, Linsky M (2009) The practice of adaptive leadership: tools and tactics for changing your organization and the World. Harvard Business Press, Boston, MA
12. Jones P (2013) Design for care: innovating healthcare experience. Rosenfeld Media, New York
13. Brown T (2008) Design thinking. Harv Bus Rev 86(6):84–92
14. Rogers KH, Luton R, Biggs H, Biggs R, Blignaut S, Choles AG et al (2013) Fostering complexity thinking in action research for change in social-ecological systems. Ecol Soc 18(2):31
15. Caron D (2009) It's a VUCA World. http://www.slideshare.net/dcaron/its-a-vuca-world-cips-cio-march-5-2009-draft. Accessed 23 Sept 2012
16. Polanyi M (1958) Personal knowledge. Towards a post-critical philosophy. Routledge, London
17. Polanyi M (1983) Tacit dimension. Peter Smith Publisher Inc., Gloucester, MA
18. Cohen WM, Levinthal DA (1990) Absorptive capacity: a new perspective on learning and innovation. Adm Sci Q 35(1):128–152
19. Miller WL, Morris L (1999) 4th generation R&D - managing knowledge, technology, and innovation. Wiley, New York
20. Howell WS (1982) The empathic communicator. Wadsworth Publishing Company, University of Minnesota, St. Paul, MN
21. Argyris C, Schön DA (1974) Theory in practice: increasing professional effectiveness. Jossey-Bass, California SF
22. Raelin JA (2001) Public reflection as the basis of learning. Manag Learn 32(1):11–30.
23. Snowden D (2002) Complex acts of knowing: paradox and descriptive self-awareness. J Knowl Manag 6(2):100–111
24. Kurtz CF, Snowden DJ (2003) The new dynamics of strategy: sense-making in a complex and complicated world. IBM Syst J 42(3):462–483
25. Goldratt EM (1990) What is this thing called THEORY OF CONSTRAINTS and how should it be implemented? The Northern River Press. Great Barrington, MA
26. Schneider M, Somers M (2006) Organizations as complex adaptive systems: implications of complexity theory for leadership research. Leadersh Q 17(4):351–365
27. Albert S, Ashforth BE, Dutton JE (2000) Organizational identity and identification: charting new waters and building new bridges. Acad Manage Rev 25(1):13–17
28. Fulop L, Mark A (2013) Relational leadership, decision-making and the messiness of context in healthcare. Leadership 9(2):254–277
29. Bapat V (2017) Why the lowly dandelion is a better metaphor for leaders than the mighty banyan. Harv Bus Rev Digital Articles 3/23/2017:2–4

30. Nonaka I (1988) Toward middle-up-down management: accelerating information creation. Sloan Manage Rev 29(3):9–18
31. Nonaka I (1994) A Dynamic Theory of Organizational Knowledge Creation. Organization Sci 5(1):14–37
32. Beresford MJ (2010) Medical reductionism: lessons from the great philosophers. Q J Med 103:721–724
33. Morin E (2008) On complexity. Hampton Press, New Jersey
34. Hosking D, Fineman S (1990) Organizing processes. J Manag Stud 27(6):583–604

Addendum 1

Medical Reductionism: Lessons from the Great Philosophers - Mark Beresford [32]

Recent years have seen significant improvements in the treatment of disease, many of which are the result of a better understanding of the intricate components and processes involved in cell biology. For example, our knowledge of cell proliferation pathways is becoming ever more detailed leading to the development of an increasing number of novel targeted therapies. Medicine is following a philosophy of "reductionism": deconstructing a complex process into its component parts to enable better comprehension. Although this approach has obvious advantages in that identifying specific component malfunctions might lead to more effective and less toxic treatments, there are potential dangers in becoming too reductionist in our philosophy. The advantages and disadvantages of reductionism have long been debated by philosophers and thinkers and there is much to learn by revisiting some of their arguments with reference to the field of medicine.

The History of Reductionism

The earliest reductionist philosopher was Thales, born around 636 BC at Miletus in Asia Minor. He hypothesised that the universe was made out of water-water being the fundamental substance of which all others were composed. Reductionism was later re-introduced by Descartes in Part V of his Discourses.[1] He suggested that the world was like a clockwork machine, which could be understood by taking it to pieces and studying the individual components. Reductionism has since developed to encompass at least three related but distinguishable themes: ontological, methodological, and epistemic. In biological science, ontological reductionism is the idea that each system is constituted by nothing but molecules and their interactions and also establishes a hierarchy of chemical, biological, and physical properties. Methodological reductionism is the idea that biological systems are most fruitfully investigated at the lowest possible level and epistemic reductionism suggests that knowledge of a higher domain can be always reduced down to a lower more fundamental level. In modern cancer research, it is often methodological reductionism that predominates.

There are, however, potential problems with a reductionist approach:

(i) Reductionism often arouses distrust: although reductionism aims to make things more intelligible, in reality the common understanding of the many tends to be replaced by the better understanding of the few. When a disease is explained in molecular and submolecular levels, it becomes difficult for the layperson to conceptualise. We see this in medical science, where even dedicated researchers are unable to have a full understanding of the cellular pathways outside of their immediate field of interest.

(ii) Reductionism risks oversimplification of a process: in reducing something down do we merely eliminate certain aspects from our description of it?

There becomes a point where the reduction becomes disassociated from the phenomenon it is trying to explain and exclusively reductionist research strategies can be systematically biased and overlook salient biological features. Again this is evident in medicine—although many "targeted" agents are now used in the clinic, it is fair to say that in most cases the benefits to patients have been relatively modest, despite sound theoretical principles and laboratory data.

(iii) Reductionist explanations can sometimes lead to confusion over cause and effect: this is the classic "chicken and egg" problem. For example, is a disordered proliferation pathway the cause or result of a malignancy—which came first? We may not be targeting the root cause of the problem.

1. Descartes R. The Philosophical Writings of Descartes in 3 vols. Translated by Cottingham J, Stoothoff R, Kenny A, Murdoch D. Cambridge, UK, Cambridge University Press, 1988.

Addendum 2

Frames and Habits of Mind for Complexity Thinkers - Kevin Rogers et al. [14]

We find that the most important competencies that enable effective use of this integrative learning framework are psychological. They are ways of thinking that allow one to unlearn reductionist habits while adopting and embedding those more conducive to working in complex systems. We have adapted the educational learning concept of "Habits of Mind" developed by Arthur Costa and colleagues (Costa 1991, Costa and Kallick 2008) to foster intelligent thinking in school children.

A habit of mind is a pattern of intellectual behaviour that leads to productive actions. Habits of mind are seldom used in isolation but rather in clusters that collectively present a pattern of behaviours. When people are confused by dilemmas, or come face-to-face with uncertainties, their response is determined by the patterns of intellectual behaviour upon which they can draw. This implies that people should maintain an awareness of, and make conscious choices about, which patterns of intellectual behaviour (habits of mind) are most appropriate to use under which circumstances. A certain level of competency is then required to use, carry out, and sustain the behaviours effectively, and also to reflect upon, evaluate, and modify them for future use under different conditions.

Moving one's self, or a group of stakeholders, from one position of competency to another is unlikely to happen unless thinking and doing are bounded by particular intellectual patterns. We recognise three broad frames of mind, each of which encompasses a set of habits of mind that are critical to leading participative planning and decision-making in complex social-ecological systems. These frames of mind are openness, situational awareness, and a healthy respect for, what we term, the restraint/action paradox.

Openness (See Text Box 1)

To embrace and effectively engage with complexity requires a certain psychological openness from individuals and institutions, especially when in transition from a predominantly reductionist paradigm. This openness can be described as a willingness to accept, engage with, and internalise the different perspectives, even paradigms, to be encountered when dealing with diverse participants in an interdisciplinary situation. An open frame of mind requires conscious acceptance that notions such as ambiguity, unpredictability, serendipity, and paradox will compete strongly, and legitimately, with knowledge, science, and fact. In essence, it means that while navigating challenges of a complex social-ecological system, one holds one's own strong opinions lightly (Pfeffer and Sutton 2006) and engages as both facilitator and learner.

Box 1: *Habits of mind that promote patterns of openness in behaviour*

- Hold your strong opinions lightly and encourage others to do the same
- Be prepared to identify and accept the intervention of surprise, serendipity, and epiphany
- Encounter every person with equal respect, listen for their specific needs, knowledge, and ways of knowing
- Be open to both/and options
- Do not reject ambiguity or paradox. They are to be expected and their acceptance as legitimate can often avoid dispute
- Cultivate, honor, and affirm the legitimacy of multiple perspectives and outcomes. Be ready to chart your way through them to learn about multiple legitimate outcomes: there are many ways of skinning the cat
- Accept everyone as colearners, not experts or competitors
- Encourage cooperation and consensus: the best way to get what you need is to help others get what they need

Situational Awareness (See Text Box 2)

One of the critical differences between complexity-based and reduction-based thinking is the importance of context and scale in complex systems. Each issue or system attribute can appear quite different, and interactions have quite different outcomes, under different contexts and at different scales (Levin 1998, Dollar et al. 2007). Spatial and historical context are very important, but so too are the different participants' value systems and how they lead to different outcomes. We use the acronym V-STEEP (Values—Social, Technical, Economic, Environmental, and Political) (Rogers and Luton 2011) to guide us when scoping context. An awareness of the complex context in which an adaptive challenge exists, and of how it changes in time and space, is critical to effectively navigating through it. In essence, one must cultivate a state of anticipatory awareness and constant mindfulness of the VSTEEP environment when navigating complex systems.

Box 2: *Habits of mind that promote patterns of situational awareness in behaviour*

- Discern when a change is sufficient to require renegotiation or review
- Consider the importance of relationships and interactions between entities and not just the entities themselves
- Become conscious of and accept change agents and processes
- Be time and place specific: without it you cannot properly identify the appropriate context or define problems and solutions

- Be aware of contingencies, scale, and history: they all play a role in mapping the present and the future
- Surface the collective principles and values that will bound decision situations and help keep decision-making consistent from one context to the next
- Use these principles to guide decision-making, rather than relying on facts and numbers, which will change with context
- Reflect often: formally, informally, individually, and collectively

---

A Healthy Respect for the Restraint/Action Paradox (See Text Box 3)

Leadership and decision-making in a complex system constitute a balance between the risks associated with practicing restraint and taking action. On the one hand, if the context requires it, one needs to consciously practice restraint and create space that allows the emergence of ideas, trust, opportunity, and even epiphany to loosen the tangled problem knot. There is a strong need for a certain slowness (Cilliers 2006) in taking time to allow emergence to unfold. On the other hand, one needs the courage to take action in a mist of uncertainty because, in a complex system, the consequences of our actions are never entirely predictable, and no matter how good our knowledge, there is never an objective "right" decision. Being conscious of, and comfortable with, this paradox is critical to successfully fostering and practicing adaptive leadership in social-ecological systems.

These three frames of mind are interdependent, with openness as the foundation or most critical one of the three as it can enable or constrain the other frames. To some extent, adequate situational awareness is not possible without openness to a diversity of perspectives. In a complex system, one simply cannot afford a one-sided perspective. Knowing when to act and when to practice restraint depends on one's awareness of changing dynamics in the system, but it also requires openness to the unexpected. The more specific habits of mind are more easily contextualised, remembered, and taught when grouped under these frames, but they are not confined to use under one frame. As one becomes more competent in their use, they are easily moved or modified from one context to the next. This list of habits is a living list that is continually honed as we learn more from explicitly applying complexity thinking to social-ecological problem situations.

Box 3: *Habits of mind that promote patterns of a healthy respect for the restraint/action paradox* Decisiveness/willingness to act under tension

- Encourage courage. Do not be afraid of intelligent mistakes
- Avoid paralysis from the paranoia of omission, and/or fear of simplicity
- Have the courage to seize the just-do-it moment
- Accept that there is no one right place to start or end. Do so when it is sensible and useful
- Have courage to take action from which you can learn. Even mistakes lead to learning
- Cultivate an awareness of the natural inclination to avoid discomfort and have the courage to push beyond it

Restraint under tension

- Discern when to trust the facilitation process and stand back quietly, giving the group dynamic space and allowing emergence
- Avoid premature convergence—avoid being too quick to make judgments and choices. Keep options on the table long past their apparent usefulness. Many will find context later in the process
- Avoid overconfidence about being ready to take action in a data-driven "predict and act" mode
- Know when to rest. Open and participatory engagement exposes vulnerabilities, requires humility, and takes energy
- Getting ahead of the game leaves participants unsettled and opens opportunities for dissent. Provide participants ample time for healing and replenishment

Cilliers, F. P. 2006. On the importance of a certain slowness. *Emergence: Complexity and Understanding* 8:106–113.Costa 1991

Costa, L., and B. Kallick. editors. 2008. *Learning and leading with habits of mind.* Product # 108008, Association for supervision and curriculum development, Alexandria, Virginia, USA.

Dollar, E. S. J., C. S. James, K. H. Rogers, and M. C. Thoms. 2007. A framework for interdisciplinary understanding of rivers as ecosystems. *Geomorphology* 89:147–162. http://dx.doi.org/10.1016/j.geomorph.2006.07.022

Levin, S. A. 1998. Ecosystems and the biosphere as complex adaptive systems. *Ecosystems* 1:431–436. http://dx.doi.org/10.1007/s100219900037

Pfeffer, J., and R. I. Sutton. 2006. Evidenced-based management. *Harvard Business Review* 84:62–74.

Rogers, K. H., and R. Luton. 2011. *Strategic adaptive management as a framework for implementing integrated water resources management in South Africa.* Report No. KV 245/10. Water Research Commission, Pretoria, South Africa.

Addendum 3

Leadership Without Easy Answers - Ronald Heifetz [1]

Distinguishing Adaptive from Technical Work (pp. 73–88)

The practice of medicine illustrates the distinction between technical and adaptive problems, and the dynamics these problems generate. Patients come to physicians with symptoms and signs of illness. They hope that their doctor will be able to "fix" the problem, but they do not know if their hopes are well-founded. Often, the physician can indeed cure the illness. If a person has an infection, there are many times when the physician can say, "I have an antibiotic medication that will almost definitely cure you without any effort or life adjustment needed on your part. The medication is virtually harmless. I can give you one shot, or a week of pills, whichever you prefer". For the purposes of our discussion, we can call these technical situations Type I-situations in which the patient's expectations are realistic: the doctor can provide a solution and the problem can be defined, treated, and cured on the basis of (1) using the doctor's expertise, and (2) shifting the patient's burden primarily onto the doctor's shoulders. The patient appropriately *depends* on the doctor's know-how, and the doctor *depends* on the patient's trust, satisfaction, and willingness to arrange payment.

These Type I situations are somewhat mechanical: one can actually go to somebody and "get it fixed". Many medical and surgical problems are of this sort, and many of them are life-saving. From the doctor's point of view, these provide gratifying moments when she can say, "Finally somebody has brought me a problem that I can solve!" Although the patient's cooperation is crucial in these situations, the weight of problem-defining and problem-solving rests with the physician. The patient looks to her to provide a prescription that at once will offer direction (take this medicine), protection (the medicine will overcome the infection), and order (you should be able to resume normal activity within the week).

Of course, many situations that bring people to doctors are not so technical. We can separate these adaptive situations into Types II and III. In Type II situations, the problem is definable but no clear-cut solution is available. The doctor may have a solution in mind, but she cannot implement it. And a solution that cannot be implemented is not really a solution; it is simply an idea, a proposal. The patient must create the solution in Type II situations, though the doctor may play a central role. Heart disease sometimes presents a Type II problem. The patient can be restored to more or less full operating capacity, but only if he takes responsibility for his health by making appropriate life adjustments. In particular, he will have to consider the doctor's prescriptions for long-term medication, exercise, diet program, and stress reduction. He will have to choose among these. Type II situations can be managed in a mechanical way only partially by the physician. She diagnoses and prescribes, but her recommendations will have side effects requiring the patient's evaluation of the tradeoffs. What new balance should he reach between cutting down the intensity of his job, getting exercise, or eating better? The patient has to recognise his own problem enough to provoke adaptive change. The responsibility for meeting the problem has to be shared.

In these situations, the doctor's technical expertise allows her to define the problem and suggest solutions that may work. But merely giving the patient a technical answer does not help the patient. Her prescribing must actively involve the patient if she is to be effective. The patient needs to confront the choices and changes that face him. The doctor's technical answers mean nothing if the patient does not implement them. Only he can reset the priorities of his life. He has to learn new ways. And the doctor has to manage the learning process in order to help the patient help himself. The dependency on authority appropriate to technical situations becomes inappropriate in adaptive ones. The doctor's authority still provides a resource to help the patient respond, but beyond her substantive knowledge, she needs a different kind of expertise—the ability to help the patient do the work that only he can do.

Type III situations are even more difficult. The problem definition is not clear-cut, and technical fixes are not available. The situation calls for leadership that induces learning when even the doctor does not have a solution in mind. Learning is required both to define problems and implement solutions. Chronic illness and impending death from any cause often fit this category. In these situations, the doctor can continue to operate in a mechanical mode by diagnosing and prescribing remedies (and a "remedy" of some sort can usually be found). Yet doing so avoids the problem-defining and problem-solving work of both doctor and patient.

In Type II and III situations, *treating the illness* is too narrow a way for the patient and the physician to define the task. It applies a technical formulation to a nontechnical problem. When critical aspects of the situation are probably unchangeable, the problem becomes more than the medical condition. For example, if the patient's diagnosis is an advanced stage of cancer in which the likelihood of cure is remote, it may be useless-indeed, a denial of reality-to define the primary problem as cancer. Cancer, in this case, is a *condition*. To the limited extent it can be treated at all, it is only part of the problem. To define cancer as the primary problem leads everyone involved to concentrate on finding solutions to the cancer, thus diverting their attention from the real work at hand. The patient's real work consists of facing and making adjustments to harsh realities that go beyond his health condition and that include several possible problems: making the most out of his life; considering what his children may need after he is gone; preparing his wife, parents, loved ones, and friends; and completing valued professional tasks. Table 1 summarises the characteristics of the three types of situations.

Table 1 Situational types

Situation	Problem definition	Solution and implementation	Primary locus of responsibility for the work	Kind of work
Type I	Clear	Clear	Physician	Technical
Type II	Clear	Requires learning	Physician and patient	Technical and adaptive
Type III	Requires learning	Requires learning	Patient > physician	Adaptive

Unfortunately, neither doctors nor patients are inclined to differentiate between technical and adaptive work. Indeed, the harsher the reality, the harder we look to authority for a remedy that saves us from adjustment. By and large, we want answers, not questions. Even the toughest individual tends to avoid realities that require adaptive work, searching instead for an authority, a physician, to provide the way out. And doctors, wanting deeply to fulfill the yearning for remedy, too often respond willingly to the pressures we place on them to focus narrowly on technical answers.

...

Implications

Although Plato set the precedent, analysing leadership with a medical metaphor presents some difficulties. Doctor-patient relationships differ fundamentally from the relations of business executives, politicians, and public managers to their respective constituencies. Large social systems like organisations or polities present the manager with substantially more complex patterns than does the doctor-patient dyad. In a medical setting, a problem will lack clarity because the patient has not yet reasoned and separated the problem into Type I and II components. In a complex social system, a problem will lack clarity because a multitude of factions will have divergent opinions about both the nature of the problem and its possible solutions. One faction's fix is another faction's adaptive challenge. Competing values are often at stake. Furthermore, in a large social system the scientific experts often disagree even on the fundamental outlines of a problem, particularly at the early stages of problem definition.[7] Each faction will have its own expert. For example, witness the public debate about so scientific a question as global warming. Does global warming present a problem needing attention? Which scientist should we trust?[8]

Moreover, in medical illness, the patient has the problem. But in organisational and public life, there will be many relevant parties to a problem, diffusing responsibility for it. The critical strategic question becomes: 'Whose problem is it? And the answer is not so obvious. For example, who should take responsibility for drug abuse: police, parents, schools, clergy, taxpayers' the army' or some combination of these?

Still, medicine and politics present similar dilemmas. ... First, an authority figure exercising leadership has to tell the difference between technical and adaptive situ-

---

[7]Robert Tucker suggests that "The validity of definitions of the situation may be a matter of degree. There is a possibility, theoretical if not practical in any particular case, of a more inclusive diagnosis that would make room for some, if not all, of the purposes and concerns of both sides." Tucker, *Politics as Leadership*, p. 53.

[8]See Thomas C. Schelling. "Climate Change: Implications for Welfare and Policy," in the National Academy of Sciences study, *Changing Climate: Report of the Carbon Dioxide Assessment Committee* (Washington, DC: National Academy Press, 1983), pp. 449–482; and more recently John Broome, *Counting the Cost of Global Warming* (Cambridge, England: White Horse Press, 1992), Chaps. 1 and 2, who refutes Schelling based on more recent scientific findings.

ations because they require different responses. She must ask the key differentiating question: *Does making progress on this problem require changes in people's values, attitudes, or habits of behaviour?* If people recognise the problem and can repeat a well-worked solution, then she can engage an authoritative response with practical efficiency and effect. ... In situations that call for adaptive work, however, social systems must learn their way forward. Even when an authority has some clear ideas about what needs to be done, implementing change often requires adjustments in people's lives.

Hence, with adaptive problems, authority must look beyond authoritative solutions. Authoritative action may usefully provoke debate, rethinking, and other processes of social learning, but then it becomes a tool in a strategy to mobilise adaptive work *towards* a solution, rather than a direct means to institute one. ...

As suggested, this requires a shift in mindset. When using authoritative provocation as part of a strategy, one must be prepared for an eruption of distress in response to the provocation and to consider early on the next step. One has to take the heat in stride, seeing it as part of the process of engaging people in the issue. In contrast, the mindset which views authoritative action as a solution to an adaptive problem would logically view an aggravated community *as* an extraneous complication to making headway, rather than an inherent part of making progress. Operating with that mindset, an authority figure would likely respond defensively and inappropriately when the community retaliates.

Second, ... having an authority relationship with people is both a resource for leadership and a constraint. Authority is a resource because it can provide the instruments and power to hold together and harness the distressing process of doing adaptive work. Authority is a constraint because it is contingent on meeting the expectations of constituents. Deviating from those expectations is perilous. ...

Third, as learning takes place, Type III situations may be broken down partially if not completely into Type II and Type I components. This involves both process and technical expertise. When an authority distinguishes conditions from problems, she can bring tractable issues to people's attention. By managing attention to issues instead of dictating authoritative solutions, she allows invention. People create and sort through alternative problem definitions, clarify value trade-offs, and test potential avenues of action. Creativity and courage can sometimes transform adaptive challenges into technical problems by expanding people's technical capabilities.

Addendum 4

The Five Steps of Focusing - Eliyahu Goldratt [25]

The message of this book is not bottlenecks or cutting batches. It's not even how to arrange the activities of the factory floor. As a matter of fact, the message is the same for any aspect of any company from product design and marketing to manufacturing and distribution. Everyone knows that the actions of marketing are guided by the concept of cost and margins, even more than the actions of production. And everyone knows that the best salesman in his/her company is the one who violates all the rules—which immediately implies that the rules in marketing are as wrong as those in manufacturing.

We grossly underestimate our intuition. Intuitively we do know the real problems, we even know the solutions. What is unfortunately not emphasised enough, is the vast importance of verbalising our own intuition. As long as we will not verbalise our intuition, as long as we do not learn to cast it clearly into words, not only will we be unable to convince others, we will not even be able to convince ourselves of what we already know to be right. If we don't bother to verbalise our intuition, we ourselves will do the opposite of what we believe in. We will "just play a lot of games with numbers and words." If we don't bother to verbalise our intuition, we ourselves will do the opposite of what we believe in. We will "just play a lot of games with numbers and words."

How do we listen to what we intuitively know to be right? How do we go about verbalising it?

The first step is to recognise that every system was built for a purpose. We didn't create our organisations just for the sake of their existence. Thus, every action taken by any organ—any part of the organisation—should be judged by its impact on the over-all purpose. This immediately implies that, before we can deal with the improvement of any section of a system, we must first define the system's global goal; and the measurements that will enable us to judge the impact of any subsystem and any local decision, on this global goal.

Once these are defined, we can describe the next steps in two different ways. One, in which we are using the terminology of the system that we are trying to improve. The other, using the terminology of the improvement process itself. We find that both descriptions are very helpful and only when both are considered together, does a non-distorted picture emerge.

How to sort out the important few from the trivial many? The key lies in the recognition of the important role of the system's constraints. A system's constraint is nothing more than what we all feel to be expressed by these words: anything that limits a system from achieving higher performance versus its goal. To turn this into a workable procedure, we just have to come to terms with the way in which our reality is constructed. In our reality any system has very few constraints (this is what is proven in The Goal, by the Boy-Scout analogy) and at the same time any system in reality must have at least one constraint. Now the first step is intuitively obvious:

1. Identify the System's Constraints.

Once this is accomplished—remember that to identify the constraints also means to prioritise them according to their impact on the goal, otherwise many trivialities will sneak in—the next step becomes self-evident. We have just put our fingers on the few things which are in short supply, short to the extent that they limit the entire system. So let's make sure that we don't waste the little that we have. In other words, step number two is:

2. Decide How to Exploit the System's Constraints.

Now that we decided how we are going to manage the constraints, how should we manage the vast majority of the system's resources, which are not constraints? Intuitively it's obvious. We should manage them so that everything that the constraints are going to consume will be supplied by the non-constraints. Is there any point in managing the non-constraints to supply more than that? This of course will not help, since the overall system's performance is sealed—dictated by the constraints. Thus the third step is:

3. Subordinate Everything Else to the Above Decision.

But let's not stop here. It's obvious we still have room for much more improvement. Constraints are not acts of God; there is much that we can do about them. Whatever the constraints are, there must be a way to reduce their limiting impact and thus the next step to concentrate on is quite evident.

4. Elevate the System's Constraints.

Can we stop here? Yes, your intuition is right. There will be another constraint, but let's verbalise it a little bit better. If we elevate and continue to elevate a constraint, then there must come a time when we break it. This thing that we have elevated will no longer be limiting the system. Will the system's performance now go to infinity? Certainly not. Another constraint will limit its performance and thus the fifth step must be:

5. If in the Previous Steps a Constraint Has Been Broken, Go Back to Step 1.

Unfortunately, we cannot state these five steps without adding a warning to the last one: "But Do Not Allow Inertia to Cause a System Constraint."

We cannot overemphasise this warning. What usually happens is that within our organisation, we derive from the existence of the current constraints, many rules. Sometimes formally, many times just intuitively. When a constraint is broken, it appears that we don't bother to go back and review those rules. As a result, our systems today are limited mainly by policy constraints.

We very rarely find a company with a real market constraint, but rather, with devastating marketing policy constraints. We very rarely find a true bottleneck on the shop floor, we usually find production policy constraints. We almost never find a vendor constraint, but we do find purchasing policy constraints. And in all cases the policies were very logical at the time they were instituted. Their original reasons have since long gone, but the old policies still remain with us.

The general process thus can be summarised (using the terminology of the system we seek to improve) as:

1. Identify the system's constraints.
2. Decide how to exploit the system's constraints.

3. Subordinate everything else to the above decision.
4. Elevate the system's constraints.
5. If in the previous steps a constraint has been broken, go back to step one, but do not allow inertia to cause a system constraint.

As we said before, the only way not to cause severe distortions, is to describe the same process, but this time using the terminology of the improvement process itself. Every manager is overwhelmed with problems, or as some would call it opportunities. We all tend to concentrate on taking corrective actions that we know how to take, not necessarily concentrating on the problems we should correct and the actions needed to correct those problems. Thus, if a process of ongoing improvement is to be effective, we must first of all find—WHAT TO CHANGE.

In other words, the first ability that we must require from a manager is the ability to pinpoint the core problems, those problems that, once corrected, will have a major impact, rather than drifting from one small problem to another, fooling ourselves into thinking that we are doing our job. But once a core problem has been identified, we should be careful not to fall into the trap of immediately struggling with the question of How To Cause The Change. We must first clarify to ourselves—TO WHAT TO CHANGE TO—otherwise the identification of core problems will only lead to panic and chaos.

Thus, we should also require that a manager acquire the ability to construct simple, practical solutions. In today's world, where almost everybody is fascinated by the notion of sophistication, this ability to generate simple solutions is relatively rare. Nevertheless, we must insist on it. It's enough to remind ourselves of what we have so harshly learned from reality, over and over again. Complicated solutions don't work, simple one's might. Once the solution is known, and only then, are we facing the most difficult question of—HOW TO CAUSE THE CHANGE.

Part III
Complex Adaptive Health Systems: Theory Meets Praxis

All theories are legitimate, no matter.
What matters is what you do with them.

Jorge Luis Borges (1899–1986)
Argentine writer and poet

It is the theory which decides what can be observed.

Albert Einstein (1879–1955)
German-born theoretical physicist

Part I of this book described the foundational elements that underpin the formation of a complex adaptive health system, and Part II outlined how to apply the principles of complexity sciences to the (re)design of health systems. Three examples from three very different context illustrated how—under the guidance of *committed leaders*—adherence to these principles—the shared understanding of *purpose, goals, and values* resulted in the bottom-up/top-down emergence of complex adaptive health systems:

- A primary health care system in the slums of Nairobi
- A national integrated realignment of health and community services to contain HIV/AIDS in Brazil
- A community-owned, community-run, and community-focused health system for the Alaska Native and American Indian people in the greater Anchorage area

This next part of this book will explore how to better understand the structure and dynamics of health system organisations. Fundamentally this will require a change in mindset; continuing to use the prevailing one is unlikely to gain fundamentally different understandings.

Fig. 1 An array of dots [1]

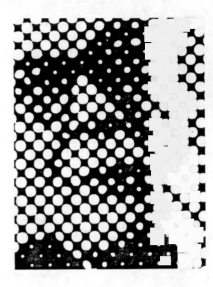

Passioura's Visual Parable[1]

Figure 1 shows an array of dots [1]. If we were asked to make a study of these dots, we would probably start by looking for pattern in them. We would note that their centres form a square array whose rows are at 45° to the horizontal, that most of the dots are circular, that there is a bimodal distribution of their size, and that dots of a given size tend to be clustered together. We might note that some of the dots appear to be malformed, and if we have tenured appointments we might have time to reflect that by using such a pejorative word as "malformed" we have already developed expectations about our observations, that is, that we have started to make theory—dots should be circular, and if they are not, it is an error.

It is clear then that there is plenty of pattern here. But is there significant pattern? What does "significant" mean? Have we been making the right observations? Could the large and small dots be a two-letter alphabet similar to that of the Morse code, so that we should be looking for lineal rather than areal pattern? There seems to be no way to find out.

But if we look at an extended field of the dots as shown in Fig. 2, and if we blur our eyes to the extent that the dots almost disappear, they suddenly gain significance, and do disappear. We are no longer looking at dots. We are now looking at the face of a man who is smoking a pipe. Figure 1 is now seen to be a picture of his eyes, nose, and mouth, and almost all our previous discussion on arrays, and rows, and size, and shape, is now seen to be irrelevant. All that matters is the gross distribution of the different-sized dots to give the illusion of light and shade. The significance of the dots can be seen only by abandoning almost all the detailed information we

---

[1]Passioura JB. Accountability, Philosophy and Plant Physiology. Search 1979;10(10):347–350.

Fig. 2 An array of dots? [1]

have about them, and only by changing the language that we use to describe them. We cannot discuss their significance by restricting ourselves to words like size, and shape, and array. We have to use words like light, and shade, and nose, and mouth.

It is this transition from one language to another that epitomises the way our minds deal with layered systems. And it is by perceiving the world as being organised into conceptual layers that we manage to make sense of it; the use of such terms as "molecular level", "cellular level", ["organ level", "person level", "primary care level", "secondary care level", "tertiary care level", "community level", "regional level", and "whole health system level"], attests to that. . . . What follows is a description of the main properties of layered systems, or hierarchically organised systems as they are sometimes called. The account is based on that of Mesarovic MD. and Macko D. (1969) ['Foundations for a scientific theory of hierarchical systems,' in Hierarchical Structures (L. L. Whyte, A. G. Wilson and Donna Wilson, eds.). American Elsevier, New York. pp. 29–50].

Properties of Layered Systems

1. Each level has its own language, concepts, and principles. In our discussion of Fig. 2 we used words belonging to three different levels: "array" and "dot" belong to the lowest (i.e. least organised) level; "light" and "shade" belong to the middle level, and summarise the important features of the organisation of the dots; "nose" and "mouth" belong to the highest level, and summarise important features of the organisation of light and shade. Our understanding of a layered system is, in part, measured by our ability to inter-translate the languages of adjacent layers. Translating to a lower layer provides us with explanations, translating to a higher layer provides us with the significance, of the phenomenon we are studying.

2. *Discovery at a given level is stimulated by thinking of adjacent levels. We have seen that to discover a face while concentrating on the dots of Fig. 1 is virtually impossible. Yet had we been told that the organisation of the dots represents light and shade, our discovery of the face would probably have been facilitated as we blurred the figure for the first time. Similarly, our appreciation of the significance of the dots in terms of light and shade might concentrate our attention on an important feature that we have not previously considered, namely the spatial frequency. If the array of dots were on a finer grid, we would be able to see more detail in the picture.*

3. *Interaction between levels is not symmetric: a higher level requires all lower levels in order to operate effectively, but not vice versa. If we transformed Fig. 1 by cutting it up into several pieces and rearranging them, we would still have an array of dots, even though they formed a meaningless pattern. But if we transformed the dots by, say, squashing them so that they formed thin overlapping lines instead of discrete areas, we would have neither dots nor picture.*

4. *Higher levels result from constraints being imposed on lower levels. Randomly arranged dots would give no picture. It is only after the dots have been constrained to form groups that a picture can arise. A group of large dots gives a patch of light; a group of small ones, a patch of shade.*

5. *A constraint is expressed in the language of the higher level. Dots are grouped (constrained) to form a patch. One could express the grouping in terms of the size and position of individual dots, but such a description would be tedious and befuddling and would give no clue to the significance of the constraint.*

Implications for Understanding Complex Adaptive Health Systems

Readers are reminded that every system consists of a number of subsystems and is itself part of a larger supra-system. Passioura alludes to the important relationships between systems levels; subsystem levels provide **explanations** for the characteristics of the system level of interest, the supra-system level explains the **significance** of the system level to the whole (Table 1).

These interrelationships highlight that *breaking systems into their components is flawed with danger as the parts do no longer contain the properties of the whole system*. Missing this point can lead to erroneous interpretations of the system's behaviour and not infrequently results in overly simplistic managerial interventions.

In line with Passioura's notions we also have to distinguish the understanding of issues along a continuum of changing contexts (Fig. 3). Deconstructing *what we know* into its constituents is explanatory and associated with a high level of certainty. However, *what we would like to know* about an issue can only be envisaged and will result in novel insights.

Table 1 Health system phenomena at different levels of organisation

	Primary care	Person	Community
Supra-system level SIGNIFICANCE	Resource allocation for secondary/tertiary care	Community morbidity and mortality	Socioeconomic determinants of health
System level DESCRIPTION	First point of care	Personal health experience	Social capital
Subsystem level EXPLANATION	Nurses and doctors practicing in the community	Personal morbidity family support environmental exposures	Number of friends community halls sporting facilities, etc.

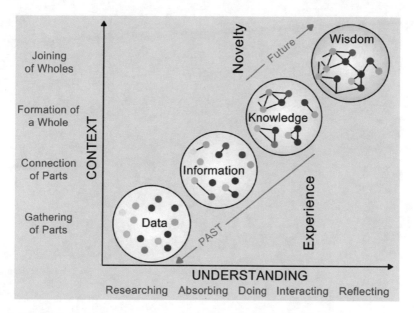

Fig. 3 The continuum of understanding and context. Real understanding arises from being able to link diverse knowledge domains. Adopted from: Cleveland H. "Information as Resource", The Futurist, December 1982, p. 34–39

The following two chapters consider two broad approaches to understanding *complex adaptive systems (organisations)*:

- A posteriori *approaches* that illuminate the historical features of the system—its structure and its outcomes, and by deduction its driver(s)
- *Prospective approaches* that provide insights to the possible future achievements of the system, i.e. its potential dynamic behaviour, given what is known so far

These two approaches are then applied to the problem of obesity. Only an appreciation of the interdependence between all "*partial insights*" allows an "*overall understanding*" of the problem, i.e. the obesity epidemic as a whole is "*greater and different*" to the "*sum of its parts*".

Further Readings

Morin E (2008) On complexity. Hampton Press, New Jersey

Chapter 9
Analysing "the Workings" of Health Systems as *Complex Adaptive Systems*

Overview. Complex adaptive systems can be analysed in two very different ways:

- Looking *backwards* asking: which of its structures and behaviours allowed its current state to emerge (the *what* and *why* questions)
- Looking *forward* asking: changes to which of its structures and behaviours may most likely shape dynamics that achieve a future desired outcome (the *how* questions)

Looking backwards decomposes the system. Decomposition of systems can produce:

- Health atlases that describe the distribution of various health services like the location of hospitals, community practices, specialist medical and allied services, etc. in a geographic area
- Geospatial distribution maps superimpose a variety of different data onto a map and visually highlight their linkages. For example, researchers have found a strong relationship between socioeconomic characteristics, the distribution of fast food outlets, and obesity rates across different suburbs
- Creating geospatial maps for different time periods can show progress in combating particular issues of concern like the improvements in the battle against sleeping sickness in the Democratic Republic of the Congo

Looking forward takes account of the fact that the *system as a whole*, rather than its discrete entities, produce the behaviours and outcomes one observes and desires. Looking forward is the realm of modelling. A model is a "simplified version of reality", it contains those "agreed upon" variables regarded as "responsible to cause" the behaviours and outcomes of the system.

Modelling in the first instance is a *learning tool*—it allows all involved in model building to gain a deep insight into the system's structure and function. In the second instance it is a *decision-making tool*—it invites the exploration of "what-if"

© Springer International Publishing AG 2018
J.P. Sturmberg, *Health System Redesign*, DOI 10.1007/978-3-319-64605-3_9

scenarios to help find the "*best possible*" approach to solving a problem. Modelling provides decision makers a "safe space" to explore the long-term effects of potential solutions on the system's behaviours and outcomes.

However, modelling is not a panacea; as Rittel emphasised, every solution to a wicked problem is a "one shot solution"; modelling helps decision makers to "give it the best shot possible".

Points for Reflection

- How can one analyse the function and performance of a health system or a healthcare unit?
- Systems are constantly changing. How can one best "predict" the impact of decisions on the long-term behaviour/outcomes of a system?
- If you participated in the analysis of the structure and function of a health system/health system unit:

  - How did this affect your understanding of the system and its behaviour?
  - How did you arrive at "the necessary changes that needed to be made"?
  - What outcomes did these changes achieve?

- If you participated in modelling the structure and function of a health system/health system unit:

  - How did this affect your understanding of the system and its behaviour?
  - How did you arrive at "the necessary changes that needed to be made"?
  - What outcomes did these changes achieve?

How can we better understand the systems in systems nature of health and health care like a *patient* and a *patient in his family and community context*, a *medical practice* as an organisation and a *medical practice in a particular location* or a *hospital* and a *hospital in a particular geographic location* (Fig. 9.1)? Traditional approaches aim to deconstruct the system with the aim to understand each part in turn. However, an understanding of "*the parts*" is usually not sufficient to understand the "*system as a whole*" and its dynamic behaviours.

This chapter outlines a number of techniques that facilitate a deeper understanding of a complex adaptive system or a complex adaptive organisation. There are two broad methodologies:

- A posteriori *approaches* that illuminate the historical features of a system or organisation—its structure and its outcomes, and by deduction its driver(s)
- *Prospective approaches* that provide insights to the possible future achievements of a system or organisation—its potential dynamic behaviours, given what is known so far

First a reminder—a health system consists of many subsystems that can be *simple, complicated*, or *variably complex*. Therefore it is important to firstly identify which type of subsystem one is dealing with before selecting a particular analytic tool (Table 9.1).

And second—there are many different approaches to understand the complexities in health systems (Table 9.2). As the health system is a *complex adaptive system* approaches from engineering, business, economics, defence and aviation are only applicable for specific subsystems of the health system, like preoperative check-lists

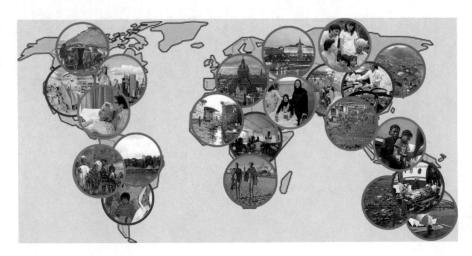

Fig. 9.1 Health and healthcare contexts. The nested nature of healthcare—the person and the person in the context of his family (*green circles*), medical practice in the context of the healthcare system (*red circles*), and the personal environment in the context of one's place of living (*blue circles*)

Table 9.1 Simple, complicated, complex, and complex adaptive subsystems in a health system

	Simple	Complicated	Complex	Complex adaptive systems
Types of Systems	Mechanical systems		Complex (dynamic) systems	
Examples in community health care	Flu vaccination	Managing a 2nd degree burn	Community Care for frail elderly, linking care domains; medication management of polypharmacy	Collaboration in GP clinic; Multimorbidity management
Examples in hospital health care	Laboratory testing; surgery	Hip replacement; Acute psychiatric unit	Bed management in a hospital; Staff management of a hospital	Intensive care unit
Examples in health sub-system		Protocols, e.g. handwashing policy	Managing an epidemic; Managing a natural disaster	Mental health; Health financing
Structure of System	One-to-one relationships E.g. nurse giving Flu shot	One-to-many relationships E.g. surgeon managing a theatre team; E.g. nurse unit manager ensuring staff records every patient incidents regardless how trivial	Many-to-many and system-to-system relationships (nested systems) Subsystems can have simple, complicated, and complex components E.g. the value of services listed in the MBS (simple) however the fees charged by individual doctors to different patients in their practice is highly variable and depends on many factors (complex adaptive)	
Outcomes	Linear; E.g. measured as percentage of eligible population being vaccinated	Mostly predictable; E.g. measured as number and type of in theatre complications _(Linear)_	Alter with history and initial conditions; Unpredictable/emergent; E.g. contextual description of the SES characteristics of population groups, the detailed description of delivery of an intervention and the observed outcomes (e.g. harm reduction of illicit drug use); Non-linear and feedback; Complex - Chaotic	
Generalizability	Yes	Yes	No	No

Table 9.2 Characteristics of complexity approaches

Systems approaches from	Description	Activities	Examples	Addresses structure	Addresses process	dynamics	Direction of analysis/interactions
Engineering [1]	An approach that involves anticipating ineffective processes that jeopardize quality, and designing interventions to overcome such shortcomings	• Plan-Do-Study-Act (PDSA) • Situation-Background-Assessment-Recommendations (SBAR) • Stochastic modelling • House of Quality • Statistical process control charts with lean six sigma [http://www.leansixsigmatraining.net/toyota-production-system/]	• Hospital-acquired pressure • Ulcer prevention • Falls prevention	✓	✓	✗	⇓
Business [2, 3], Economics and Knowledge management		• Knowledge Discovery from Data (KDD) • Expert-based Cooperative Analysis (EbCA) • Outcome management analysis • Causality analysis • Lean approach to health logistics • Quality improvement model (IHI-QI) • Six sigma • Toyota production system	• Population mapping • Service mapping • Addressing waist in the health system • Safety in healthcare	(✓)	(✓)	✗	⇓ ⇑
Defence, Aviation and other High-risk sectors [4]	Develops a zero-defect culture based on the recognition that highly technical operations depend on the interaction of systems, subsystems, agents and contexts	• Root cause analyses • SWARMing • TeamSTEPPS [5]	• Safety in healthcare • Staff interaction training	✓	(✓)	(✗)	⇓
Computer sciences	Simulation modelling [6]	Decision support systems (DSS) System dynamics modelling Agent-based modelling	Information and knowledge access	✗ ✓	✓ ✓	✓ ✓	⇓ ⇑

✓ = yes, (✓) or (✗) = variable, ✗ = no, ⇐ = backwards, ⇒ = forwards

adopted from aviation. In addition many of these techniques look backwards; they aim to identify what led to the current outcomes. However, health system redesign aims to make improvements for the future and is the domain of *modelling and simulation*. While modelling and simulation cannot predict the future they allow a better understanding of potential benefits and risks in the context of the best understanding of the system's structure and dynamics at this point in time.

9.1 A Posteriori *Approaches* to Understanding Health Systems as Complex Adaptive Systems

"Looking backwards" provides answers to the question: "*what are the structures and actions in the system we work in*" that have produced the "*outcomes we observe*" (and may or may not be happy with). A posteriori approaches lend themselves to reflect on a system's or organisation's **existing** structures, interactions, and drivers.

9.1.1 History of Decomposing Simple/Complicated Systems

Decomposing works well for *designed systems* like cars, computers, or production chains. Being able to decompose these type of systems allows improvement in the structure and/or function of each part, and when reassembling the parts one has *recreated the same system* with altered system part characteristics—for all intense and purposes the system may now function better or worse. Redesigning simple/complicated systems requires the authority and the provision of resources by *managers*.

9.1.2 The Dangers of Decomposing Complex Adaptive Systems

However, the health system is a *complex adaptive—NOT a simple/complicated—system*; its stakeholders constantly learn based on the feedback they receive. In addition, depending on their place and role in the system, they focus on *specific but limited agendas* (for an example, see Table 9.3). To recap, organisations:

- Have no *stable state; nonlinear dynamics* make their behaviour appear random/chaotic
- Their agents are *independent*, influenced by their environment, emotional states, and social rules
- Their agents have *conflicting goals and behaviours*; they need to adapt to each other's differences

Table 9.3 Stakeholders and Their Varying Interests in Health Care

Stakeholder	Risk management	Prevention	Detection	Treatment
Public Delivery	e.g. Buy insurance	e.g. Stop smoking	e.g. Get screened System Clinicians[a]	Clinicians and providers[b]
Government	Medicare, Medicaid, Congress	NIH, Government CDC, DoD, et al.	NIH, Government CDC, DoD, et al.	NIH, Government CDC, DoD, et al.
Non-Profits		American Cancer Society, American Heart Association, et al.	American Cancer Society, American Heart Association, et al.	American Cancer Society, American Heart Association, et al.
Academia	Business schools	Basic science disciplines	Technology and medical schools	Medical schools
Business	Employers, insurance companies, HMOs		Guidant, Medtronic, et al.	Lilly, Merck, Pfizer, et al.

[a]The category of clinicians includes physicians, nurses, and other health care professionals
[b]The category of providers includes hospitals, clinics, nursing homes, and many other types of testing and treatment facilities [1]

- Their agents *learn and change* their responses and behaviours based on *iterative feedback* leading to *self-organisation and emergence*; outcomes can be innovation or disasters
- As a large CAS has *no single point of control* ("no one is in charge") organisations like a health system can only be influenced **but never** controlled
- No individual has either the *authority nor resources* to re/design the system

Given these characteristics of large CAS, Rouse **cautions against the decomposition of complex adaptive systems**. He stresses that decomposition of such systems entails a high likelihood of losing important information about interactions amongst phenomena of interest [7]. Such loss invariably leads to "not seeing the woods for the trees" resulting in erroneous conclusions, or put in Mencken's words: *For every complex problem there is an answer that is clear, simple, and wrong.*

9.1.3   Analysing the Structure/Components of a Health System

Analysing the structure/components of a health service provides valuable insights into service organisation and resource allocation. It allows descriptive comparisons between health system organisation and/or outcomes across different contexts.

However, a structural decomposition of services cannot provide any information about its function like:

- Is this particular system configuration effective and efficient
- Is it conducive to collaboration between service providers

- How does the social and physical environment contribute to good/poor health
- Are health and social services accessible and culturally appropriate
- Does it enable patients to better cope with their problems

9.1.3.1   Health Atlas

Salvador-Carulla et al. [8] proposed a methodology to map existing (mental) health services across different countries in Europe considering meso- and micro-level characteristics (location, service types). Each country provided structured data on their population, SES indices, general information on their mental health policies, mental health service components, and geographic data. The methodology is described in detail in the paper; the output of the decomposition is shown in Fig. 9.2 (top) for the availability of residential mental health services at different scales, and in Fig. 9.2 (bottom) for different types of mental health services in the Helsinki region.

9.1.4   Exploring Contributing Factors

Epidemiological approaches are designed to identify potential contributing factors to an outcome of interest. These approaches are useful in identifying hot spots of poor health, environmental contributors, or socioeconomic factors. While these are not causally explanatory, they all provide important pointers to shape policy decision-making and service redesign.

Of note, most issues are outside the direct health system domain. Health professionals see the *consequences* of policy decisions, social and environmental circumstance, and the availability/lack of availability of healthcare and social services; however, they have *no direct ability* to modify these. Effective health system redesign thus requires interdisciplinary and across scale collaboration between all domains that impact on the health of individuals and communities.

9.1.4.1   Geospatial Mapping

The example of the mental health atlas is a static form of geospatial mapping. A more dynamic picture emerges when overlaying various factors thought to contribute to a health outcome onto the same map. Figure 9.3 shows the geographical distribution of childhood obesity in Berlin and the distribution of three explanatory variables—socioeconomic status, percentage of non-German population, and number of fast food restaurants/1000 inhabitants. Figure 9.4 highlights the *nonlinear* (log) risk relationship between the variables on obesity [9]. Clearly one policy

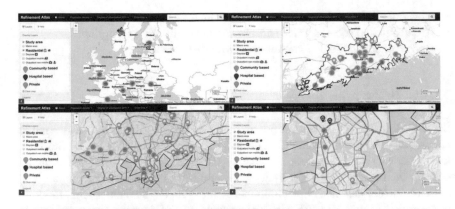

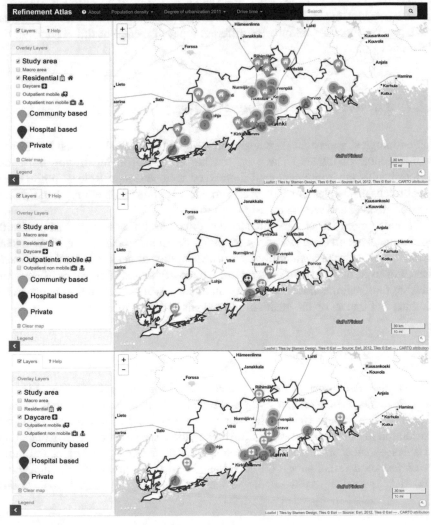

Fig. 9.2 Comparison of residential mental health services at different scales of resolution—Europe (*top left*), Helsinki region (*top right*), inner city Helsinki (*bottom left*), and at a street level of a neighbourhood (*bottom right*) (*top*); Availability of different types of mental health services in the Helsinki (*bottom*) (http://www.psychiatry.univr.it/refinement/atlas/atlas.html#)

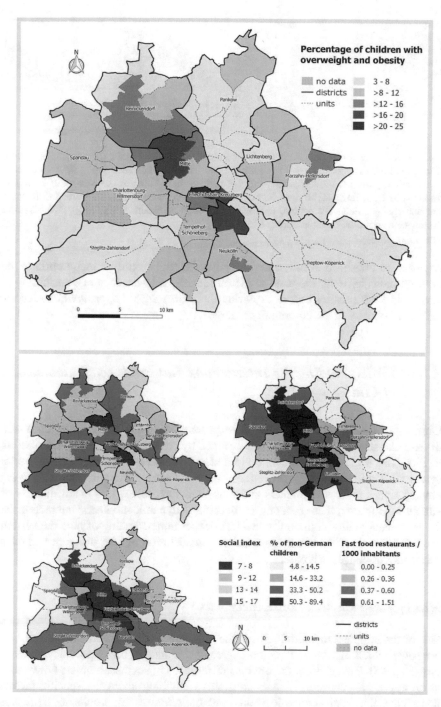

Fig. 9.3 Geospatial distribution of childhood obesity in Berlin and three explanatory variables—socio-economic status, percentage of non-German population, and number of fast food restaurants/1000 inhabitants. Reproduced from Lakes T, Burkart K. Childhood overweight in Berlin: intra-urban differences and underlying influencing factors. International Journal of Health Geographics [14] (Creative Commons Attribution 4.0 International License)

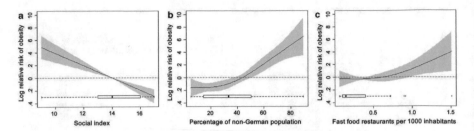

Fig. 9.4 Relationship between overweight and obesity and social index (**a**) percentage of non-German children (**b**) and fast food restaurants density (**c**). *Grey areas* depict 95% confidence intervals. *Boxplots* of the particular predictor variable are shown at the *bottom of each plot* (reproduced from Lakes T, Burkart K. Childhood overweight in Berlin: intra-urban differences and underlying influencing factors. International Journal of Health Geographics [14] (Creative Commons Attribution 4.0 International License)

approach to obesity prevention for the city of Berlin would be inappropriate; the findings indicate firstly the need to identify locally relevant factors contributing to obesity in each locality before exploring the *most adapted **approaches*** to reduce childhood obesity in the community at large.

9.1.5   Understanding the Interactions that Produced Outcomes of Concern

Observable system outcomes, like life-expectancy in a city or the prevalence of a disease like sleeping sickness, can be explored by considering potential contributing factors. These may be socioeconomic and environmental, or the result of health system function (planning, prevention, or provision). Generally these analyses employ linear regression models and thus limit themselves to a small number of variables. However, these outcomes reflect many dynamic *nonlinear* interactions at the individual and/or community level. A deeper understanding of how the system produced the observed outcomes requires consideration of how different variables relate and influence each other.

9.1.5.1   Life-Expectancy Differences in a City

One of the simplest methodologies is the mapping of life-expectancy along a city bus route which highlights the high degree of variance in life-expectancy across a city (Fig. 9.5). This reflects the obvious differences in socioeconomics; however—as an aggregate measure—it does not tell us anything about the specific factors underlying low socioeconomic status and their *interacting nonlinear dynamics* which exacerbate the problem.

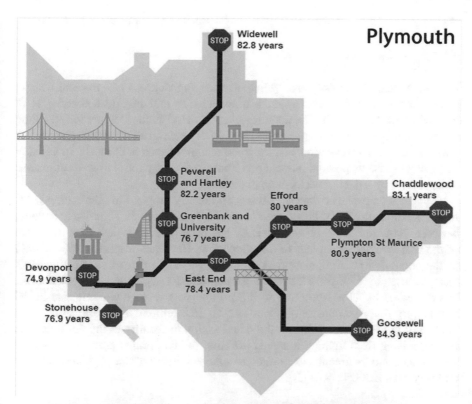

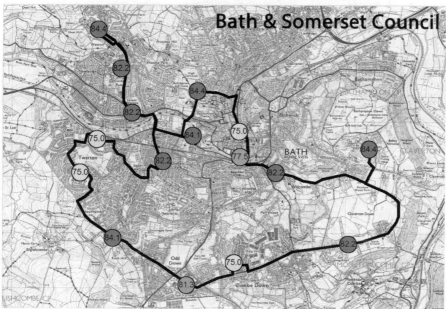

Fig. 9.5 Life-Expectancy along a metropolitan bus route—a schematic representation. Plymouth's life-expectancy bus route by neighbourhood (2011–2013), www.plymouth.gov.uk/thrive_bus_route_by_neighbourhood.pdf and a geospatial representation (Bath & North East Somerset Council—Life Expectancy http://www.bathnes.gov.uk/services/your-council-and-democracy/local-research-and-statistics/wiki/life-expectancy)

9.1.5.2   Time-Series Comparison

Human African trypanosomiasis (HAT) or sleeping sickness is a tropical disease caused by protozoa trypanosoma and is transmitted by the tsetse fly. Untreated, HAT invariably results in death. The main reservoir for HAT in the Democratic Republic of the Congo are humans, so prevention mainly depends on mass screening of at-risk populations, passive detection, and the treatment of infected individuals. In addition controlling tsetse fly populations can contribute to disease control in areas of intense transmission by reducing vector-human contact.

Comparing prevalence data over time can identify progress in eliminating HAT. In the Democratic Republic of the Congo HAT has been in significant decline; between 2000 and 2012 the risk of HAT has been reduced to less than one-third of the land area and about half of the population. However, despite a 10% increase in the population, the population at high and very high risk of contracting HAT has decreased by 45% from 2.8 to 1.5 million and the population at moderate risk has decreased by 21% from 10.5 to 8.2 million with a corresponding rise in the low to very low risk population from 19.8 to 26.8 million. The national trend in decline of HAT was not uniform; the deterioration in security in the north-eastern region, arising from fighting amongst different militia groups, prevented rigorous surveillance and treatment and resulted in a large increase of the population at high and very high risk (Fig. 9.6) [10].

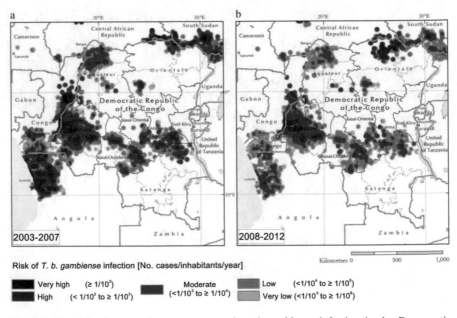

Fig. 9.6 The risk of contracting trypanosoma brucei gambiense infection in the Democratic Republic of the Congo, (**a**) 2003–2007 and (**b**) 2008–2012. Reproduced from Lumbala C, Simarro PP, Cecchi G, Paone M, Franco JR, Kande Betu Ku Mesu V, et al. Human African trypanosomiasis in the Democratic Republic of the Congo: disease distribution and risk. International Journal of Health Geographics [10] (reproduced with permission from the authors)

9.1.6 Evaluating System Outcomes in Light of a System's Purpose, Goals, and Values

Decomposing complex adaptive systems in the above ways may allow one to deduce an organisation's underlying driver, derived from its agreed purpose, goals, and values statements. These can then be compared against the initial intentions as documented, e.g. in policy or institutional value and mission statements. This approach contributes to accountability based on outcomes rather than the adherence to simplistic process markers.

9.2 A Prospective Approach to Understanding Health Systems

Looking backwards provides insights into the "whats and hows" but not the "whys" that produced the outcomes we observe.

Locking forward to improve the health system requires a different mindset; as Peter Drucker emphasised there is a difference between *doing things right and doing the right thing*,[1] or before him Albert Einstein describing *insanity as doing the same over and over again and expecting a different result*.

System analysis of a *value-focused health system* should focus on out-puts/outcomes of the system's behaviour. This requires a mind shift—outputs/outcomes no longer are the result of the workings of a discrete organisational group *but* the organisation as a whole. Rouse [7] contrasts the CAS approach to understanding organisational behaviour from traditional approaches as shown in Table 9.4.

Based on these insights Rouse [1] suggests four approaches to analysing the health systems as a CAS:

- Measurements and projections of system states in terms of current and projected value flows, as well as current and projected problems

---

[1] When we look at the models of quality and we frequently point to the Japanese and what they have done to the automobile. There is no doubt that they have improved the quality of the automobile, but it is the wrong kind of quality. Peter Drucker made a very fundamental distinction between doing things right and doing the right thing. The Japanese are doing things right but they are doing the wrong thing. Doing the wrong thing right is not nearly as good as doing the right thing wrong. You see the automobile is destroying urban life around the world, just visit Mexico City, Santiago or any of those major cities where you find congestion and pollution so bad that children have to be kept home from school, they are not allowed outdoors because the pollution is so intense, and then we are talking about the quality of the automobiles that drive it. It is the wrong concept of quality, quality ought to contain the notion of value not merely efficiency. There is a difference between efficiency and effectiveness. Quality ought to be directed at effectiveness. The difference between efficiency and effectiveness is the difference between knowledge and wisdom. But, unfortunately we have not got enough wisdom to go around.

transcript: If Russ Ackoff had given a TED Talk … https://www.youtube.com/watch?v=OqEeIG8aPPk)

Table 9.4 Comparison of organisational behaviour [7]

	Traditional system	Complex adaptive system
Roles	Management	Leadership
Methods	Command and Control	Incentives and inhibitions
Measurement	Activities	Outcomes
Focus	Efficiency	Agility
Relationships	Contractual	Personal commitments
Network	Hierarchy	Heterarchy
Design	Organisational design	Self-organisation

- Measurements and projections of system performance in terms of current and projected value, costs, and metrics (e.g. value divided by cost), as well as current and projected options for contingencies
- Observations of system stakeholders in terms of the involvement and performance of each stakeholder group
- Capabilities for measurement, modelling, and display of system states, including agile "What … If?" experimentation and adaptation

9.2.1   Mind Models

Before considering modelling as a tool to address Rouse's challenge, it is necessary to revisit *how* we think about the health system and what it reveals about our personal assumptions of reality and our ability to manage.

9.2.1.1   Personal Behaviours

Humans behave in predictable, albeit not always rational ways. For the most part we tend to use *intuitive approaches* to decision-making, and only much less frequently use a *cognitive*—analytic, structured, and disciplined—*approach*. In organisations decisions are frequently made by individuals despite knowing that group decision-making consistently outperforms the former [11].

9.2.1.2   Mindsets and Reality

Snowden [12] proposed the framework of *multi-ontology sense making* as a way to understand mindsets and their relationships to reality. He points out that we experience the world at times as ordered and predictable and at others as un-ordered and unpredictable. In turn our responses are either based on rules or heuristics resulting in a 2×2 table (Fig. 9.7). The importance lies in knowing the location

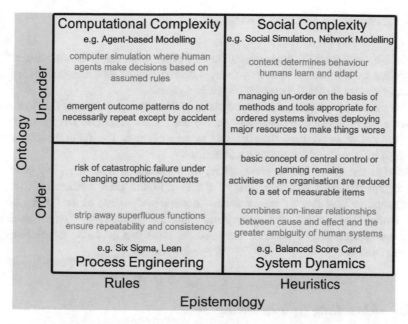

Fig. 9.7 The ontology-epistemology matrix. Each quadrant describes a particular complexity concept, representative complexity tools, and their benefits and risks—(based on Sheppard F, Williams M, Klein VR. TeamSTEPPS and patient safety in healthcare [5].)

of a problem as each requires different but specific approaches to find solutions, and as each solution carries its own specific risks.

Applying this multi-ontology sense making approach to group-based problem solving provides the necessary requisite level of diversity for both interpretation of the problem and ways to respond. In Snowden's words: *Requisite diversity means ensuring the acceptance of a sufficient number of divergent perspectives to enable the sensing of weak signals and avoidance of the all-too-common pattern entrainment of past success, while maintaining a sufficient focus to enable decisive and appropriate action. Above all, it is about ensuring cognitive effectiveness in information processing and thus gaining cognitive edge, or advantage* [6].

In general terms managing ordered systems tends to favour efficiency and stability suitable for mechanistic problems. However, in living systems *stability* and thus *effectiveness* results from *adaptability to changing contexts.*

It should now be clear that simple "industrial" approaches to health system problems and health system redesign are generally inappropriate and frequently futile. Understanding the differences between the four approaches is a prerequisite for *prospective* approaches to managing health system and health service problems.

9.3   Modelling System Problems

Modelling is a rapidly emerging field[2] offering a better understanding of the behaviour of complex adaptive systems, i.e. understanding the effects of interdependencies and feedback between a system's agents.

Problems in an organisation can be classified as either *problems of the "system as a whole"* or *problems in a particular part of the system*. Problems emerge over time, they are not planned, they simply arise as a function of the dynamic interactions amongst its members' behaviours and actions.

Models are simplified representations of "systems as wholes". They provide a visual representation of those parts of the system and their relationships that we understand to have created the current—"observable"—state of the "real system". The model then can be interrogated and modified to see how it *might* evolve in the future (Addendum 1 outlines three critical steps that guide the development of system models).

9.3.1   Modelling as a Learning Tool

George Box said: *Essentially, all models are wrong, but some are useful.* Its particular usefulness arises from model building as a *stakeholder engagement activity*. Implemented in that way "modelling" is a learning tool, it harnesses the common understanding of those working in the system/organisation (Fig. 9.8).

The importance of failing to reach a common understanding about the problem to be modelled is well recognised. It is particularly important to understand the *different perspectives and interpretations of the problem*, and to consider the possible implications of potential problem solutions, as one may end up with:

1. *Convoluting the problem given that differences in perspectives are* **not identifiable**
2. *Oversimplifying the problem given that differences in perspectives are* **not resolvable**
3. *Oversimplifying the problem given that differences in perceptions are* **not resolved correctly**
4. *Reducing the problem situation to a well-defined problem that is* **not relevant** *to the case at hand* [emphasis added] [13]

---

[2]http://www.systemswiki.org/index.php?title=The_Future_of_Health_Systems_Modeling
5 min with ... Professor Nate Osgood—The Australian Prevention Partnership Centre https://www.youtube.com/watch?v=Y6vQNV-av2g

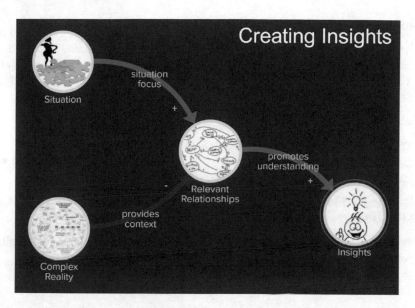

Fig. 9.8 Creating Insights. Modified screenshot, Gene Bellinger—https://stw.kumu.io/creating-insights (Creative Commons Attribution License)

9.3.2   Modelling: Elaborating on a System's Dynamics

Besides of gaining insight into the nature of the system, "modelling" (as a computational exercise) provides an understanding of the system's *dynamic* behaviour. Figure 9.9 shows a structural model that aims to understand the constraints on aged-care services in a community.

Currently the system has 1000 nursing home beds and 90 community social care workers delivering care packages to the elderly in the community. Figures 9.10 and 9.11 show the dynamic behaviour of the model over two time frames—1 year and 3 years. The example highlights that a short-term view can hide significant long-term consequences. This is a common "decision-maker's trap"—they often overlook time delays between the implementation of change and change in system performance.

9.3.2.1   What … If? Number of Patients Waiting for Services

Consider three scenarios:

- Doubling the number of nursing home beds
- Doubling the social care workforce
- A combination of a 50% increase in nursing home beds and social workforce

Doubling the number of nursing home beds:

- In the short-term decreases the waiting time for a nursing home bed for acute care patients, but over time waiting times for acute care patients will rise again
- This approach will not alter the increasing waiting time of acute care patients for an aged-care package

Doubling the social care workforce:

- Will steady the wait for acute care patients awaiting an aged-care package
- It will also result in a doubling of the number of patients receiving aged-care packaged who currently wait for nursing home admission

Combining a 50% increase in nursing home beds and social care workforce provides the greatest benefit:

- In the short-term this approach will half the number of acute care patients waiting for an aged-care package and in the long-term reduce it to about a quarter
- It will delay the rise **but not** the number of acute care patients waiting for nursing home admission

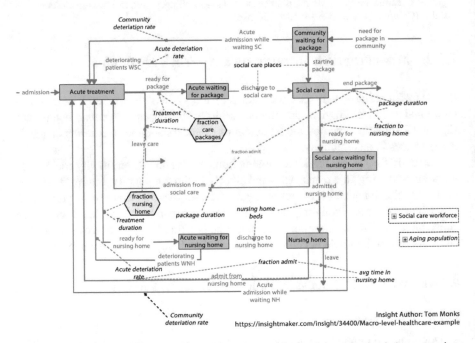

Fig. 9.9 Example of a macro-level health system model aimed to understand the constraints on community aged-care services. Model developed by Tom Monks in Insightmaker https://insightmaker.com/insight/34400/Macro-level-healthcare-example (Creative Commons Attribution License)

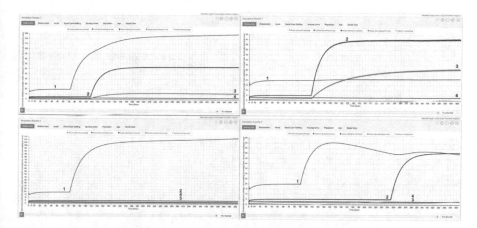

Fig. 9.10 Community outcomes over 1 year—short-term impacts

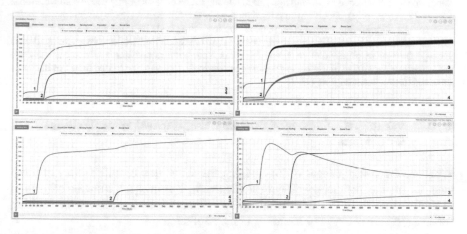

Fig. 9.11 Community outcomes over 3 years—long-term impacts. 1000 nursing home beds, social care workforce size = 90 (*top left*), 1000 nursing home beds, doubling social care workforce size = 180 (*top right*), Doubling nursing home beds (2000), social care workforce size = 90 (*bottom left*). Combining changes: increasing nursing home beds to 1500 and increasing social care workforce size to 130 (*bottom right*). **1** = acute care patients waiting for aged-care package, **2** = acute care patients waiting for nursing home admission, **3** = community receiving social care waiting for nursing home admission, **4** = community waiting for an aged-care package. Note: y-axis scale changes, the "*thick lines*" in the plots show oscillation between time points

- It will reduce the number of people receiving aged-care packages awaiting nursing home admission
- BUT after 3 years the numbers waiting will have risen again to baseline levels

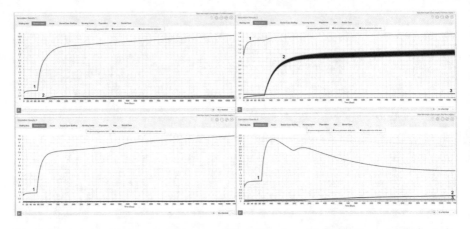

Fig. 9.12 Patient outcomes—deterioration while waiting for services. 1000 nursing home beds, social care workforce size = 90 (*top left*), 1000 nursing home beds, doubling social care workforce size = 180 (*top right*), Doubling nursing home beds (2000), social care workforce size = 90 (*bottom left*). Combining changes: increasing nursing home beds to 1500 and increasing social care workforce size to 130 (*bottom right*). **1** = patients deteriorating while waiting for aged-care package, **2** = acute admissions while waiting for nursing home admission, **3** = acute admissions while waiting for an aged-care package. Note: y-axis scale changes, the "*thick lines*" in the plots show oscillation between time points

9.3.2.2   What ... If? Number of Patients Being Harmed While Waiting for Services

What are the consequences of maintaining the status quo or making any of these changes on the patient's well-being? Figure 9.12 shows the number of patient deteriorating in the community who require hospital admission while either waiting for an aged-care package or a nursing home admission:

- Doubling the number of nursing home beds substantially reduces the number of patients deteriorating in the community
- BUT increases the number of admissions for those awaiting an aged-care package
- Doubling the number of aged-care packages has no impact on the number deteriorating in the community
- BUT prevents the need for hospital admission
- ***Combined increases*** in nursing home beds and aged-care packages results in ***halving*** the number of people deteriorating in the community ***in the short-term***, reducing to a ***quarter in the long-term***
- AND a marked reduction in patients requiring hospitalisation while waiting for nursing home admission
- The number requiring admission while waiting for an aged-care package remains stable

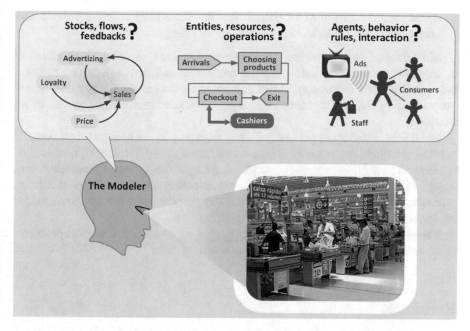

Fig. 9.13 Choosing a modelling technique—what question requires an answer, image courtesy of AnyLogic®: The three methods in simulation modeling; available at: http://www.xjtek.com/files/book/The_three_methods_in_simulation_modeling.pdf

9.3.3   Modelling Techniques

To reiterate, principally models are a *simplified representation of reality*. The model design depends on the lens used (Fig. 9.13):

- Are we interested in exploring feedback within the system (e.g. continuity of care for patients with chronic disease)
- Are we interested in understanding the process flow through a particular unit within the health system (e.g. achieving 4 h rule of patients being seen in the emergency department)
- Are we interested to understand how individuals are affected by events in the health system (e.g. spread of an epidemic, progression of a disease)

There are three principle simulation modelling approaches to explore the function of a system:

- System dynamics modelling (SD-model: stocks, flows, feedback—macro-level, often top-down perspective)
- Discrete event modelling (DE-model: entities, resources, operations—meso-level, often workflow perspective)

- Agent-based modelling (AB-model: agents, behaviours, rules, interactions— micro-level, often individual and/or bottom-up perspective)

Modelling allows the testing of all perceivable health system interventions in a "safe environment"; whilst even good models cannot predict definite outcomes, they provide a good approximation of potential benefits and pitfalls like unexpected outcomes and impacts in related system domains, as demonstrate in the above example.

Modelling is an expert field only slowly emerging in the health system domain. While good modelling not only depends on a "good model", it also requires sophisticated and powerful modelling tools like AnyLogic® (http://www.anylogic.com/). AnyLogic's strength is the ability to simultaneously explore system structures, processes, and agent behaviours within the same model, allowing the simultaneous exploration of multiple stakeholder perspectives.

The next chapter presents a number of system approaches that address problems at the micro, meso, and macro level of the health system.

References

1. Padula W, Duffy M, Yilmaz T, Mishra M (2014) Integrating systems engineering practice with health-care delivery. Health Syst. 3(3):159–164
2. Haque W, Urquhart B, Berg E, Dhanoa R (2014) Using business intelligence to analyze and share health system infrastructure data in a rural health authority. JMIR Med Inform 2(2):e16
3. Scoville R, Little K (2014) Comparing lean and quality improvement. IHI white paper. Institute for Healthcare Improvement, Cambridge, MA
4. Hudson P (2003) Applying the lessons of high risk industries to health care. Qual Saf Health Care 12(suppl 1):i7–i12
5. Sheppard F, Williams M, Klein VR (2013) TeamSTEPPS and patient safety in healthcare. J Healthc Risk Manag 32(3):5–10
6. Marshall DA, Burgos-Liz L, Ijzerman MJ, Osgood ND, Padula WV, Higashi MK, et al (2015) Applying dynamic simulation modeling methods in health care delivery research—the SIMULATE checklist: report of the ISPOR simulation modeling emerging good practices task force. Value Health 18(1):5–16
7. Rouse WB (2008) Health care as a complex adaptive system: implications for design and management. The Bridge 38(1):17–25
8. Salvador-Carulla L, Amaddeo F, Gutiérrez-Colosía MR, Salazzari D, Gonzalez-Caballero JL, Montagni I, et al (2015) Developing a tool for mapping adult mental health care provision in Europe: the REMAST research protocol and its contribution to better integrated care. Int J Integr Care 15:e042
9. Lakes T, Burkart K (2016) Childhood overweight in Berlin: intra-urban differences and underlying influencing factors. Int J Health Geogr 15(1):1–10
10. Lumbala C, Simarro PP, Cecchi G, Paone M, Franco JR, Kande Betu Ku Mesu V, et al (2015) Human African trypanosomiasis in the Democratic Republic of the Congo: disease distribution and risk. Int J Health Geogr 14:20
11. Higgins G, Freedman J (2013) Improving decision making in crisis. J Bus Contin Emer Plan 7(1):65–76
12. Snowden DJ (2005) Multi-ontology sense making: a new simplicity in decision making. Inform Prim Care 13(1):45–53

13. Lynch C, Padilla J, Diallo S, Sokolowski J, Banks C (2014) A multi-paradigm modeling framework for modeling and simulating problem situations. In: Tolk A, Diallo SY, Ryzhov IO, Yilmaz L, Buckley S, Miller JA (eds) Proceedings of the 2014 Winter Simulation Conference: IEEE, p 1688–1699
14. Lakes T, Burkart K (2016) Childhood overweight in Berlin: intra-urban differences and underlying influencing factors. Int J Health Geogr 15(1):1–10

Addendum 1

Three Types of System Diagrams

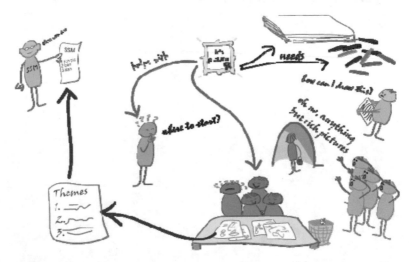

Rich picture diagram. Image courtesy of Ramage M and Shipp K. Expanding the Concept of 'Model': The Transfer from Technological to Human Domains within Systems Thinking

Rich pictures are unstructured pictures and usually drawn by hand. They depict all the major aspects of a problem of interest.

The aim of a rich picture diagram is to capture the full extent of the issues without giving any thought to their groupings or relationships, however, some related aspects of relationships between different issues are frequently illustrated through relative positions or simple lines connecting those issues.

Multiple cause diagrams are used to explore why changes or events happen.

The purpose of the diagrams is to examine the multiple causes behind particular events and processes. Here one looks primarily at the causal chain behind processes. Developing a multiple cause diagram may identify important feedback loops that can provide insights into the multiple causes of a system's behaviour and how to make undesirable behaviour less likely.

Influence diagrams are a type of systems map that show the relationships between the components within the system. They highlight the relationships and influences between the system's components.

An extension of influence diagrams are sign graph diagrams (not shown). Analysing the relationships between the components can tell if the component at the beginning of an error will cause a change in the same (indicated by a "+") or opposite (indicated by a "−") direction in the component at the tip of the arrow. Furthermore influence loops—technically known as feedback loops—become apparent and provide further insight into the dynamics of the system's behaviour.

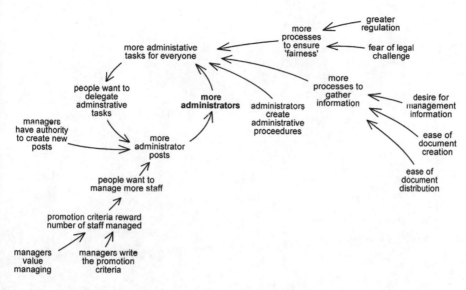

Multiple cause diagram. Image courtesy of Ramage M and Shipp K. Expanding the Concept of 'Model': The Transfer from Technological to Human Domains within Systems Thinking

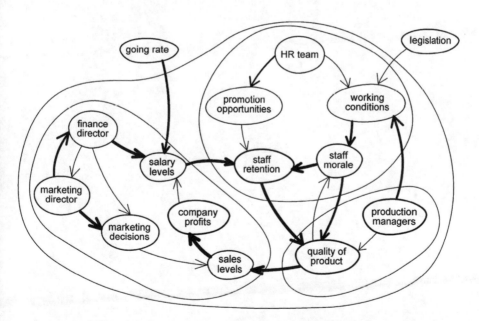

Influence diagram. Image courtesy of Ramage M and Shipp K. Expanding the Concept of 'Model': The Transfer from Technological to Human Domains within Systems Thinking

Chapter 10
Health System Redesign: Applying Complex Adaptive Systems Approaches

Overview. Health system redesign, as argued in this book, is based on three fundamental assumptions:

- The philosophy of medicine—the *value of health services* arises from its *impact on the health of the people* we treat
- The *person/patient is at the centre* of a functional complex adaptive health system
- A seamlessly integrated health system has to understand its *purpose, goals, and values* to devise its unique "*simple (operating) rules*". These together determine the core driver for the "*system as a whole*" as exemplified by the Mayo Clinic's motto: "*The needs of the patient come first*"
  This overarching principle does not prevent a health system's subsystems to adopt their own drivers. However, they need to contribute to the seamless integration of meeting the health system's overall objectives

This chapter illustrates how people/person-centred complex adaptive systems thinking and interventions can guide the redesign of novel approaches at every organisational level.

At the service delivery (micro) level:

- *Clinical care in the consultation.* Drawing causal loop diagrams can provide important insights into the dynamics of a person's illness. The deeper understanding about the linkages between the biological, social, emotional, and cognitive state of the person's current illness experience allows a clinician to more effectively integrate the management of the personal, environmental, and medical domains
- *Preventing avoidable hospitalisation of the frail elderly.* Monitoring the daily changes in frail elderly patients' health experiences can identify those at risk of avoidable hospitalisation. The main reason resulting in avoidable hospitalisation, surprisingly, is the perception of *lack of social support* rather than actual deterioration in organ specific function

© Springer International Publishing AG 2018
J.P. Sturmberg, *Health System Redesign*, DOI 10.1007/978-3-319-64605-3_10

- *Guidelines can be unworkable.* When identified, a process known as *"positive deviance"* allows those affected to quickly develop novel approaches that achieve the desired outcomes. *Positive deviance* entails (1) to acknowledge that there is a problem, (2) that every individual is part of the problem, (3) that there are barriers to change, and (4) that collective conversations amongst all involved will result in better solutions

At the community (meso) level:

- *Health system redesign at the community level, particularly in disadvantaged ones, requires community consultation.* Since *health is a personal experience* understanding what impacts on the people's and community's health is essential. For example, the most disadvantaged community in Sydney identified community development and renewal, employment skills and opportunities as well as community safety as the top priorities for the improvement of their health
- *Community health invariably requires a multi-pronged approach.* The *"Shape up Somerville"* initiative exemplifies this approach. The nutrition department worked with schools to improve pupils' nutrition knowledge and adapted the canteen's food offerings. The next step engaged the City Council to improve walk and cycle ways as well as play and sports grounds. Optimisation of the school bus routes allowed more kids to safely walk to the next bus stop rather than needing to be driven to school, and working with food outlets identified those willing to offer healthy food choices

At the policy (macro) level:

- *Health systems need to clearly define their purpose, goals, and values.* Purpose, goals, and value statements are the foundations that guide the behaviours and actions of a health system's agents and thus affect the function of the "health system as a whole"
- *As the system emerges over time its purpose and values remained unchanged.* What changed are its specific goals in light of newly identified needs

All these examples have one thing in common, they all focus on the *person/patient*. This focus provides the necessary space required to allow for the essential complex adaptive work amongst all to realise *best possible health experiences*. This approach invariably results in:

- More effective and efficient care delivery
- Greater satisfaction of all involved in health care
- Achieves equity
- Makes the system more sustainable

Points for Reflection

These points of reflection are best addressed after reading this chapter.

- Who is at the centre of your health system?
- Does your health system *meet the needs of the person/patient*?
- How could you achieve care at the consultation and community level that would *meet the needs of the person/patient*?
- What are some of the enablers and inhibitors to achieving the goal of *meeting the needs of the person/people* in the community?

This chapter of the book aims to illustrate how *complex adaptive systems thinking* can indeed make a difference to the improvement of all kind of health system issues.

The main point to highlight again is: any system needs to understand its **purpose**, **goals**, **values**, and **"simple rules"**. Together they define the **core driver** of the system. Adherence to the core driver is a prerequisite for change in parts of the system to seamlessly integrate with the "system as a whole", and thus allow it to truly function as a *complex adaptive health system.*

While the purpose and goals of a health system can be easily agreed upon, defining *common values* for a health system is much more difficult to achieve. Aiming for a *value-focused* health system has emerged as the catch-cry for health system reform over the past decade; yet, what constitutes "value" remains contentious (see Addenda to Chap. 5). The importance of defining common values for our health systems cannot be overemphasised as it is the *definition of value* that defines how the health system approaches health care and health system redesign.

The philosophy of medicine clearly states that the *value of health services arises from its impact on the health of the people we treat* [1]. Economic and political philosophies may see this rather differently, value for money sounds a noble aim but political reality often distorts this to favour those who cry out loudest, be it people, patients, health professionals, or industry.

The argument pursued is that a *functional complex adaptive health system* would put the *person/patient at its centre* [1–7], a view now more broadly embraced.[1] Hence, within the limited scope of this book, we showcase a few examples that address how *people/person-centred complex adaptive systems thinking* can influence the way we approach problems at the nano, micro, meso, and macro level of organisation.

---

[1] At the *NEJM Catalyst* event *New Risk, New Business Models* held in Boston, October 6, 2016, Dr Rushika Fernandopulle made these observations and drew the following observations: Attempts made by incumbent health plans and systems to address problems such as high costs and poor outcomes have not been wholly successful. Even new processes, rewards, technology, and culture changes meant to improve health care are still largely built *for the old system.* Despite lots of rhetoric, the real effort is almost always small and incremental. About 12 years ago, I realised that these small, incremental changes were not going to work. The problem is that our current health care system focuses on transactions. Last I checked, those don't heal anyone. What heals people—the reason we all went into medicine—is relationships. To form those relationships, we must remove transactions, and to do that, we have to change everything. Change the payment model, change the delivery model, change the technology platform, maybe **more importantly** change the culture. (http://catalyst.nejm.org/videos/relationship-based-care-change-everything/?utm_campaign=Connect+Weekly&utm_source=hs_email&utm_medium=email&utm_content=39615521&_hsenc=p2ANqtz--5tkREDH1pZUnaiETiCgF1p3zHuFRfJ2T3xjcaoReqBDKolXNZ-_4wiS4_d2uXAZQtnxo2yFwBsBiV--RC84XahREgxA&_hsmi=39615521)

10.1 Micro-Level Problems

Micro-level problems arise in the context of direct patient care. Three examples outline how to improve patient outcomes by adopting *complex adaptive systems thinking*:

- How do external factors impact on clinical disease presentation
- How can primary care providers prevent avoidable hospital admissions
- How to replace redundant guidelines for infection control with adaptive solutions that can work for everyone in a particular environment

10.1.1 Dynamic Changes in Disease Progression

Simply drawing a multiple cause and sign graph diagram illuminates how a patient's deteriorating health results as much from the interdependent variables of his social context as basic physiology.

Consider the following case study: 63-year-old John is married, recently retired, and has three grown-up children no longer living at home. His relationship with his wife is strained, and he is greatly concerned about the relationship and work stresses experienced by his children. He has come in to see his general practitioner/family physician for a routine check-up. His medical history includes hypertension treated with an ACE-inhibitor and impaired glucose tolerance along with mild obesity. He has ceased smoking 12 months ago. Diet and regular exercise have helped him to control both his blood pressure and blood glucose levels.

Today John's BP is 175/105 and his weight has increased by 5 kg (BMI 28.7). His random blood sugar level is 13.5 mmol/L (244 mg/dl). After hearing these results, he admits that he has been "a bit slack" in looking after himself for the past few months.

Where to from here? If you take a *disease-focused mindset* you take his explanation at face value, increase his medications, and encourage him to return to his previous lifestyle behaviours. Or you could take a *person-centred approach* to understand the deeper reasons for his deterioration.

A *person-centred approach* involves exploring the context of John's deterioration. A complex adaptive systems thinking approach can enhance the family physician's person-centred consultation approach by illuminating the linkages between the social, emotional, cognitive/semiotic, and physiological aspects of his illness. To assist with this task, you can draw a causal loop diagram to understand the interconnected issues and feedback loops affecting his disease progression (Fig. 10.1). A causal loop diagram thus gives the primary care clinician new insights into John's illness experience. It opens a new narrative approach to help John

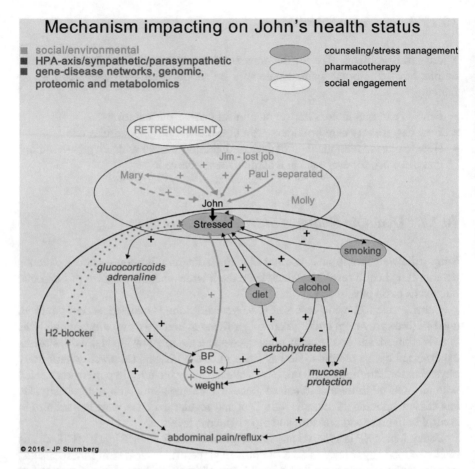

Fig. 10.1 Causal loop diagram of John's illness experience. John's current health status is influenced by three broad domains—his external environment, his personal situation, and his response to it, and the physiological responses resulting from his lifestyle choices. Note how feedback loops between variables from different environments influence different aspects of the physiology and health experience. Social and environmental factors (*green font*), physiological stress responses (*red font*), biological responses (*purple font*), counselling/stress management (*red circles*), poly/pharmacy (*blue circles*), and social interventions (*yellow circles*), adapted from Sturmberg JP. Systems and complexity thinking in general practice. Part I—clinical application [31]

make sense of his illness, identify new intervention points, and explore alternative treatment approaches in order to modify his illness experience.[2]

First, note the context of John's deterioration; the central issue for his deterioration relates to his stresses triggered by social events—his retirement, marital

---

[2]For a step-by-step approach to developing this causal loop diagram see Sturmberg JP. Systems and complexity thinking in general practice. Part I—clinical application [31].

frictions and his children's marital and work difficulties—to emotionally and cognitively cope he has increased his alcohol consumption and started smoking again. All of these challenges trigger the physiological stress response, activating the hypothalamus–pituitary–adrenal axis to release hormones (cortisol, adrenaline) which increase blood pressure and glucose levels. The combined effects of elevated stress hormones, increased alcohol consumption, and smoking explain the—now reported—new symptom of dyspepsia. These events form feedback loops resulting in further increase in John's stress levels, exacerbating the physiological, social, and behavioural variables.

Missing these context driven factors in John's illness will result in unintended consequences associated with the traditional disease-focused doctor-centric approach to the consultation. Increasing medication dosages may reduce blood pressure and lower the blood glucose levels but run the risks of polypharmacy, drug side effects, diminished quality of life, and overtreatment. When the stress levels regress to the mean, the higher medication doses increase the risks of transient hypotension, falls, and erectile dysfunction.

Sharing the causal loop diagram with John is a powerful educational tool to facilitate a shared understanding about the complexities, i.e. the interconnected dependencies of John's life and patho/physiology, impacting on his current health experiences. This shared understanding can help identify the best leverage points for restoring physiological homeostasis [8], sense of coherence [9], and resilience [10] in order to optimise healthy living [11]. Jointly exploring his map starts a therapeutic conversation for shared and informed decision-making about selecting family, behavioural, pharmacological, and therapeutic interventions [12].

The causal loop diagram approach helps one to understand the subjective and objective aspects of John's current health state and enables the formulation of the most appropriate management strategies. A complexity mindset considers more than just disease-specific interventions which exist for almost every condition and frees family physicians and patients from the erroneous expectation that there is a formula or guideline for optimising positive outcomes. Many aspects of managing illness involve interventions of a socioeconomic and environmental nature. Engaging patients in dialogues forms a partnership with their physician [12] that helps to:

- Develop a coherent narrative explanation of their illness experience
- Assess real-time impacts of assessments and interventions
- Achieve shared treatment decisions including compromises aimed at achieving desired outcomes
- Consider potential—positive and negative—unintended consequences resulting from either taking or not taking a full history, performing or not performing a physical examination, ordering or not ordering investigations, and suggesting or not suggesting therapeutic interventions

10.1.2   Care for the Frail Elderly: Preventing Avoidable Hospitalisation

Avoidable hospital admission is a major issue for many western health services [13]. The frail elderly are at a particularly high risk of hospitalisation. However, the frail elderly are not a homogenous cohort [14]; each person has unique personal and clinical features that can trigger a sudden decline in health necessitating urgent care, which may be medical, emotional, or social in nature. There are multiple discernible phases or patterns across the illness and disease journey over time, which are associated with considerable expenditure variation. Stages of the patient journey vary according to the dynamics and interconnected feedback loops among the bio-psycho-social, health care, and environmental domains as well as chronic disease and/or frailty progression [15, 16]. Identifying patterns of impending need for care combined with readily provided tailored care has the potential to prevent most avoidable hospitalisations.

Avoiding hospitalisation occurs at the interface between the micro and meso levels of care. Meeting a person's medical, emotional, social, and cognitive needs requires input from the person's local health professionals as well as community and social care services (Fig. 10.2).

10.1.2.1   Monitoring the Health Trajectory of the Elderly and Frail

Most frail elderly, while principally cared for on an ongoing basis by a primary care physician, are often only seen episodically when their health has significantly deteriorated. This example from Ireland illustrates how ongoing telephone-based monitoring of the health experiences of an at-risk population can reduce avoidable hospitalisation (Fig. 10.3). The service is run by lay health workers who maintain ongoing semi-structured conversations with at-risk patients; responses are summarised according to health concerns, self-rated health, and well-being and entered into a computer programme with build-in predictive modelling capabilities (Patient Journey Record system (PaJR)). Health workers receive real-time feedback that guides decision-making regarding the most appropriate ongoing management at this point in time—no action required, review with local health professional or immediate need for medical review. Evaluation has shown that many avoidable hospitalisations result from needs arising from fears of social isolation and missing timely support from community services [15, 17]. The daily telephone contacts provide important social care which is strongly related to reduced mortality in the frail elderly [18].

PaJR is an example how the reconfiguration of available local services might contribute to a more effective and efficient health service. While it may involve greater investment in some "non-medical services" it generates substantial savings for the health service at large.

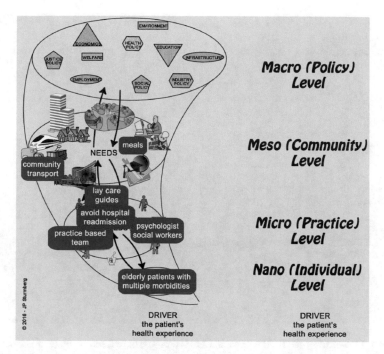

Fig. 10.2 The PaJR system deals with a particular part of the health system, the frail elderly at high risk of avoidable hospitalisation. The main actors in the system are the person at the nano (individual) and the primary care service at the micro level. Many people's deterioration relates to lack of social services residing at the meso (community) level. The benefits of aligning patient needs not only maintains or improves patients' health and well-being, it also saves scares hospital related resource use

10.1.3   MRSA-Control: Facilitating Adaptive Change in an Institutional Setting

MRSA is a perpetual problem in institutional care settings. Usually formal infection control guidelines and protocols have failed to achieve the desired outcomes as they fail to understand the context in which staff is expected to implement them. Staff in one hospital was concerned about the risks and negative consequences of spreading MRSA between patients and initiated an *adaptive change* process (Fig. 10.4).

Solving this problem required health professionals to engage in making *adaptive changes* to their own behaviours. Making change to reach a "workable" solution (this approach to adaptive change management is known as "positive deviance" [19]) requires:

- In the first instance to acknowledge there is a problem
- That every individual is part of the problem
- That there are barriers to change

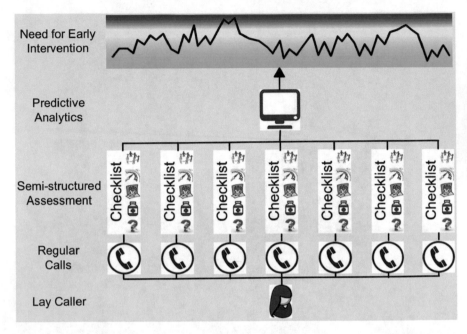

Fig. 10.3 Flowchart of the PaJR approach. Care is person-centred, semi-structured assessment of well-being, change in medication use, self-assessed health, confidence in managing, and social support are key variables of the dynamics of health. Change in the patterns of these parameters can predict the likelihood of deterioration in health in the next few days. Early intervention can re-stabilise health and thus avoids preventable hospital admission

- That a better solution will emerge from collective conversations amongst all involved

This case study demonstrates a bottom-up approach to solving a local problem within a specific part of the healthcare system [20]. Positive deviance utilises people's understanding of the problem and the barriers to change through collective conversations. The process requires the full engagement and support of an organisation's leadership across organisational levels and between service networks. Results are emergent "workable" solutions *valid only in this environment at this point in time*. In the setting of this case study the success of bottom-up change encouraged other units to tackle their particular problems utilising positive deviance approaches.

10.1.3.1   Achieving local change—the importance of context

Current policy statements rarely reflect the importance of *context on behaviour* to improve organisational function and outcomes [21–23]. It is a major reason for failures to achieve and/or maintain sustained change within organisations. Lindberg and Schneider [20] emphasise the importance of understanding the human dynamics

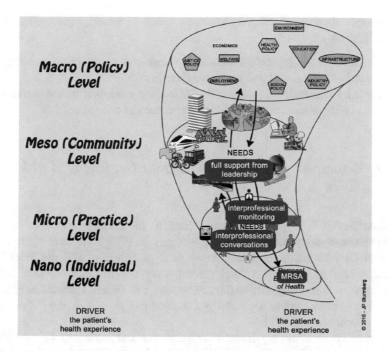

Fig. 10.4 Responding to a local issue. Prevailing MRSA prevention guidelines were recognised to put patients and staff in a rehabilitation ward at risk of accidents and infection spread. Staff concern initiated a conversation between staff and management that resulted in the "*bottom up*" emergence of "*workable guidelines*" for this local context

and qualities associated with change in complex human systems, including changes shaped by power, fear, attachment, and paradox. They outline one of many "techniques" [20, 24–26] to lead a change process. This approach facilitates an understanding of the multiple facets of the problems people face, and allows them to learn and grow, and to find the *best possible, i.e. best adapted, solutions* for their *unique context*.

This case study illustrates how to successfully change ONE particular problem at the care delivery level, even in otherwise highly fragmented or dysfunctional healthcare systems. Principally, one can achieved "process related changes" in any local situation, like a rehabilitation ward, when concerned staff at the nano/micro level of care delivery adopt a patient-centred care focus.

10.2   Meso Level Problems

Meso level problems arise as a consequence of community dysfunction. At this level care needs are broader than just the delivery of healthcare services and entail the need for social care and community development. Two examples outline how to improve individual and community health outcomes by adopting a *complex adaptive systems thinking* approach:

- People in a severely socioeconomically deprived community co-designed a community environment that *promotes their health*
- Community leadership co-designed a cascading community development programme to implement community health promotion and prevention

10.2.1   Community 2168: When Citizens Get Engaged with Change

The Community 2168 project[3]—a reference to the local postcode of the most disadvantaged Sydney suburb of Miller—began in 1999 with three agencies, the Liverpool City Council, the State Department of Housing, and the local health service. It was designed as a "major community renewal and capacity building partnership". It was a response to the community's feeling of abandonment in light of the crisis in public safety triggered by the closure of their bank, the police station, and other local services [27].

Community 2168 set up forums for residents and local service providers—including local NGOs, police, the council, and housing, health, and community services—to come together to identify the community's most pressing problems and devise ways of dealing with them. The project team realised that the citizens were the ones who best understand the relationships between their local environment, housing, social infrastructure, education, safety of roads and recreational facilities, etc., on their health.

The people in Miller identified that community development would provide greater benefit for their health than merely increasing the number of health services. They experienced family dysfunction and mental health and drug and alcohol problems as a consequence of the vicious cycle of community deprivation and hopelessness.

10.2.1.1   Moving Forward for Miller: The Strategic Plan 2015–2018

Based on these insights the Community 2168 Project put forward a 3-year strategic direction to guide *what* the project will do and *how* it will do it. Seven domains emerged—the focus on "health and well-being" being at the bottom of the list:

- Community Building, Engagement, Participation, and Communication
- Community Pride and Harmony
- Urban Renewal

---

[3]http://www.liverpool.nsw.gov.au/community/our-community/living-in-2168

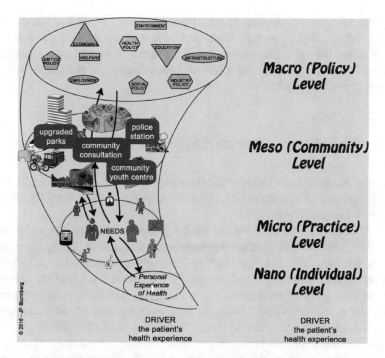

Fig. 10.5 Community 2168, whilst having a health improvement goal, focused largely on the community. Engaging community members with community service providers identified the necessary local change to be addressed as a prerequisite for health improvements. Of note, this project succeeded without the need of policy level change or major investments into healthcare delivery services

- Employment and Skills Development
- Education and Training
- Community Safety
- Health and Well-being

This project tackles the root causes of the poor health of the people in Community 2168—socioeconomic inequality. *Investing* in community development is a more effective and efficient way to improve the health of this community. The project team coordinated necessary *health system improvements* required to achieve *better health* rather than simply expanding—in a top-down fashion—healthcare services to manage the consequences of socioeconomic inequality underlying the community's poor health (Fig. 10.5).

Unfortunately health and social services operate from different government departments which rarely coordinate their efforts. Here all identified services work collaboratively with local communities to restore the lost trust in government agencies by implementing actions that address the most pressing needs first. Working together prevents unnecessary bureaucratic "knee-jerk responses" to either push for punitive welfare reforms in light of the community's "recalcitrant behaviours" or equally unnecessary service restructuring perceived to be the reason for the lack of progress. Both responses waste *scarce health and social service resources* that are better *invested* into services and infrastructures that allow people and communities to grow and thereby improve their health (in economic terms, this approach *generates profits*).

10.2.2   The Shape up Somerville (SUS) Project

Somerville is a socioeconomically disadvantaged community northwest of Boston. It had a high rate of childhood obesity which was the starting point for the *Shape Up Somerville* (SUS) project.[4]

In 2002 the CDC initially funded the project as an obesity prevention project for first to third graders through environmental change. In 2005, based on the project's success, SUS was adopted by the City of Somerville and since has employed a *systems change* agenda: engage all sectors and levels of the community including local government, businesses, schools, non-profits, healthcare, grass-roots organisations, and individuals, to create policy change that promotes community-wide health and well-being, health equity, and social justice [28, 29].

Shape up Somerville is an example of a health professional led multi-level community development project for better health. While the focus is on the improvement of the health of everyone living in the community its implementation is a stepwise one driven by the principle of community engagement involving citizens, community groups, and local government leaders. The first step aimed at improving the food in school canteens—an initiative led by dieticians, followed by improving access to the school bus by making it safe for children to walk to their nearest bus stop. The emergent properties of these interventions resulted in children insisting on healthier food at home, restaurants adapting their menus offering healthier meal choices, and the council repairing playgrounds, walkways, and bicycle lanes (Fig. 10.6).

This initiative emerged as a powerful force that influenced the values of a community and focused all in pursuing the issues that needed to change to achieve an ongoing improvement in the health of individuals and the community at large.

---

[4]http://www.somervillema.gov/departments/health/sus

http://www.nutrition.tufts.edu/index.php?q=research/shapeup-somerville

Shape Up Somerville: Building and Sustaining a Healthy Community with Collective Impact https://www.youtube.com/watch?v=aBHz-GzDX8c

Shape Up Somerville: NECN— Call to Revolution https://www.youtube.com/watch?v=71V12zS7nQU

Mayor Joe Curtatone Speaks at White House for First Lady Obama's Let's Move Program 2.9.10 https://www.youtube.com/watch?v=viIJLjVrUcg

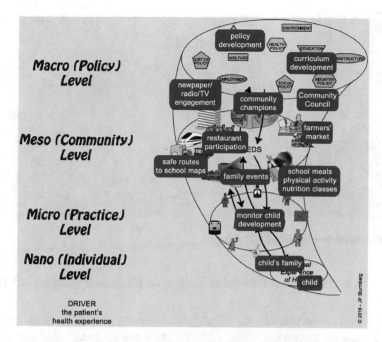

Fig. 10.6 Shape up Somerville started at the interface between the meso and micro levels of care. Reducing childhood obesity is a *systemic* problem, it requires as much an individual as a family and community focus. The project succeeded as it aligned all agents around the common focus on improving the health of their community's children

These two examples show the importance of galvanising citizens to "*do the adaptive work that needs to be done*" [24], creating the common purpose, goals, and values that allow the needed changes to be formulated and solutions implemented; while health focused, much of the work that needed to be done was simultaneously done by health professionals, local government workers, and community members. In both cases leadership was team-based; leading was distributed to achieve desired outcomes in the most effective and efficient way.

10.3 Macro-Level Problems

Macro-level problems arise in the policy domain and deal with "health system as a whole" problems. Chapter 7 described the design of three health system in three different context—the vortex images below just serve as a reminder (Fig. 10.7).

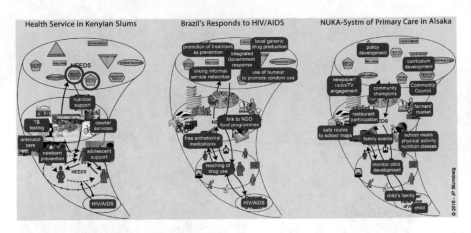

Fig. 10.7   Macro-level health system reform

10.4   Value Focused *Complex Adaptive* Health System Reform

As the examples in this chapter highlight it is easily possible to shift the focus of healthcare on the person/patient. The *focus on the person/patient* provides the necessary space for essential complex adaptive interactions between all involved in their care.

Required interactions will necessarily vary dependent on the nature of the problem and/or circumstances—some will be managed by simple or complicated, others by complex and complex adaptive approaches (Table 10.1).

Responding to problems with the appropriate strategy invariably results in:

- More effective and efficient care delivery
- Greater satisfaction of all involved in health care
- Achieves equity
- Makes the system more sustainable

However, it must be recognised that not all organisations have the same capacity to make changes; the capacity to change depends to a large degree on the organisation's prevailing dynamics. Organisations that are:

- **Highly ordered** systems, such as *very bureaucratic organisations*, tend to fail because of their rigidity; they resist requisite adaptation
- **Highly chaotic** systems also tend to fail, as they have *too few stable components* to buffer them and small forces tend to result in system disruption
- **Complex dynamic** systems that are *simultaneously ordered and disordered* are more able to meet challenges and more resilient to weather distractions

Adopting the Cynefin approach [30] as previously described can help organisational leaders to facilitate the necessary adaptive change required to move towards a more adapted health system.

Table 10.1 What constitutes *value*—perspectives from different stakeholders

Types of Systems	Simple	Complicated	Complex	
	Mechanical systems		Complex (dynamic) systems	Complex adaptive systems
Examples in community health care	Flu vaccination	Managing a 2nd degree burn	Community Care for frail elderly, linking care domains; medication management of polypharmacy	Collaboration in GP clinic; Multimorbidity management
Examples in hospital health care	Laboratory testing	Hip replacement surgery	Bed management in a hospital; Acute psychiatric unit	Intensive care unit; Staff management of a hospital
Examples in health sub-system		Protocols, e.g. handwashing policy	Managing an epidemic; Managing a natural disaster	Mental health; Health financing
Structure of System	One-to-one relationships; E.g. nurse giving Flu shot	One-to-many relationships; E.g. surgeon managing a theatre team; E.g. nurse unit manager ensuring staff records every patient incidents regardless how trivial	Many-to-many and system-to-system relationships (nested systems) Subsystems can have simple, complicated, and complex components E.g. the value of services listed in the MBS (simple) however the fees charged by individual doctors to different patients in their practice is highly variable and depends on many factors (complex) adaptive)	
Outcomes	Linear; E.g. measured as percentage of eligible population being vaccinated (Linear)	Mostly predictable; E.g. measured as number and type of in theatre complications	Alter with history and initial conditions; Unpredictable/emergent; E.g. contextual description of the SES characteristics of population groups, the detailed description of delivery of an intervention and the observed outcomes (e.g. harm reduction of illicit drug use); Non-linear and feedback; Complex - Chaotic	
Generalizability	Yes	Yes	No	No

The next chapter will explore how different lenses on the same health problem—obesity—expand our understanding of a "complex problem". All lenses provide invaluable perspectives, however, only *shared deliberation* amongst all stakeholders can provide the best possible understanding of the problem in its entirety, and thus a "systems-based resolution".

References

1. Pellegrino E, Thomasma D (1981) A philosophical basis of medical practice: towards a philosophy and ethic of the healing professions. Oxford University Press, New York/Oxford
2. Leutz WN (1999) Five laws for integrating medical and social services: lessons from the United States and the United Kingdom. Milbank Q 77(1):77–110
3. Sturmberg JP, O'Halloran DM, Martin CM (2010) People at the centre of complex adaptive health systems reform. Med J Aust 193(8):474–478
4. Sturmberg JP, Martin CM, Moes M (2010) Health at the centre of health systems reform - How Philosophy Can Inform Policy. Perspect Biol Med 53(3):341–356
5. Sturmberg JP, O'Halloran DM, Martin CM (2012) Understanding health system reform - a complex adaptive systems perspective. J Eval Clin Pract 18(1):202–208
6. Valentijn PP, Schepman SM, Opheij W, Bruijnzeels MA (2013) Understanding integrated care: a comprehensive conceptual framework based on the integrative functions of primary care. Int J Integr Care 13:e010
7. Sturmberg JP, O'Halloran DM, Martin CM (2013) Health care reform - the need for a complex adaptive systems approach. In: Sturmberg JP, Martin CM (eds) Handbook of systems and complexity in health. Springer, New York, p 827–853
8. Sturmberg JP, Bennett JM, Picard M, Seely AJE (2015) The trajectory of life. Decreasing physiological network complexity through changing fractal patterns. Front Physiol 6:169
9. Antonovsky A (1993) Complexity, conflict, chaos, coherence, coercion and civility. Soc Sci Med 37(8):969–974
10. Rutter M (1985) Resilience in the face of adversity. Protective factors and resistance to psychiatric disorder. Br J Psychiatry 147(6):598–611
11. Reeve J, Lloyd-Williams M, Payne S, Dowrick C (2009) Towards a re-conceptualisation of the management of distress in palliative care patients: the self-integrity model. Prog Palliat Care 17(2):51–60
12. Launer J (2002) Narrative-based primary care: a practical guide. Radcliffe Medical Press Ltd, Oxford
13. Busby J, Purdy S, Hollingworth W (2015) A systematic review of the magnitude and cause of geographic variation in unplanned hospital admission rates and length of stay for ambulatory care sensitive conditions. BMC Health Serv Res 15:324
14. Hutchinson AF, Graco M, Rasekaba TM, Parikh S, Berlowitz DJ, Lim WK (2015) Relationship between health-related quality of life, comorbidities and acute health care utilisation, in adults with chronic conditions. Health Qual Life Outcomes 13:69
15. Martin CM, Grady D, Deaconking S, McMahon C, Zarabzadeh A, O'Shea B (2011) Complex adaptive chronic care - typologies of patient journey: a case study. J Eval Clin Pract17(3): 520–524
16. Martin C, Biswas R, Joshi A, Sturmberg J (2011) Patient Journey Record Systems (PaJR): the development of a conceptual framework for a patient journey system. In: Biswas R, Martin CM (eds) User-driven healthcare and narrative medicine. IGI-Global, Hershy, PA, p 75–92
17. Martin CM (2014) Self-rated health: patterns in the journeys of patients with multi-morbidity and frailty. J Eval Clin Pract 20(6):1010–1016

18. Mazzella F, Cacciatore F, Galizia G, Della-Morte D, Rossetti M, Abbruzzese R, et al (2010) Social support and long-term mortality in the elderly: role of comorbidity. Arch Gerontol Geriatr 51(3):323–328
19. Lawton R, Taylor N, Clay-Williams R, Braithwaite J (2014) Positive deviance: a different approach to achieving patient safety. BMJ Qual Saf 23:880–883
20. Lindberg C, Schneider M (2013) Combating infections at Maine Medical Center: insights into complexity-informed leadership from positive deviance. Leadership 9(2):229–253
21. Fulop L, Mark A (2013) Leading in healthcare - foregrounding context: the theory and practice of context - introduction to the special issue. Leadership 9(2):151–161
22. Seelos C, Mair J (2012) Innovation is not the holy grail. Stanf Soc Innov Rev 10(4):44–49
23. Ham C, Dixon A, Brooke B (2012) Transforming the delivery of health and social care: the case for fundamental change. King's Fund, London
24. Heifetz R (1994) Leadership without easy answers. Harvard University Press, Cambridge, MA
25. Snowden DJ, Boone ME (2007) A leader's framework for decision making. Harv Bus Rev 85 (11):69–76
26. Fulop L, Mark A (2013) Relational leadership, decision-making and the messiness of context in healthcare. Leadership 9(2):254–277
27. Sweet M (2011) Understanding miller: inside story [internet]. www.inside.org.au. Published 28 March 2011
28. Economos CD, Curtatone JA (2010) Shaping up Somerville: a community initiative in Massachusetts. Prev Med 50(Suppl 1):S97–S98
29. Economos CD, Hyatt RR, Must A, Goldberg JP, Kuder J, Naumova EN, et al (2013) Shape Up Somerville two-year results: a community-based environmental change intervention sustains weight reduction in children. Prev Med 57(4):322–327
30. Kurtz CF, Snowden DJ (2003) The new dynamics of strategy: sense-making in a complex and complicated world. IBM Syst J 42(3):462–483
31. Sturmberg JP (2007) Systems and complexity thinking in general practice. part 1 - clinical application. Aust Fam Physician 36(3):170–173

Chapter 11
Obesity—A Multifaceted Approach: One Problem—Different Models—Different Insights and Solutions

Overview. Obesity decreases people's well-being and contributes to the early development of diseases like diabetes, heart disease, and arthritis. Obesity is rising rapidly as much in the developed world as in low and middle income countries. Government and non-government funders of health care fear that this epidemic of obesity will threaten the viability of health systems.

What can be done to stop the epidemic from spreading? What can be done to help obese people to reduce their weight and prevent the early onset of debilitating diseases like diabetes, heart disease, and arthritis?

What we know:

- Obesity, especially around the waist and in the belly, increases the body's inflammatory load; inflammation is the principle mechanism for the complications of obesity
- Our weight reflects the balance between our food intake and our physical activity
- Obesity spreads within our social networks; being around obese people leads to an increase in our own body weight
- Children of overweight parents are much more likely to become overweight themselves; the main reason for this are the learned patterns of behaviour in relation to shopping, food consumption, and physical activity
- Outdoor activities have significantly reduced with the rise of electronic entertainment for both children and adults
- Obesity is much more common in socioeconomically deprived communities
- Socioeconomically deprived communities have poorer access to healthy foods but easy access to junk food
- Politics reign over policies; political decisions have favoured industry interests over health interests
- Industrial food production has increased the volume of foods grown but in many cases, has decreased the quality of these foods
- Junk food advertising dominates in all forms of media (newspapers, TV, internet), and specifically targets children and adolescents

© Springer International Publishing AG 2018
J.P. Sturmberg, *Health System Redesign*, DOI 10.1007/978-3-319-64605-3_11

Solving the obesity epidemic requires an understanding of the interdependencies of the more than 100 variables and 300 links of the obesity network. The network variables can be grouped into seven broad domains: (1) metabolic pathways, (2) individual activity patterns, (3) individual food consumption patterns, (4) an individual's coping skills, (5) a person's social and (6) physical environments, and (7) the food production, marketing, and distribution system.

Solving the obesity epidemic requires a *seamlessly integrated policy* approach based on clearly defined goals, shared values, and common implementation rules. Such an approach will take *account of the system wide implications of change* to any variable in any of the seven domains. It will evaluate the implications of any change on the person, the community, and society as a whole.

How can we develop systemic solutions to the obesity epidemic? Interventions can be grouped at the personal, community, and societal level, however, the greatest likelihood of success results from coordinated approaches across these levels. Interventions to consider include:

At the person level:

- Improve food and physical activity education in parenting groups, schools, and work places
- Increase physical activities, decrease sedentary activities
- Improving shopping and cooking skills

Personal level interventions require support at the community level:

- Improve access to safe walk and cycle ways, play grounds, and sports fields
- Improve healthy food choices in stores and restaurants
- Replace "junk food" with fresh foods in the school and work environments
- Provide easily accessible, cost-effective and reliable public transport
- Foster the development of community gardens to improve access to fresh foods especially in socioeconomically disadvantaged communities

Community level interventions need to be supported at the whole of society level:

- Promotion/advertising of healthy eating and physical activity
- Incentives to support local fresh food production, like community gardens
- Development and implementation of production rules that ensure the delivery of high quality plant and animal foods
- Phasing out of "junk food" advertising modelled on the approach to tobacco
- Using tax system mechanisms to support healthy food production and penalise "junk food" production
- Investing in infrastructure that supports safe physical activity in local communities
- System wide assessment of investments into health against savings in healthcare

Successful change management must consider the inevitable emergence of resistance to change as change entails threats to the vested interests inherent in the prevailing status quo.

Points for Reflection

- Considering obesity as a systemic problem, who are the key agents that control the status quo?
- Obesity results from personal, community, and societal behaviours. How are they related to each other?
- What kind of interventions could be considered at each level?
- To be successful in achieving lasting change, strategies need to seamlessly integrate across and between personal, community, and societal levels. What strategies could be employed to facilitate this change?

Obesity, and in particular childhood obesity, is a problem that currently occupies the minds of benchtop researchers, people, health professionals, industry, insurers and politicians as well as policymakers. All are concerned with the *one problem*, all have developed *different models* to understand the problem, and all have found *different insights and solutions*. While all provide valuable insights on part of the problem (which in that sense is reductionist), few have attempted to outline a systemic approach to manage the problem as a *whole* [1–3].

Appreciating the complexities of obesity and avoiding erroneous strategic decision-making requires:

- An appreciation that obesity causes span the nano to macro-level continuum
- An evaluation of the strength and limitations of partial obesity model
- An exploration how partial models fit into an "obesity as whole" model

11.1 The Pieces of the Obesity Puzzle

Obesity is a complex problem. This chapter cannot provide a comprehensive picture of all the complexities, rather, it aims to point to some key issues that have been explored using systems thinking approaches:

- Physiological aspects
- Social aspects
- Industry aspects

before outlining an "obesity as a whole" model and its implication for systemic solutions considering:

- Biomedical approaches
- Social and environmental approaches
- Policy approaches

11.1.1 Physiological Aspects

11.1.1.1 Low-Grade Inflammation of White Adipose Tissue

Benchtop research has identified the physiological changes associated with obesity [4–6]. These findings indicate that increasing weight gain results in an inflammatory response in adipose tissue. The resulting increase in pro-inflammatory cytokines leads to insulin resistance preventing glucose uptake by muscle cells and inhibition of neoglucogenesis in the liver as well as endothelial inflammation in blood vessels. The consequences of the inflammatory processes are clinically seen in the rise of blood glucose levels, free fatty acids, and pro-inflammatory markers like CRP, TNF-α, and IL-6 (Fig. 11.1). Reversing obesity by diet and exercise reduces these pathophysiological changes [7–9].

Fig. 11.1 Simplified system dynamics model of the *"Physiology of Obesity"*. Obesity results in an increase in the metabolically active white adipose tissue resulting in an increased production of inflammatory molecules responsible for insulin resistance (*solid arrows*) and the inhibition of the protective effects of adiponectin (*dashed arrows*)

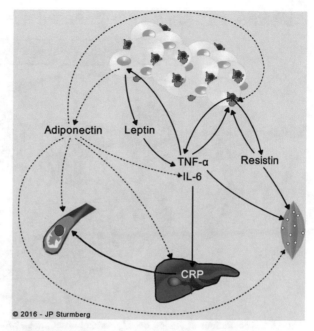

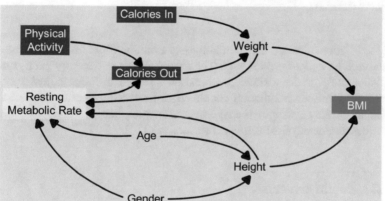

Fig. 11.2 Agent-based model of body mass index. Modifiable variables (*red boxes*) that affect BMI (*green box*), resting metabolic rate is a function of age, height, and gender (*yellow box*)

11.1.1.2 "My-BMI"

At the person level overall nutritional state is reflected in a person's body mass index (BMI) calculated from his weight and height. Weight reflects energy balance (caloric intake and use), and height is genetically determined by gender and—in childhood and adolescents—age. Caloric output is a function of resting metabolic rate[1] and physical activity (Fig. 11.2).

---

[1] Metabolic rate is usually estimated by the Schofield equation from height, weight, age, and gender.

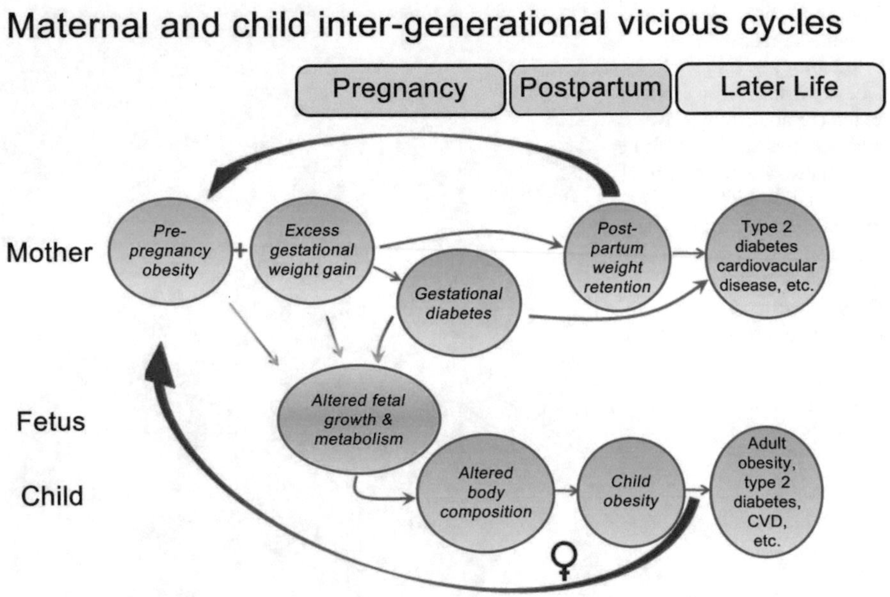

Maternal and child inter-generational vicious cycles

Fig. 11.3 The vicious cycle of obesity spread from mother-to-child (image courtesy of Dr Matthew W Gillman)

These relationships are the foundations to examine different weight loss strategies through an agent-based model. The model allows one to vary each parameter either separately or in various combinations. Hence one can adjust the model parameters to various population characteristics as well as testing the most likely benefits of different weight management strategies like the effects of different weight loss and/or physical activity interventions [10].

11.1.2   Social Aspects

11.1.2.1   The Social Spread of Obesity

At the micro-level obesity starts early in life [11, 12] and, as children become adults, its spread is perpetuated by "mother-to-child" transmission (Fig. 11.3) [11].

Christakis and Fowler [13] showed that social influences—social norms, social capital, and stress—promote obesity throughout social networks. In addition evidence emerged for adult-to-adult, adult-to-child, and child-to-child influences that promote obesogenic behaviours [14].

The researchers developed a model (Fig. 11.4) to investigate the effects of social relationships and found a stronger link between adult-to-child than child-to-child

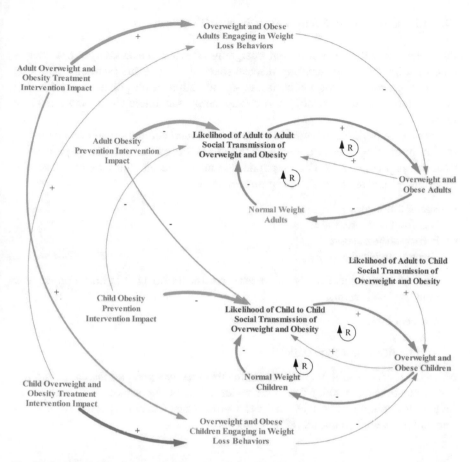

Fig. 11.4 Causal loop diagram of adult and child social transmission of obesity. The figure shows the elements of the system model to test hypotheses regarding child and adult social transmission of unhealthy behaviours causing overweight and obesity. Adult level elements are shown in green and child level elements are shown in purple. "R" indicates reinforcing feedback loops. Prevention intervention impact for children and adult levels are shown with negatively labelled arrows to social transmission. Intervention impact lines are shown at different widths to indicate differences in relative magnitude of impact. The *thickest lines* are shown regarding adult-to-adult impact and child-to-child impacts. *Lines of medium thickness* are shown regarding adult-to-child impact. The *thinnest lines* are shown regarding child to adult impact (reproduced from Frerichs LM, Araz OM, Huang TTK. Modeling social transmission dynamics of unhealthy behaviours for evaluating prevention and treatment interventions on childhood obesity [14]. (Creative Commons Attribution License))

social transmission rate, and that interventions focusing on adults rather than children were more effective in preventing children becoming obese.

These findings are highly significant and highlight how modelling can prevent the investment of efforts and resources into doomed projects.

11.1.2.2 Community Factors Associated with Obesity

Prevention is better than cure, but designing effective prevention programmes is much harder than implementing disease-specific curative interventions. The first step in a prevention programme is the identification of all potential contributing factors, the second to identify the relationships and interactions between these factors.

A research project conducted in an Australian rural community identified the key factors promoting obesity amongst children resulting in a community prevention systems map (Fig. 11.5). Four separate domains were identified as key areas for designing effective prevention programmes [15]:

- Social influences
- Fast food and junk food
- Participation in sport
- General physical activity

The epidemiological study of obesity across Berlin [14] is an example how community level factors:

- Socioeconomics
- Ethnicity
- Availability of fast food outlets

affect the level of health in different segments of a city's population. These findings nicely illustrate that looking for "one size fits all" solutions cannot work. Rather they help to design tailored policies and interventions best suited to specific community and environmental conditions (Fig. 11.6).

11.1.3 Industry Aspects

11.1.3.1 Obesity: The Conflicted Politics of the Food System

Obesity at large is a symptom of our economic orientation and organisation [17–19]. Enterprises of all kind focus on only *their side of the ledger* (paraphrased as "what's in it for me"),[2] however, every ledger has two sides—my gain is your loss. Such a "win-lose" framework creates *unsustainable states* in which everyone ultimately loses [20]. It is the role of government to *balance vested interests for the greater good of its citizens*—Fig. 11.7 highlights some of the challenges and some of the responses of industry, individuals, and communities. A detailed understanding of

---

[2]The cooperation law states that it is the company directors' fiduciary duty to ensure profit maximisation for their shareholders.

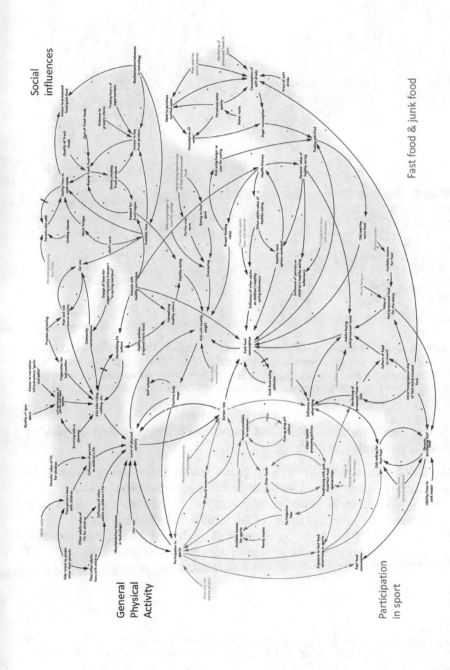

Fig. 11.5 Causal loop diagram of cause of childhood obesity in a rural community (reproduced from Allender S, Owen B, Kuhlberg J, Lowe J, Nagorcka-Smith P, Whelan J, et al. A community based systems diagram of obesity causes [15]. (Creative Commons Attribution License))

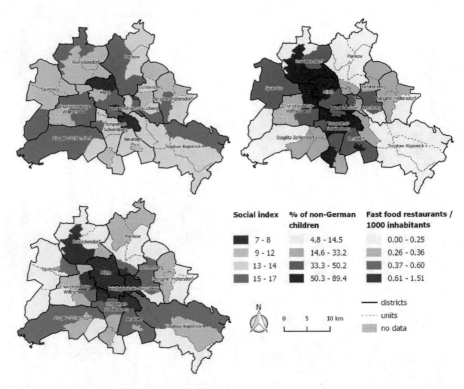

Fig. 11.6 Geospatial distribution of childhood obesity in Berlin in relation to three community level factors—socioeconomics, ethnicity, and availability of fast food outlets (reproduced from Lakes T, Burkart K. Childhood overweight in Berlin: intra-urban differences and underlying influencing factors [16]. (Creative Commons Attribution 4.0 International License))

the food system's interrelationships and interactions can help to minimise making undesirable policy choices like[3]:

- The link between biofuels and food prices indicates how policy decisions in one domain easily can have variable undesirable but unintended consequences—biofuels have increased land clearing, reduced the diversity of agricultural production, and contributed to half of the increase in food prices [21]
- The emergence of community gardens is an unplanned (unexpected) response of especially socioeconomically deprived communities to the unaffordability of fresh foods [22–24]

---

[3]The systemic nature of the food system has been highlighted by the Institute of Medicine in its recent publication: IOM (Institute of Medicine) and NRC (National Research Council). 2015. A framework for assessing effects of the food system. Washington, DC: The National Academies Press.

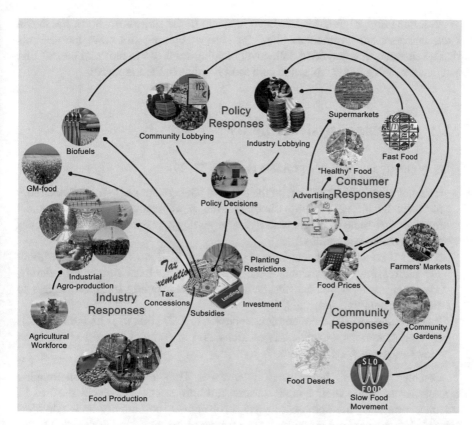

Fig. 11.7 The conflicted politics of the food system. Every policy decision will lead to particular response by different stakeholders. The figure is necessarily an oversimplification and cannot show all linkages and feedback loops. Note how the support of the biofuel industry had an unintended and undesirable impact on food prices. While food price pressures, especially in socioeconomically disadvantaged communities led to the emergence of community gardens, environmental and food quality concerns allowed the parallel emergence of the *slow food movement*

- Government's fiscal constraints preference short term food industry growth over long-term healthcare consequences, e.g. the food industry denying to be a major source of the obesity crisis nevertheless offering to increase their efforts to reformulate food production despite this posing significant technical difficulties and requiring significant investments [25–27]
- Globally, deregulation of the food system results in speculation in food commodities, and despite an increase in food crops, food prices as well as hunger rises, hence the call to implement a *food sovereignty* system [25] and fostering biodiversity as a means to sustainable agriculture [28]
- Other issues: health risks—growing problem of antibiotic resistance from animal feed additives; environmental risks—soil damage, weed and fertiliser pollution, loss of biodiversity; socioeconomic risks—loss of small farms as a result of an industrial model of crop production [29]

Unfortunately political leaders have succumb to the short-termism of the media cycle that demands "immediate fixes" for every symptom—this collusion prevents that all citizens get engaged in collectively finding solutions to the "real issues" that guarantee reliable, affordable, and safe food supplies in the long term.

11.2   A Whole of System Approach to Obesity

Obesity clearly is a complex problem [1, 8, 19, 27, 29]:

- It cannot be solved by calling on the obese to take greater *personal responsibility* for their health [27] or by directing even more resources into biomedical research that focuses on its underlying physiology, weight related morbidities, and pharmacotherapeutics
- Nor can it be solved by altering the *obesogenic food environment* [27] without also addressing the stressors of the person's external environmental—family, education, socioeconomics, the build environment, public transport, access to affordable healthy food, etc. [3]
- It will require an all of government approach [19, 27] that uses its familiar tools of tax concessions, subsidies, regulations, and investment support to create an *anti-obesogenic* food system

Complex problems have no *easy answers*. They require systems thinking approaches to guide their course towards resolution. The focus will need to be on three domains, the socio-ecological environment, community and individual lifestyle behaviours, and individual management of the condition (Table 11.1).

The full complexities of obesity are outlined in the Foresight report [1] which identified more than 100 variables with more than 300 connections (Fig. 11.8). The variables of the model cluster around seven broad domains (Fig. 11.9):

- Biology/physiology
- Individual activities
- Food consumption
- Individual psychology
- The activity environment
- The social environment
- Food production

The model also identified that the strength of feedback between variables in the model varies. These differences point to potential barriers and enablers to be considered for policy developments and intervention designs. The Foresight report identified key intervention strategies (Fig. 11.10) into various obesity system domains including:

- Education
- Media campaigns supporting healthy eating

Table 11.1 Systems-based approaches to reverse the obesity epidemic

	Socio-ecological approaches	Lifestyle approaches	Health services approaches
Approaches	Approaches that shape the economic, social, and physical (built and natural) environments	Approaches that directly influence behaviour (reducing energy intake and increasing physical activity)	Health Services approaches (focus on the individual person in his immediate and community context, utilisation of biomedical interventions)
Focus	Focus on economic and social policy factors and community development	Focus on community attitudes and expectations require community development strategies	Focus on the individual person in his immediate and community context, utilisation of biomedical interventions
E.g.	• Food environments • Physical activity environments • Socioeconomic environments (including taxation, employment, education, housing, and welfare)	• Eating • Physical activity • Healthy food choice offers in food outlets • Improved physical environment, public transport options	• Managing and reducing existing weight problems in individuals • Working with families to prevent overweight or obese children becoming overweight or obese adults

- Shifting macro-economic drivers
- Modifying food production processes and food supply
- Exposing children to good eating experiences early in life
- Improving healthcare options for obese people
- Creating the physical environment to support physical activity
- Modifying workplace environments to provide healthy food choices in their canteens and foster physical activities
- Encourage the responsible use of technology in daily life

Each of these strategies has the potential to improve a particular aspects of the obesity puzzle. However, as experience has shown, interventions that solely focus on one particular aspect of the puzzle typically achieve little and/or no lasting change. Successful system improvements require an a priori exploration of potential effects as well as side effects of focused interventions on the behaviour of the "system as a whole".

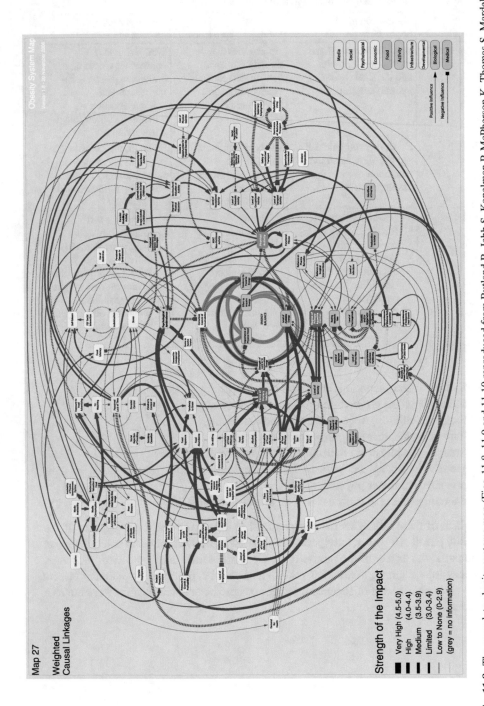

Fig. 11.8 The complete obesity systems map (Figs. 11.8, 11.9 and 11.10 reproduced from Butland B, Jebb S, Kopelman P, McPherson K, Thomas S, Mardell J, et al. Foresight. Tackling obesities: future choices—Project report [1]. (Open Government Licence v3.0))

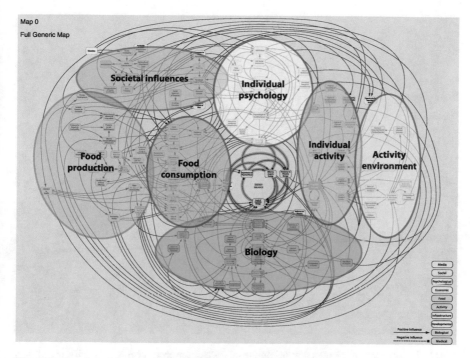

Fig. 11.9 Overlay of the seven broad system domains of the obesity system

11.3   System Redesign to Tackle "The Epidemic of Obesity"

2-D representations of complex multi-layered problems like obesity may detract from "more readily seeing" the multidirectional and multidimensional relationships between the various aspects of the problem. The 3-D representation of obesity in the health vortex model (Fig. 11.11) highlights some of the layered dependencies of the obesity problem as well as emphasising the need for all agents to maintain their focus on the "core of the problem"—the person, and the person's experience of the condition:

- How does it affect him
- How does he believe he ended up being overweight
- How does he envisage to overcome the problem
- How does he understand the obstacles that may stand in the way of change

11.3.1   Sources of Resistance

The latter should help to overcome some of the false and unhelpful conceptual dichotomies in the debate about the obesity epidemic:

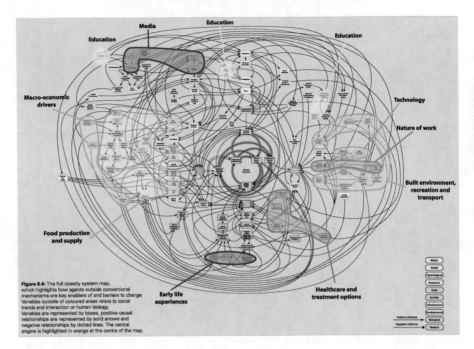

Fig. 11.10 Overlay of 11 intervention points comprising nine strategies to modify the obesity system's behaviour

- *Individual blame versus an obesogenic society*
- *Obesity as a disease versus sequelae of unrestrained gluttony*
- *Obesity as a disability versus the new normal*
- *Lack of physical activity as a cause versus overconsumption of unhealthy food and beverages*
- *Prevention versus treatment*
- *Overnutrition versus undernutrition* [18]

An integrated approach to tackle obesity must address individual, health service, community service, education, industry, and policy domains.[4] This can only be achieved by adopting the common organisational framework of defining purpose, goals, shared values, and "simple (or operating) rules"; they form the basis on which a seamlessly integrated system (Fig. 11.9) can emerge.

---

[4]*Systems Thinking and Evaluation* is a brief animated talk to show health systems planners and evaluators how to recognise interdependencies and avoid foreseeable "mistakes" in planning obesity interventions (https://www.youtube.com/watch?v=2vojPksdbtI).

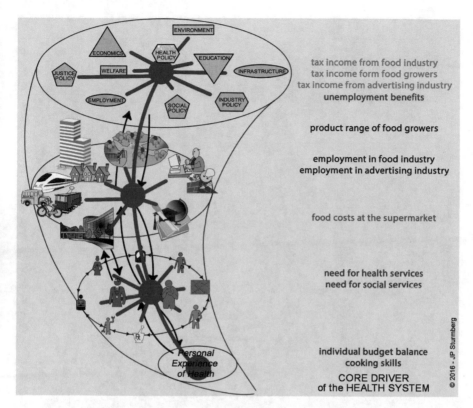

tax income from food industry
tax income form food growers
tax income from advertising industry
unemployment benefits

product range of food growers

employment in food industry
employment in advertising industry

food costs at the supermarket

need for health services
need for social services

individual budget balance
cooking skills
CORE DRIVER
of the **HEALTH SYSTEM**

© 2016 - JP Sturmberg

Fig. 11.11 A seamlessly integrated policy approach to manage the "epidemic of obesity" will take into account all issues at all levels of system organisation

11.3.2   Broadening the Public Debate

The outlined systems approaches to understand and manage the multiple issues of the obesity epidemic should help to broaden the public debate in the pursuit of equitable and sustainable solutions for all stakeholders. However, resistance to change is inevitable, as Banchoff [30] pointed out:

> Actors who benefit from a given set of institutions and policies tend to rally around the status quo, reinforcing a path-dependent process. ... They can also frame the terms of legislative debate by ruling in and out certain policy alternatives and generating rhetorical resources for defenders of incremental, as opposed to far reaching, policy change. (pp. 201–2)

11.3.3   Recognising Roots of Resistance

To overcome such resistance Nader [31] offers a framework that links key agents to key interventions in "the fight" against obesity (Fig. 11.12):

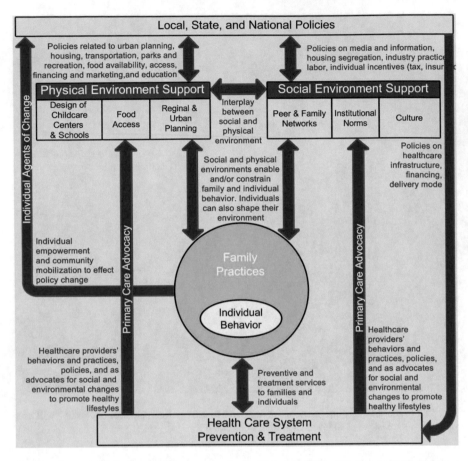

Fig. 11.12 An integrated policy response to obesity (based on Nader PR, Huang TTK, Gahagan S, Kumanyika S, Hammond RA, Christoffel KK. Next steps in obesity prevention: altering early life systems to support healthy parents, infants, and toddlers [31])

- Preventive and treatment services to families and individuals
- Social and physical environments enable and/or constrain family and individual behaviour. Individuals can also shape their environment
- Healthcare providers' behaviours and practices, policies, and as advocates for social and environmental changes to promote healthy lifestyles
- Individual empowerment and community mobilisation to effect policy change
- Interplay between social and physical environment
- Policies related to urban planning, housing, transportation, parks and recreation, food availability, access, financing and marketing, and education
- Policies on media and information, housing segregation, industry practices, labour, individual incentives (tax, insurance)
- Policies on healthcare infrastructure, financing, delivery mode

11.3.4 Managing System Redesign to Tackle "The Epidemic of Obesity"

System redesign to tackle "The Epidemic of Obesity" does require a detailed understanding of its various underlying mechanisms, it requires a deep understanding of the interconnections and interdependencies of its many systemic features, but most of all, it requires a broad public discourse to shape *"healthy eating for healthy weight"*.

References

1. Butland B, Jebb S, Kopelman P, McPherson K, Thomas S, Mardell J et al (2007) Foresight. Tackling obesities: future choices - project report. Government Office for Science, London
2. Ebbeling CB, Pawlak DB, Ludwig DS (2002) Childhood obesity: public-health crisis, common sense cure. Lancet 360(9331):473–482
3. Skinner AC, Foster EM (2013) Systems science and childhood obesity: a systematic review and new directions. J Obes 2013:10
4. Kershaw EE, Flier JS (2004) Adipose tissue as an endocrine organ. J Clin Endocrinol Metab 89(6):2548–2556
5. Bastard J-P, Maachi M, Lagathu C, Kim MJ, Caron M, Vidal H et al (2006) Recent advances in the relationship between obesity, inflammation, and insulin resistance. Eur Cytokine Netw 17(1):4–12
6. Kargi AY, Iacobellis G (2014) Adipose tissue and adrenal glands: novel pathophysiological mechanisms and clinical applications. Int J Endocrinol 2014:614074
7. Esposito K, Pontillo A, Di Palo C, Giugliano G, Masella M, Marfella R et al (2003) Effect of weight loss and lifestyle changes on vascular inflammatory markers in obese women: a randomized trial. J Am Med Assoc 289(14):1799–1804
8. Nicklas BJ, Ambrosius W, Messier SP, Miller GD, Penninx BW, Loeser RF et al (2004) Diet-induced weight loss, exercise, and chronic inflammation in older, obese adults: a randomized controlled clinical trial. Am J Clin Nutr 79(4):544–551
9. Bruun JM, Stallknecht B, Helge JW, Richelsen B (2007) Interleukin-18 in plasma and adipose tissue: effects of obesity, insulin resistance, and weight loss. Eur J Endocrinol 157(4):465–471
10. Hennessy E, Ornstein JT, Economos CD, Herzog JB, Lynskey V, Coffield E et al (2016) Designing an agent-based model for childhood obesity interventions: a case study of childobesity180. Prev Chronic Dis 13:E04
11. Gillman MW, Ludwig DS (2013) How early should obesity prevention start? N Engl J Med 369(23):2173–2175
12. Gortmaker SL, Taveras EM (2014) Who becomes obese during childhood - clues to prevention. N Engl J Med 370(5):475–476
13. Christakis NA, Fowler JH (2007) The spread of obesity in a large social network over 32 years. N Engl J Med 357(4):370–379
14. Frerichs LM, Araz OM, Huang TTK (2013) Modeling social transmission dynamics of unhealthy behaviors for evaluating prevention and treatment interventions on childhood obesity. PLoS ONE 8(12):e82887
15. Allender S, Owen B, Kuhlberg J, Lowe J, Nagorcka-Smith P, Whelan J et al (2015) A community based systems diagram of obesity causes. PLoS ONE 10(7):e0129683
16. Lakes T, Burkart K (2016) Childhood overweight in Berlin: intra-urban differences and underlying influencing factors. Int J Health Geogr 15(1):1–10

17. Swinburn BA, Sacks G, Hall KD, McPherson K, Finegood DT, Moodie ML et al (2011) The global obesity pandemic: shaped by global drivers and local environments. Lancet 378(9793):804–814

18. Kleinert S, Horton R. Rethinking and reframing obesity. The Lancet.385(9985):2326–2328.

19. Ludwig DS, Pollack HA (2009) Obesity and the economy: from crisis to opportunity. J Am Med Assoc 301(5):533–535

20. Gortmaker SL, Swinburn BA, Levy D, Carter R, Mabry PL, Finegood DT et al (2011) Changing the future of obesity: science, policy, and action. Lancet 378(9793):838–847

21. Chakravorty U, Hubert M-H, Moreaux M, Nøstbakken L (2016) The long run impact of biofuels on food prices. Scand J Econ 119(3):733–767

22. Nelson T (1996) Closing the nutrient loop. World Watch 9(6):10–17

23. Hanna AK, Oh P (2000) Rethinking urban poverty: a look at community gardens. Bull Sci Technol Soc 20(3):207–216

24. Ferris J, Norman C, Sempik J (2001) People, land and sustainability: community gardens and the social dimension of sustainable development. Soc Policy Adm 35(5):559–568

25. Rosset P (2011) Preventing hunger: change economic policy. Nature 479(7374):472–473

26. Scott C, Hawkins B, Knai C (2017) Food and beverage product reformulation as a corporate political strategy. Soc Sci Med 172:37–45

27. Kersh R (2009) The politics of obesity: a current assessment and look ahead. Milbank Q 87(1):295–316

28. Food and Agriculture Organization of the United Nations (2016) Sustainable agriculture for biodiversity, biodiversity for sustainable agriculture. Food and Agriculture Organization

29. Frood S, Johnston LM, Matteson CL, Finegood DT (2013) Obesity, complexity, and the role of the health system. Curr Obes Rep 2(4):320–326

30. Banchoff T (2005) Path dependence and value-driven issues: the comparative politics of stem cell research. World Polit 57(2):200–230

31. Nader PR, Huang TTK, Gahagan S, Kumanyika S, Hammond RA, Christoffel KK (2012) Next steps in obesity prevention: altering early life systems to support healthy parents, infants, and toddlers. Child Obes 8(3):195–204

Part IV
Person-Centred, Equitable, and Sustainable Health Systems: Achieving the Goal

"If we don't figure out a way to create equity, real equity, of opportunity and access, to good schools, housing, health care, and decent paying jobs, we're not going to survive as a productive and healthy society."

Tim Wise (born 1968)
American anti-racism activist and writer

"When you change the way you look at things the things you look at change."

Max Planck (1958–1947) - German theoretical physicist
Nobel Prize in Physics in 1918

Paraphrasing Max Plank, *changing the way we look at the health system allows us to see the issues affecting health systems—their contexts and behaviours—in a different light*.

Part I described the foundational elements to understand the complex adaptive nature of health systems:

- The key features of complexity sciences
- Understanding the structure and dynamics of complex adaptive systems through visualisation
- Understanding the nature of health as an "adaptive subjective experiential state"

Part II introduced the principles of systems-based health system redesign based on:

- Shared understanding of purpose, goals, and values
- Committed leadership that translates the shared understandings into "simple (operating) rules"
- Provided examples that illustrated the application of these principles to "real world" health system and healthcare system problems

Part III linked the theory of complex adaptive systems approaches to its praxis. These challenges included:

- Understanding the strength and weaknesses of various analytic tools
- The role of modelling in system redesign
- Maintaining the focus on the person/patient to allow the emergence of "best" adapted health systems in different contexts

The final part of this book will look at **health system redesign** *from a design thinking* perspective. Design is concerned with resolving problems *between the state of affairs as it is and the state it ought to be* [1]; design thinking thus applies the principles of design to the way people *see things working*.

As a strategy, design thinking deliberately engages all affected stakeholders in an iterative process to solve, i.e. help them **make sense**, of the wicked problems that stand in the way of *how things ought to be*.

Design thinking is now widely regarded *as an essential tool for simplifying and humanising* [2] the way we live, work, and engage with our environment. It offers a way to involve the diverse stakeholders of the health and healthcare system to work towards a health and healthcare system that *meets the needs of our people/patients*.

As argued throughout this book we need a health care system that focuses on *health* rather than healthcare [3–5]. McGinnes [3] eloquently refers to the interdependencies of our personal and social circumstances and their effects on our health and healthcare needs:

> Ultimately, the health fate of each of us is determined by factors [genes, social, environment, behaviour and medical care] acting not mostly in isolation but by our experience where domains interconnect. Whether a gene is expressed can be determined by environmental exposures or behavioral patterns. The nature and consequences of behavioral choices are affected by our social circumstances. Our genetic predispositions affect the health care we need, and our social circumstances affect the health care we receive.

We need a redesigned health and healthcare system that focuses on *health*, the *status quo of disease management systems* is no longer acceptable or sustainable. The principle focus of redesign is the enhancement of *users' experiences, especially their emotional ones* [2]. The literature, economic reality, and political necessity point to three key parameters for changing the way we look at health and healthcare systems; they *ought to be*:

Person-centred

Equitable

Sustainable

Design thinking allows us collectively to envision person-centred, equitable, and sustainable health and healthcare systems. The emphasis here is on the pleural as the emerging outcomes will initially be *local health and healthcare system prototypes*. Over time they will develop into "best adapted" systems given their local constraints and reflect the best local way to maintain and restore the health of people and communities.

Sceptics must confront the well-documented misconceptions (Table 1) that it is the biomedical approach that results in better health and longer life [3]. The design thinking process should allow their engagement and *change the way they look at things so they can appreciate things from a changed perspective.*

Table 1 Issues, perceptions, and misperceptions about the health system, compiled from McGinnis JM, Williams-Russo P, Knickman JR. The Case For More Active Policy Attention To Health Promotion [3] [emphasis added]

Issue	Fact	Additional comments
Health improvements over time	• The major contributions to improved health in England over the previous 200 years came more from *changes in food supplies, sanitary conditions, and family size* than from medical interventions [6]	
Effect of medicine on life expectancy	• Since 1950 medicine has accounted for about *three of the total of seven years* by which life expectancy has increased [7]	• Participants in the study rarely attributed increased life expectancy to public health measures or improvements in social health determinants. In contrast, subjects believed that medical care, by far, played the predominant role and attributed medical care for causing 80% of the life expectancy increase [8]
Leading Determinants of Health	• Drawing on the power of the extensive studies [9] of the past generation, we can now speak about our health prospects as being shaped by our experiences in five domains: • **Genetic and gestational endowments**—only about 2% of deaths in the USA may be attributed to purely genetic diseases • **Social circumstances**—health is powerfully influenced by education, employment, income disparities, poverty, housing, crime, and social cohesion	• Socially isolated persons have a death rate *two to five times higher* than that of those who maintain close ties to friends, family, and community [11] • …each *1% rise in income inequality* (the income differential between rich and poor) is associated with something on the order of a *4% increase in deaths among persons on the low end*, which prods us to sort out the pecuniary elements of deprivation from the biological, behavioural, and psychological consequences of place [12]

(continued)

Table 1 (continued)

Issue	Fact	Additional comments
	• **Environmental conditions**—The places where we live and work can present hazards in the form of toxic agents, microbial agents, and structural hazards • **Behavioural choices**—The daily choices we make with respect to diet, physical activity, and sex; the substance abuse and addictions to which we fall prey; our approach to safety; and our coping strategies in confronting stress are all important determinants of health • **Medical care**—Improvements in the quality or use of medical care have a relatively limited ability to reduce deaths. Over the course of the twentieth century, about five of the thirty years of increased life expectancy could be attributable to better medical care [10]	• The Institute of Medicine (IOM), for example, suggests that *medical errors alone may account for 44,000–98,000 deaths annually, or about 2–4% of all deaths* [13]
The interconnected factors of health and illness/disease	• The health of populations is the product of the *intersecting influences* from these different domains [genes, social, environment, behaviour and medical care], *influences that are dynamic* and that *vary in their impact depending upon* when in the life course they occur and upon the effects of preceding and subsequent factors [14]	• On a population basis, using the best available estimates, the impacts of various domains on early deaths in the USA distribute roughly as follows: *genetic predispositions, about 30%; social circumstances, 15%; environmental exposures, 5%; behavioural patterns, 40%; and shortfalls in medical care, 10%*
The current drivers of health policy	• Quite distinct from the issues of evidence and complexity is *old-fashioned interest-group dynamics*. The interest groups that make health their highest priority and thus lobby hard for resources are those focused on research and treatment related to specific chronic diseases	• The result is a vacuum of political accountability for maintaining population health—in effect, a *diffusion of responsibility for health*

(continued)

Table 1 (continued)

Issue	Fact	Additional comments
Barriers to health system redesign	• **Redistributive investments in health**—Interest-group dynamics, of course, play large roles in considerations of ways to change social conditions and the physical environment. Changing social inequalities and even investing tax dollars in social and community programs always represent zero-sum activities where those with more resources need to share with those with few resources. It takes more than just evidence that social change would improve health to convince the general public that such redistributive investments should be undertaken. *These choices are very much about ideology and social values* • **Social preferences**—In comparing investments in behavioural change to investments in medical care, the added issue of lifestyle and habits comes into play. *The public clearly wants medical care when illness occurs; this is a well-articulated social preference.* However, many people do not want to change their health-threatening behaviour even when they are quite aware of the risks they are taking. In these cases, arguments to invest in public programs to encourage behavioural change need to consider *what social factors predispose people to choose health-threatening behaviour*	• Often, careful consideration indicates that people are induced to adopt unhealthy behaviour in subtle and not so subtle ways. Simple examples include eating unhealthy foods *because of the absence of supermarkets in low-income neighbourhoods*, adopting sedentary lifestyles *because of unsafe neighbourhoods or environments* that make walking dangerous or unappealing, and smoking cigarettes or overusing alcohol *because of the influence of advertisements*
Shifting the emphasis of the healthcare system	• In 2010, the Healthy People goals were broadened to issues of *functional status* and *quality of life* and placed particular emphasis on *reducing disparities* among groups [15]	

(continued)

Table 1 (continued)

Issue	Fact	Additional comments
The need for public engage-ment	• A focused, engaged public needs to understand the payoffs to *healthier lifestyles* and *improved social conditions* that *reduce stress* and *improve well-being*	• …people need to be convinced that interventions to change lifestyles and social conditions are available and not too burdensome
Drivers for a people-centred health policy approach	• …we [need to] build [incentives] into policy initiatives for healthier lifestyles, environments, and social conditions	• An array of legal and public policy interventions is available to improve population health: economic incentives and disincentives, information interventions, direct regulation, indirect regulation through the tort system, and deregulation [16]

References

1. Rittel HWJ, Webber MM (1973) Dilemmas in a general theory of planning policy sciences. Pol Sci 4(2):155–169
2. Kolko J (2015) Design thinking comes of age. Harv Bus Rev 93(9):66–69
3. McGinnis JM, Williams-Russo P, Knickman JR (2002) The case for more active policy attention to health promotion. Health Aff (Millwood) 21(2):78–93
4. Sturmberg JP, O'Halloran DM, Martin CM (2010) People at the centre of complex adaptive health systems reform. Med J Aust 193(8):474–478
5. Sturmberg JP (2015) If you want health, have a HEALTH system: changing the agendum. Eur J Pers Cent Healthc 3(2):175–181
6. McKeown T (1976) The modern rise of population. Edward Arnold, London
7. Bunker JP (2001) The role of medical care in contributing to health improvements within societies. Int J Epidemiol 30(6):1260–1263
8. Lindsay GB, Merrill RM, Hedin RJ (2014) The contribution of public health and improved social conditions to increased life expectancy: an analysis of public awareness. J Community Med Health Educ 4:5
9. McGinnis JM (2001) United States. In: Koop CE, Pearson CE, Schwarz MR (eds) Critical issues in global health. Jossey-Bass, San Francisco, pp 80–90
10. U.S. Department of Health and Human Services (1994) Public Health Service. For a healthy nation: returns on investments in public health. Washington: U.S. Government Printing Office, Contract No.: 0-16-045143-4
11. Berkman LF, Glass T (2000) Social integration, social networks, social support, and health. In: Berkman LF, Kawachi I (eds) Social epidemiology. Oxford University Press, New York, pp 137–173
12. Wolfson M, Gravelle H, Wilkinson RG, Kaplan G, Lynch J, Ross N et al (1999) Relation between income inequality and mortality: empirical demonstration diminishing returns to aggregate level studies. Two pathways, but how much do they diverge? Br Med J 319(7215):953–957
13. Smedley BD, Syme SL (eds) (2000) Promoting health: intervention strategies from social and behavioral research. National Academy Press, Washington
14. Institute of Medicine (2001) Health and behavior: the interplay of biological, behavioral, and societal influences. National Academy Press, Washington

15. McGinnis J, Richmond JB, Brandt EN Jr, Windom RE, Mason JO (1992) Health progress in the United States: results of the 1990 objectives for the nation. JAMA J Am Med Assoc 268(18):2545–2552
16. Gostin JD (2000) Legal and public policy interventions to advance the population's health. In: Smedley BD, Syme SL (eds) Promoting health: intervention strategies from social and behavioral research. National Academy Press, Washington, pp 390–416

Chapter 12
... how things ought to be

Overview. Health systems *ought to be seamlessly integrated* to meet any person's health needs wherever they live, whenever they fall ill, and whatever the condition might be.

This view is slowly gaining acceptance, and this view is slowly being conceptualised within medical organisations like the WHO. There is a growing recognition that we *ought to redesign* our health systems around people/patient, and that our health services *ought to deliver* "good health" (however, what constitutes "good health" is often not defined).

The WHO-Europe has recognised:

- That there are multiple pathways to good and poor health
- That these pathways follow nonlinear patterns and therefore make health outcomes hard to predict
- That health results from complex interactions between many different types of determinants

The literature, economic reality, and political necessity consistently point to three key attributes that *ought to be evident* for a health and healthcare system to become seamlessly integrated:

- Person-centredness
- Equity
- Sustainability

Person-centredness

Person-centredness is broader than just the focus on the person, it also requires a focus on his physical and social environments. While some might find the focus on the person, rather than the population, problematic, *it ought to be recognised* that many of the problems seen in the individual reflect the broader problems in his community.

© Springer International Publishing AG 2018
J.P. Sturmberg, *Health System Redesign*, DOI 10.1007/978-3-319-64605-3_12

Person-centred approaches to care embrace the person, his family, and his community as interdependent. Therefore solutions to an individual's issues frequently will require the input of professionals from different sources.

Equity

Equity in healthcare assures access to health (and social) services according to a person's needs.

As Virchow already emphasised—health professionals have a responsibility to make the health system equitable. Fortunately health professional organisations increasingly recognise this responsibility and advocate for equity measures in their policy agendas.

Equity needs to be distinguished from equality. Equity in healthcare "*does not mean that everyone receives the same care. Instead, it means that care aims to achieve optimal outcomes for all groups of patients, even if achieving optimal outcomes means that care differs from person to person, and group to group*".

Healthcare needs are nonlinearly distributed across the community—most people are healthy most of the time without the need for any form of healthcare. However, healthcare delivery in most countries remains grossly inequitable. Tudor Hart described it as the "inverse care law"—*the availability of good medical care tends to vary inversely with the need of the population served.*

Sustainability

Achieving sustainability of the health and healthcare system has become an imperative; Nobel laureate economist Robert Fogel predicts that the expenditure on health will reach 20–25% of GDP by the year 2025.

Prevailing tendencies to achieve sustainability by limiting services or redistributing costs for healthcare on those in need of care will ultimately be counterproductive. Sustainability has been defined as the balance between social, environmental, and economic concerns. Hence, sustainable solutions must be affordable to individuals and society, acceptable to all constituents and adaptable as needs change over the life trajectory.

Person-centredness and equity have been identified as two key approaches that make health and healthcare systems sustainable.

Points for Reflection

- What *ought* a health system look like?
- What *ought* a healthcare system look like?
- What is patient centredness? Why does it matter?
- What is equity? Why does it matter to health systems?
- What is sustainability? How can it be ensured in health and healthcare systems?

> *"The way things are does not determine the way they ought to be."*
>
> Michael Sandel (born 1953)—American political philosopher,
> Professor of political philosophy at Harvard University

Health systems ought to be seamlessly integrated to meet any person's health needs across all organisational levels of health and healthcare related services (Fig. 12.1).

Like argued throughout this book, the WHO has now also emphasised that *health* should be the *focus for the design* of a coherent health system, one that takes account of the multiple external contributors to individual and personal health in society.

Pathways to good and poor health can be nonlinear and hard to predict, and health is increasingly understood as a product of complex, dynamic relations among distinct types of determinants. The health[1] system alone does not have the tools to solve all our health challenges.

The highest levels of government and society must recognise that health is a common objective and that achieving it requires coherence.

Zsuzsanna Jakab, WHO Regional Director for Europe

- Zsuzsanna Jakab implicitly alludes to the fact that health systems have the key defining characteristics of *complex adaptive systems and their dynamics*—complexity, nonlinearity, and non-determinism
- She emphasises that we need a broad public discourse to reach a mutual understanding about the *nature of health*—and by implication the kind of health and healthcare system able to provide us with the *state of health we desire*
- Her observation also alludes to the nature of the challenge, one that *design thinking* describes as the challenge to resolve an issue "*between the state of affairs as it is and the state it ought to be*" [1]

The next chapter will explore potential ways of getting there, but first one needs to consider what the main attributes of a redesigned health and healthcare system ought to be. The literature, economic reality, and political necessity consistently point to three key attributes:

Person-centredness
Equity
Sustainability

Accordingly, a redesigned health and healthcare system *ought to deliver* person-centred care that improves personal health experiences, provide such care in an equitable fashion based on need, and do so in an effective, efficient, and sustainable fashion.

---

[1] What Zsuzsanna Jakab really means here is the more narrow "*healthcare system*".

Fig. 12.1 A seamlessly integrated health system ought to be person-centred, equitable, and sustainable in its quest to meet any person's health needs across all organisational levels of health and healthcare related services

There is an emergent consensus for this proposition—health system *ought to*:

- Put the *person at the centre of the system*[2] and manage his illness and disease with a *personomics*[3,4] mindset
- Focus on *inequities in society and healthcare*[5,6]
- *Provide everyone in need* with accessible and affordable healthcare, a prerequisite for making the system *sustainable*[7]

Health and healthcare system redesign ought to achieve a system that reflects the *complex adaptive personal nature of health*, and the right to be *healthy in once own way* within *once own social context*. WHO-Europe [8] put it this way:

> Health is considered a human right, an essential component of well-being, a global public good and an issue of social justice and equity. Health is also increasingly recognized as a property of other systems, such as the economy, the environment, education, transport and the food system. The recognition of health as a key factor for the economic prosperity of knowledge societies is gaining ground. (page vii)

12.1   Person-Centredness

Person-centredness[8] *ought to be* the first attribute of a redesigned health and healthcare system. We need a focus on *personal health and health experience* [2–4, 9, 10] and take into account that health depends as much on one's physical

---

[2]*Despite all the rhetoric about "patient-centred care", the patient is not at the centre of things.*— David Rosenthal and Abraham Verghese [2].

[3]*It becomes absolutely clear that the established biotechnical means at our disposal must be supplemented by biographical understanding.*—Iona Heath [3].

[4]*Given the importance of the psychological, social, cultural, behavioural, and economic factors of each person, it seems only fitting that "personomics" be added to the precision medicine toolkit, and that it be used to refer to an individual's unique life circumstances that influence disease susceptibility, phenotype, and response to treatment.*—Ray Ziegelstein [4].

[5]*...the reason why poverty is unacceptable is not that the lives of the poor are shorter, but that poverty is demeaning, cruel and unjust. People should be entitled to decent living conditions not because it would make them live longer (which would be a welcome by-product) but because in a humane society the principle of fairness and justice is paramount.*—Petr Skrabanek [5].

[6]*Health systems promote health equity when their design and management specifically consider the circumstances and needs of socially disadvantaged and marginalised populations, including women, the poor and groups who experience stigma and discrimination, enabling social action by these groups and the civil society organisations supporting them.*—Lucy Gilson et.al. [6].

[7]*A sustainable health system also has three key attributes: affordability, for patients and families, employers, and the government ... ; acceptability to key constituents, including patients and health professionals; and adaptability, because health and health care needs are not static ....*—Harvey Fineberg [7].

[8]Person-centredness at an instrumental level entails: easy access to care, continuity of care preferably with a single provider, coordination of care, bidirectional communication and caring attitudes.

state as one's external context—education, employment, housing, neighbourhood and community, and geography. These external factors predetermine disease burden, health seeking behaviours, and actual health service use. A greater focus on achieving *good subjective health experiences*—independent of objective feature of health and disease—is mandatory as it determines future morbidity and mortality [11–13], and thus the economic sustainability of the system.

12.1.1 A Focus on Health

The need to refocus on health and the experience of health is increasingly recognised; e.g. Fineberg [7] argued:

> I purposely refer to a "health system" rather than a "health care system" because the solutions need to focus on the ultimate outcome of interest - that is, the population's health and each individual's health - and not only on the formal system of care designed primarily to treat illness.
>
> A successful health system has three attributes: healthy people, meaning a population that attains the highest level of health possible; superior care, meaning care that is effective, safe, timely, patient-centred, equitable, and efficient; and fairness, meaning that treatment is applied without discrimination or disparities to all individuals and families, regardless of age, group identity, or place, and that the system is fair to the health professionals, institutions, and businesses supporting and delivering care.

12.1.2 Community Engagement

Frenk [14] emphasised that the health system as a *system* involves all of us; we are all agents with a number of different roles in our respective health systems (Tab 12.1). We all benefit from it in some form when *feeling ill* or requiring *care for a disease*, and we all economically contribute to it—directly through various forms of health insurance payments, and indirectly as "healthy" or "made healthy again" citizens engaged in the economy.[9] Health system redesign thus *ought to require* community involvement, e.g. through citizen juries [15] or multi-stakeholder engagement [16] to define the health system's *purpose, goals, and values*.

---

[9]For more detail on the contribution and societal benefits of the healthcare system see: Suhrcke et al. (2005) The contribution of health to the economy in the European Union. Luxembourg: Office for Official Publications of the European Communities (http://ec.europa.eu/health/ph_overview/Documents/health_economy_en.pdf).

Table 12.1 Our various roles as agents in the health system. Frenk J. The Global System: Strengthening national health systems as the next step for global progress [14]. (Creative Commons Attribution License)

Agents within the health system include not only institutions and organisations but also the whole population:

- As patients, with specific needs requiring care
- As users, with expectations about the way in which they will be treated
- As taxpayers/service purchasers and therefore as the ultimate source of financing
- As citizens who may demand access to care as a right, and most importantly
- As co-producers of health through care seeking, compliance with treatment, and behaviours that may promote or harm one's own health or the health of others

12.1.3   Impact on Health Services

While a person-centred health system would deliver better care and better health outcomes, it won't necessarily reduce the overall disease burden of a community. As Seale [17] indicated:

> There is no evidence that with improving medical care the **overall quantity of disease** [emphasis added] in a nation diminishes. Medical advances will prevent or cure individual diseases in individuals, but it does not control the sum total of disease in any meaningful sense. The pattern of disease in the community changes, disease does not diminish or disappear. For example, the child who because of immunization does not die of diphtheria, smallpox, or tetanus at the age of 3 is cured of tuberculosis at the age of 20, lives on to be treated for diabetes at 60, becomes disabled by osteo-arthritis at 70, and finally dies of a stroke at 80. Such changes in the pattern of disease, in infinitely various ways, are happening in any community as medical advances take place. After all death for the individual is inevitable and rarely preceded by perfect health.

12.2   Equity

Equity *ought to be* the second attribute of a redesigned health and healthcare system. Equity and person-centredness are closely related concepts. Health service equity, by definition, *assures access to health (and social) services according to a person's needs* [18].

12.2.1   Equity is a Right

Equity is widely regarded as a human right. Equity means *justice according to natural law or right*. It needs to be distinguished from equality which describes the *quality or state of being equal* (Fig. 12.2).

Fig. 12.2 The "political nature" of health care—my take on the 4th box project (http://www.the4thbox.com/)—the original image has been produced by Angus Maguire for the "Interaction Institute for Social Change"

Indeed, an equity approach aims to understand and provide people with *what they need* (= fairness). In contrast, equality aims to ensure that *everyone gets the same in a particular situation* (= sameness). Equity and equality are interchangeable only when everyone starts from the same place and has the same needs.

12.2.2 Achieving Equity

Equity in healthcare "*does not mean that everyone receives the same care. Instead, it means that care aims to achieve optimal outcomes for all groups of patients, even if achieving optimal outcomes means that care differs from person to person, and group to group*" [19].

Striving to achieve equity in the provision of healthcare is a *moral* and *ethical* prerogative. As Whitehead [20] stated:

> The term inequity has a moral and ethical dimension. It refers to differences which are unnecessary and avoidable but, in addition, are also considered unfair and unjust. So, in order to describe a certain situation as inequitable, the cause has to be examined and judged to be unfair in the context of what is going on in the rest of society.

Some differences in health between people result from unavoidable factors whereas others are clearly avoidable and thus unfair [20]:

Unavoidable factors	Avoidable and thus unfair factors
• Natural, biological variation • Health-damaging behaviour if freely chosen, such as participation in certain sports and pastimes • The transient health advantage of one group over another when that group is first to adopt a health-promoting behaviour (as long as other groups have the means to catch up fairly soon)	• Health-damaging behaviour where the degree of choice of lifestyles is severely restricted • Exposure to unhealthy, stressful living, and working conditions • Inadequate access to essential health and other public services • Natural selection or health-related social mobility involving the tendency for sick people to move down the social scale (*the original ill health in question may have been unavoidable but the low income of sick people seems both preventable and unjust*)

12.2.3   The Nonlinear Distribution of Need and Equity

Healthcare needs across the community are nonlinearly distributed. As Whyte [21] has shown in relation to health in the community (Fig. 12.3), most of us are healthy most of the time, and this has not, despite improved knowledge, technology or increased funding, altered over the past 50 years [21–23]. Only about 20% of the community requires healthcare at any point in time. The majority of those only requires primary care services, around 3.2% will require secondary care and only 0.8% requires the most resource intense tertiary care sector [21–23].

These findings indicate that an equitable health system *ought to pay* greater attention to those that do not yet require healthcare system services.

For the health and healthcare system to become more equitable it *ought to also pay* more attention to the disproportionally higher needs for care at the lower end of the socioeconomic gradient. As Tudor Hart highlighted, current healthcare systems deliver care in a highly inequitable fashion (coining the term "inverse care law"): *the availability of good medical care tends to vary inversely with the need of the population served* [24].

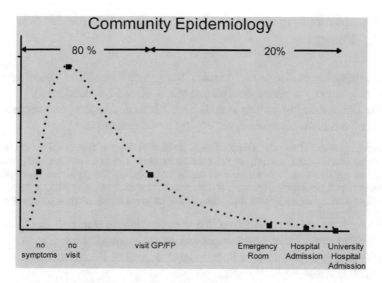

Fig. 12.3 Community epidemiology of health and healthcare needs

12.2.4   Equity as a Guiding Principle in Health and Healthcare System Redesign

Who will belong to those 20% that will be a patient next? When being a patient what will be our care needs? And on what basis should it be decided what kind of services we ought to receive?

These questions have important implications for the redesign of health and healthcare systems. The importance to address equity in the design of health and healthcare systems has previously been outline in a report by the WHO Commission on the Social Determinants of Health (Addendum 1) [6]. Hence, as contentious as it may be, an equitable health system redesign must achieve the provision of all those *health and social services* required to *fully meet a person's needs*[10] *in his community context.*

Equitable, complex adaptive health system redesigners embrace the reality that:

- Health care needs are inversely related to socioeconomic status
- The individual need for health services is largely unpredictable
- Efficient health care goes hand-in-hand with effective social care
- A mutual approach to health care financing is of benefit to society at large

The design process *ought to manage* the many entrenched interests that currently benefit from the system's "build-in" inequities (Addendum 2) [5, 24].

---

[10]For the distinction between needs and wants see Chap. 5.

12.2.5   Health Professionals Ought to Advocate for Health Equity

Health professionals for many decades have experienced the consequences of inequities in society and their detrimental health effects (Addendum 3).

In the 1850s Rudolf Virchow already highlighted that health professions must be at the forefront in tackling health destroying social inequities.

> Medicine is a social science, and politics is nothing else but medicine on a large scale. Medicine, as a social science, as the science of human beings, has the obligation to point out problems and to attempt their theoretical solution: the politician, the practical anthropologist, must find the means for their actual solution. The physicians are the natural attorneys of the poor, and social problems fall to a large extent within their jurisdiction.

Virchow is unequivocal—the health professions have a responsibility to make the health system equitable, a position not lost on the Australian Medical Association that in its position statement on Social Determinants of Health and the Prevention of Health Inequities—2007[11] states:

> Equity can be considered as being equal access to services for equal need, equal utilisation of services for equal need and equal quality of care or services for all. Central to this is the recognition that not everyone has the same level of health or capacity to deal with their health problems, and it may therefore be important to deal with people differently in order to work towards equal outcomes.

12.2.6   Implementing Equitable Care

Achieving equitable care, however, requires more than just access to the right care at the right time. It requires an extension to individual medical care; it requires a *collaborative approach* to work with community agencies to build the right conditions to overcome the social determinants of poor health, in other words, it requires systemic approaches [28–30].

It also requires governments to pay close attention to equity in their policy developments. In particular, as Starfield [30] emphasised, it requires a focus on primary care, as primary care is equity-producing. As Barbara Starfield pointed out in the context of primary care:

> [good clinical primary care depends] on specific health system policies for population[s]. Critical among these policies are attempts to **distribute resources equitably - that is, according to need** [emphasis added]; 'progressive' (as distinguished from 'regressive') financing under government control or regulation; low or no cost sharing for primary care services; and breadth of services available (comprehensiveness) within the primary care sector. Each of these policy characteristics reflects more general system characteristics:

---

[11] https://ama.com.au/position-statement/social-determinants-health-and-prevention-health-inequities-2007.

focus on distribution of health characteristics in the population - that is, an equity focus rather than just on average levels; progressivity of financing of social services in general; and consideration of population needs rather than demands (which favour the more powerful rather than the disenfranchised). That is, societies that are more equitable tend to be more equitable in many regards, because progressive governments generally promote more progressive policies across a range of social sectors.

12.3 Sustainability

The third guiding principle *ought to be* sustainability. Person-centredness and equity are two key approaches that make health and healthcare systems sustainable [31].

Sustainability of the health and healthcare systems are threatened. Nobel Laureate in economics, Robert Fogel [32], as far back as 2004 predicted that by 2025 the rapid developments in healthcare would escalate its costs to 20–25% of GDP. Indeed, many developed countries are, as he predicted, steadily moving towards this unsustainable figure.[12]

12.3.1 The Notion of Sustainability

The notion of sustainability arose in the environmental sciences and now has been broadly adopted in all domains of societal activity (Fig. 12.4). In 2005, the UN-World Summit adopted a resolution that acknowledged the interdependent features that make societal activities sustainable:

Fig. 12.4 Conceptual model of sustainability (Wikimedia Commons licence)

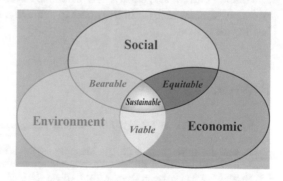

---

[12]GDP-spending on health 2014 (The World Bank—for more details see http://data.worldbank.org/indicator/SH.XPD.TOTL.ZS?view=map)
high income countries 12.3%; low and middle income countries 5.8%, the World average 9.9% US 17.1%, Maldives 13.7%, Germany 11.3%, Cuba 11.1%, Canada 10.4%, Australia 9.4%, Ecuador 9.2%, UK 9.1%, South Africa 8.8%, Brazil 8.3%, Chile 7.8%, Russia 7.1%, Luxemburg 6.9%, Kenya 5.7%, Singapore 4.9%, Senegal 4.7%, Fiji 4.5%, UAE 3.6%, Madagascar 3.0%.

These efforts will also promote the integration of the three components of sustainable development - economic development, social development and environmental protection - as interdependent and mutually reinforcing pillars. Poverty eradication, changing unsustainable patterns of production and consumption and protecting and managing the natural resource base of economic and social development are overarching objectives of and essential requirements for sustainable development [33].

Prevailing tendencies to achieve sustainability by limiting services or redistributing costs for healthcare on those in need of care will ultimately be counterproductive. Solutions require an open community wide discourse about the cost and scope of the health and healthcare system in the context of its merits, namely: quality, efficiency, acceptability, and equity [34, 35].

Sustainability arises from the complex adaptive interactions of an enterprise in its local environmental context. Fineberg [16] emphasised the three key attributes that make a health system sustainable:

- *Affordability, for patients and families, employers, and the government (recognising that employers and the government ultimately rely on individuals as consumers, employees, and taxpayers for their resources)*
- *Acceptability to key constituents, including patients and health professionals*
- *Adaptability, because health and health care needs are not static (i.e. a health system must respond adaptively to new diseases, changing demographics, scientific discoveries, and dynamic technologies in order to remain viable* [emphasis added]

Hence a health system will only be sustainable if they balance ALL social, economic, and environmental concerns in the context of person-centred and equitable care [7, 8, 36]. Addendum 4 and 5 illustrate how a not-for-profit US health system and the UK's National Health Service translate sustainability into practice.

Person-centredness, equity, and sustainability are interdependent and *ought to be managed* simultaneously in the quest to achieve a seamlessly integrated health and healthcare system.

References

1. Rittel HWJ, Webber MM (1973) Dilemmas in a general theory of planning policy sciences. Pol Sci 4(2):155–169
2. Rosenthal DI, Verghese A (2016). Meaning and the nature of physicians' work. N Engl J Med 375(19):1813–1815
3. Heath I (2011) Harveian Oration 2011 - divided we fail. Royal College of Physicians, London
4. Ziegelstein RC (2015). Personomics. JAMA Intern Med 175(6):888–889
5. Skrabanek P (1994) The death of humane medicine. London: Social Affairs Unit
6. Gilson L, Doherty J, Loewenson R, Francis V (2007) Challenging inequity through health systems. Final Report, Knowledge Network on Health Systems 2007. WHO Commission on the Social Determinants of Health, Geneva
7. Fineberg HV (2012) A successful and sustainable health system - how to get there from here. N Engl J Med 366(11):1020–1027

8. World Health Organization Regional Office for Europe (2011) Governance for health in the 21st century: a study conducted for the WHO Regional Office for Europe. World Health Organization Regional Office for Europe, Copenhagen
9. Sturmberg JP (2009) The personal nature of health. J Eval Clin Pract 15(4):766–769
10. Sturmberg JP (2013) Health: a personal complex-adaptive state. In: Sturmberg JP, Martin CM (eds) Handbook of systems and complexity in health. Springer, New York, pp 231–242
11. Idler EL, Benyamini Y (1997) Self-rated health and mortality: a review of twenty-seven community studies. J Health Soc Behav 38(1):21–37
12. Jylhä M (2009) What is self-rated health and why does it predict mortality? Towards a unified conceptual model. Soc Sci Med 69(3):307–316
13. Benyamini Y (2011) Why does self-rated health predict mortality? An update on current knowledge and a research agenda for psychologists. Psychol Health 26(11):1407–1413
14. Frenk J (2010) The global health system: strengthening national health systems as the next step for global progress. PLoS Med 7(1):e1000089
15. Mooney G, Blackwell S (2004) Whose health service is it anyway? Community values in healthcare. Med J Aust 180(2):76–78
16. Lindstrom RR (2003) Evidence-based decision-making in healthcare: exploring the issues through the lens of complex, adaptive systems theory. HealthcarePapers 3(3):29–35
17. Seale J (1962) The health service in an affluent society. Br Med J 2(5304):598–602
18. Gwatkin DR, Bhuiya A, Victora CG (2004) Making health systems more equitable. The Lancet 364(9441):1273–1280
19. Robert Wood Johnson Foundation (2014). A roadmap to reduce racial and ethnic disparities in health care. Available at: http://www.solvingdisparities.org/sites/default/files/Roadmap_StrategyOverview_final_MSLrevisions_11-3-4%20%284%29.pdf.
20. Whitehead M (1985) The concepts and principles of equity and health. Copenhagen: World Health Organization Regional Office for Europe
21. White K, Williams F, Greenberg B (1961) The ecology of medical care. N Engl J Med 265(18):885–892
22. Green L, Fryer G, Yawn B, Lanier D, Dovey S (2001) The ecology of medical care revisited. N Engl J Med 344(26):2021–2025
23. Johansen ME, Kircher SM, Huerta TR (2016) Reexamining the ecology of medical care. N Engl J Med 374(5):495–496
24. Hart J (1971) The inverse care law. Lancet I:405–412
25. Seale JR (1961) Management efficiency in the health service. Lancet 278(7200):476–480
26. Williams R (1961) The long revolution. Chatto & Windus, London
27. Fry J (1969) Medicine in three societies: a comparison of medical care in the USSR, USA and UK. Springer, New York.
28. Wong WF, LaVeist TA, Sharfstein JM (2015) Achieving health equity by design. JAMA 313(14):1417–1418
29. Association of American Medical Colleges (2016) Achieving health equity: how academic medicine is addressing the social determinants of health. Association of American Medical Colleges, Washington
30. Starfield B (2011) Politics, primary healthcare and health: was Virchow right? J Epidemiol Community Health 65(8):653–655
31. Bertakis KD, Azari R (2011) Patient-centered care is associated with decreased health care utilization. J Am Board Fam Med 24(3):229–239
32. Fogel RW (2004) The escape from hunger and premature death. Cambridge University Press, Cambridge
33. United Nations (2005) 2005 World summit outcome. Resolution adopted by the General Assembly. United Nations. http://data.unaids.org/Topics/UniversalAccess/worldsummitoutcome_resolution_24oct2005_en.pdf

34. Boxall A-M (2011) What are we doing to ensure the sustainability of the health system? Canberra, Australia: Department of Parliamentary Services, Parliament of Australia, 18 November 2011. Report No.: Contract No.: 4 2011-12. Available at: http://www.aph.gov.au/About_Parliament/Parliamentary_Departments/Parliamentary_Library/pubs/rp/rp1112/12rp04
35. Prowle M, Harradine D (2015) Sustainable healthcare systems: an international study. ACCA (the Association of Chartered Certified Accountants), London. Available at: http://www.accaglobal.com/an/en/technical-activities/technical-resources-search/2015/february/sustainable-healthcare-systems.html.
36. Coiera E, Hovenga EJ (2007). Building a sustainable health system. Yearb Med Inform 2007:11–8.

Addendum 1

Equity Principles Shape the Design of Healthcare Systems

Gilson L, Doherty J, Loewenson R, Francis V. Challenging inequity through health systems. Final report, Knowledge Network on Health Systems 2007. Geneva: WHO Commission on the Social Determinants of Health, 2007. [6]

Why health systems matter to the social determinants of health inequity

1. Health systems offer **general population benefits** that go beyond preventing and treating illness. Appropriately designed and managed, they:

   - provide a vehicle to improve people's lives, protecting them from the vulnerability of sickness, generating a sense of life security, and building common purpose within society
   - ensure that all population groups are included in the processes and benefits of socioeconomic development and
   - generate the political support needed to sustain them over time

2. Health systems **promote health equity** when their design and management specifically consider the circumstances and needs of socially disadvantaged and marginalised populations, including women, the poor and groups who experience stigma and discrimination, enabling social action by these groups and the civil society organisations supporting them.

3. Health systems can, when appropriately designed and managed, **contribute to achieving the Millennium Development Goals**.

Critical health system features that address health inequity

1. The key overarching features of health systems that generate preferential health benefits for socially disadvantaged and marginalised groups, as well as general population gains, are:

   - the leadership, processes, and mechanisms that **leverage intersectoral action** across government departments to promote population health; organisational arrangements and practices that **involve population groups and civil society organisations**, particularly those working with socially disadvantaged and marginalised groups, in decisions and actions that identify, address, and allocate resources to health needs
   - health care financing and provision arrangements that **aim at universal coverage** and offer particular benefits for socially disadvantaged and marginalised groups (specifically: improved access to health care
   - better protection against the impoverishing costs of illness; and the redistribution of resources towards poorer groups with greater health needs) and
   - **the revitalisation of the comprehensive primary health care approach**, as a strategy that reinforces and integrates the other health equity-promoting features identified above

---

Addendum 2

Factors That Entrench Inequity

These factors are known for more than 50 years but so far have been neglected in health and social system improvement efforts (first highlighted by Tudor Hart in 1971 [24])

Limiting the Role of Government in Health and Social Services Personal—Neoliberal/Libetarian Doctrine

"...the function of the State is, in general, to do those things which the individual cannot do and to assist him to do things better. It is not to do for the individual what he can well do for himself. ...I should like to see reform of the Health Service in the years ahead which is based on the assumption of individual responsibility for personal health, with the State's function limited to the prevention of real hardship and the encouragement of personal responsibility." John Seale [25]

The Psychology of the Human Double Standard—Thinking about Oneself in Favourable and about Society in Unfavourable Terms

"...we think of our *individual patterns of use in the favourable terms of spending and satisfaction, but of our social patterns of use in the unfavourable terms of deprivation and taxation* [emphasis added]. It seems a fundamental defect of our society that social purposes are largely financed out of individual incomes, by a method of rates and taxes which makes it very easy for us to feel that society is a thing that continually deprives and limits us - without this we could all be profitably spending. ...We think of 'my money' ...in these naive terms, because parts of our very idea of society are withered at root. We can hardly have any conception, in our present system, of the financing of social purposes from the social product ..." Raymond Williams [26]

Market Mechanisms are the only Way to Achieve Intelligent Planning in Health Services—The Economic Doctrine

"In a health service provided free of charge efficient management is particularly difficult because neither the purpose nor the product of the organisation can be clearly defined, and because there are few automatic checks to managerial incompetence. ...In any large organisation management requires quantitative information if it is to be able to analyse a situation, make a decision, and know whether its actions have achieved the desired result. In commerce this quantitative information is supplied primarily in monetary terms. By using the simple, convenient, and measurable criterion of profit as both objective and product, management has a yardstick for assessing the quality of the organisation and the effectiveness of its own decisions." John Seale [25]

Standing out of the Crowd—Gaining (Economic) Advantage

"In some areas, particularly the more prosperous, competition for patients exists between local hospitals, since lack of regional planning has led to an excess of hospital facilities in some localities. In such circumstances hospital administrators are encouraged to use public relations officers and other means of self-advertisement. ...This competition also leads to certain hospital 'status symbols', where features such as the possession of a computer; the possession of a 'cobalt bomb' unit; the ability to perform open-heart surgery albeit infrequently; and the listing of a neurosurgeon on the staff are all current symbols of status in the eyes of certain groups of the public. Even small hospitals of 150–200 beds may consider such features as necessities." John Fry [27]

Addendum 3

Examples of Between and Within Country Health Inequities

http://www.who.int/social_determinants/thecommission/finalreport/key_concepts/
en/

Social and economic conditions and their effects on people's lives determine their risk of illness and the actions taken to prevent them becoming ill or treat illness when it occurs.

Examples of health inequities between countries:

* the infant mortality rate (the risk of a baby dying between birth and 1 year of age) is 2 per 1000 live births in Iceland and over 120 per 1000 live births in Mozambique
* the lifetime risk of maternal death during or shortly after pregnancy is only 1 in 17,400 in Sweden but it is 1 in 8 in Afghanistan

Examples of health inequities within countries:

* in Bolivia, babies born to women with no education have infant mortality greater than 100 per 1000 live births, while the infant mortality rate of babies born to mothers with at least secondary education is under 40 per 1000
* life expectancy at birth among indigenous Australians is substantially lower (59.4 for males and 64.8 for females) than that of non-indigenous Australians (76.6 and 82.0, respectively)
* life expectancy at birth for men in the Carlton neighbourhood of Glasgow is 54 years, 28 years less than that of men in Lenzie, a few kilometres away
* the prevalence of long-term disabilities among European men aged 80+ years is 58.8% among the lower educated versus 40.2% among the higher educated

---

Addendum 4

A Sustainable Health System—US Approaches

What Does A Sustainable Health System Mean?

When we talk about a "sustainable health system", it reflects a commitment to "improving the lives of the people and communities we serve, for generations to come." Here are some ways we think about the elements of that system:

It's a system ...

- that **improves the health of our population overall**—not just the health of the patients who walk through the doors of our facilities, but people throughout our communities
- that **uses new models of care delivery** to make care more accessible, less costly, and more effective
- that **delivers care in the place and at the point of time or illness progression** to have the most impact on the continued health of the patient
- with a **workforce working in new ways**, often to the top of their license or profession, using the fullest potential of our talented and committed people
- that is **financially responsible**, investing prudently in people, infrastructure, innovation, education, and research that will truly serve patients and population health
- that **works within our communities**, as part of the fabric that holds us together
- that **values integration** and a network of care, and partners locally, regionally, and nationally to improve health and health care
- that **measures its results**, far beyond the current clinical outcomes and process measures that are in place nationally, so that we know how we are doing, how our patients are doing, and that what we are doing in terms of treatments, therapies, and procedures is effective, necessary, and of value
- that **treats patients and families as partners in care**, knowing that patients who are fully informed about the risks and benefits of treatments and procedures often make different choices and choices they are happier with than if they had left the decision up to their physician
- that **drives change and improvement**, rather than just letting change happen to it
- that **is transparent, internally and externally**, sharing our processes and our results with each other, with our patients and their families, and with other providers, to hold ourselves accountable and ultimately to make us all better

Dartmouth-Hitchcock is a nonprofit academic health system

serving communities in northern New England

http://www.dartmouth-hitchcock.org/about_dh/what_is_sustainable_health.html

---

Addendum 5

A Sustainable Health System—UK Approaches

What is Sustainable Health?

It is easy to imagine a sustainable health and care system—it goes on forever within the limits of financial, social, and environmental resources. The challenge is the current approach to delivering health and care cannot continue in the same way and stay within these limits.

A sustainable health and care system is achieved by delivering high quality care and improved public health without exhausting natural resources or causing severe ecological damage.

It may also be useful to think about the relationship between sustainability and health in three distinct ways moving from a narrow focus to a broad focus. The resources and guidance on this website focus on points 1 and 2.

A sustainable health and care system:

1—Sustainable Health and Care Sector This involves "greening" the sector with particular attention to energy, travel, waste, procurement, water, infrastructure adaptation, and buildings. This ensures resources (physical, financial, and human) used in the sector are:

- Used efficiently (e.g. buildings and homes are well insulated and use less fuel to heat)
- Used responsibly (e.g. clinical waste is disposed of safely to protect local people)

2—Sustainable Health Care

This is slightly broader (but more health care specific) than point 1 and involves working across the health system and partners to deliver health care that deliver on the triple bottom line, i.e. simultaneous financial, social, and environmental return on investment. It includes adapting how we deliver services, health promotion, more prevention, corporate social responsibility and developing more sustainable models of care.

A sustainable way of living:

3—Sustainable Health and Well-being

This is the broadest level and involves considering the sustainability of everything that impacts on health and well-being (e.g. education, farming, banking etc.).

Sustainable Development Unit

The SDU is funded by, and accountable to, NHS England and Public Health England

to work across the NHS, public health and social care system.

http://www.sduhealth.org.uk/policy-strategy/what-is-sustainable-health.aspx

Chapter 13
...and how to get there

Overview. If the pathways to good and poor health are nonlinear and therefore hard to predict, current prescriptive ways of organising and practising health and social care will be futile.

This leaves the one big questions:

- How do we achieve health and healthcare systems that *meet our needs* and has the attributes of being *person-centred, equitable, and sustainable*

Linking *systems and complexity science thinking* with *design thinking* provides a way forward in answering this question. Design thinking provides a framework to move from the current state of affairs towards the state that *ought to be*.

Its focus on enhancing the users' emotional experiences links to the health and healthcare system's focus to meet the person's/patient's needs. As a process design thinking starts with (1) understanding the nature of the problem, (2) identifying the desired outcome, and (3) freely contemplating as many solutions as possible that might achieve that goal.

Redesigning the health and healthcare system in the first instance requires:

- A willingness to take a different perspective
- The articulation of a desired state of the new system
- A willingness to take the necessary first step of engaging everyone in the conversation

...to get there

A patient-centred, equitable, and sustainable health and healthcare system requires a *whole-of-systems thinking* approach, and it requires a mindset that views the health of the community as a prerequisite for a successful and economically vibrant society. However, achieving such a health and healthcare system ultimately is a political process that requires professional as well as political leadership. It needs to engage ALL in the design process of the health system, and it requires a governance framework to oversee its implementation and running. This will not result in a "one-

© Springer International Publishing AG 2018
J.P. Sturmberg, *Health System Redesign*, DOI 10.1007/978-3-319-64605-3_13

size-fits-all" solution; in fact not seeing local adaptations reflecting the uniqueness of local circumstances would be a clear failure of the redesign efforts.

...*and the challenges*

Social change, despite all available evidence, is hard to come by, not least for the fact that change disrupts the status quo. Letting go of the prevalent profit driven motivation of many players in the healthcare delivery sectors is a major challenge. A human-centric health system redesign, while potentially meaning less high-cost services, most likely would entail more human support services. Thus, a redesigned health and healthcare system may be no less costly, but it is highly probable that the expenditure will contribute more meaningfully to the health systems ultimate goal—*meeting the needs, desires, and expectations* of those in need for health and healthcare services.

It is time to put ideology aside and focus on what matters—the *needs* and the *health* of our current and future patients.

———

The gross national product ... measures everything ... except that which makes life worthwhile.
Robert F. Kennedy (1925–1968)

Points for Reflection

- How can we start a broad-based discourse about health and health system reform?
- Who should decide what the goals of a health and healthcare system *ought to be*?
- How do we balance economic and social interests in a person-centred, equitable, and sustainable health and healthcare system?
- If health is a public good rather than a commodity or a consumable how should it be financed?

"The first step of getting somewhere is to decide that you are not going to stay where you are."
Chauncey Depew (1834–1928)—American lawyer and politician

If the pathways to good and poor health are nonlinear and therefore hard to predict, current prescriptive ways of organising and practising health and social care will be futile.

This leaves the one big challenge:

- How do we achieve a health and healthcare system that *meets our needs* and has the attributes of being *person-centred, equitable, and sustainable*

This is a question that requires, as Rittel and Webber [1] argued, planning and thus falls outside "*the classical paradigm of science and engineering - the paradigm that has underlain modern professionalism - is not applicable to the problems of open societal systems*".

These problems, they continue, need to be "*distinguished from problems in the natural sciences, which are definable and separable and may have solutions that are findable, the problems of governmental planning - and especially those of social or policy planning - are ill-defined; and they rely upon elusive political judgement for resolution. (**Not "solution." Social problems are never solved. At best, they are only re-solved-over and over again.**)* [emphasis added]"[1]

This is the point where **systems and complexity science thinking** meets **design thinking**. The former provides an understanding of the

- *structure and dynamics* of the health and healthcare system

the latter facilitates a way to engage stakeholders in the *necessary adaptive work that needs to be done* to[2]

- envision a *mutually agreeable future state* of the system

---

[1]Metaphorically, Rittel and Webber explained their point of view as: *The problems that scientists and engineers have usually focused upon are mostly "tame" or "benign" ones. ...*
Wicked problems, in contrast, have neither of these clarifying traits; and they include nearly all public policy issues - ...
There are at least ten distinguishing properties of planning-type problems, i.e. wicked ones, that planners had better be alert to .... As you will see, we are calling them "wicked" not because these properties are themselves ethically deplorable. We use the term "wicked" in a meaning akin to that of "malignant" (in contrast to "benign") or "vicious" (like a circle) or "tricky" (like a leprechaun) or "aggressive" (like a lion, in contrast to the docility of a lamb). We do not mean to personify these properties of social systems by implying malicious intent. But then, you may agree that it becomes morally objectionable for the planner to treat a wicked problem as though it were a tame one, or to tame a wicked problem prematurely, or to refuse to recognise the inherent wickedness of social problems.

[2]Interested readers are also encouraged to read Karl Weick's work on sensemaking, e.g. *Sensemaking in Organisations* [2] or *Making Sense of the Organisation* [3]. Karl Weick describes the challenge of sensemaking this way: *Sensemaking is tested to the extreme when people encounter an event whose occurrence is so implausible that they hesitate to report it for fear they will not be believed. In essence, these people think to themselves, it can't be, therefore, it isn't.*

13.1   Design Thinking

Design is concerned with resolving "[problems] *between the state of affairs as it is and the state it ought to be*" [1]; design thinking thus applies the principles of design to the way people *see things working*.

The principle focus of redesign is the *enhancement of users' experiences, especially their emotional ones* [4]. While originally developed in the context of product improvement, it is now also extensively applied to the redesign of services.

Design thinking is widely regarded as an *essential tool for simplifying and humanising* [4] the way we live, work, and engage with our environment. It offers a way to engage the diverse stakeholders of the health and healthcare system to work towards a health and healthcare system that *meets our needs as people/patients*.

13.1.1   The Origins of Design Thinking

Archer [5] first described a *systematic method for designers* highlighting that problems are complex and that their solutions require a human-centric (human values) approaches. Herbert Simon, in the late 1960s, suggested *design thinking* as a way forward to solve complex problems [6]. He concluded that *everyone designs who devises courses of action aimed at changing existing situations into preferred ones* [6].[3]

In the early 1970s Papanek [7] proposed that design knowledge ought to be used to solve societal and environmental problem. He pointed towards the moral obligations and responsibilities of design—today subsumed in the notion of "value"—observing: "*Recent design has satisfied only evanescent wants and desires, while the genuine needs of man have often been neglected.*" Unsurprisingly he likened the outcome of design thinking to that of simplifying complexity.

13.1.2   Design Thinking as a Problem-Solving Strategy

Design thinking—as a strategy—deliberately involves all affected stakeholders in an iterative problem-solving process. Its approaches **combine** insights from:

- SCIENCE (finding similarities among things that are different)
- ART (finding differences among things that are similar)

---

[3]For a detailed history of design thinking see: Stefanie Di Russo. Understanding the behaviour of design thinking in complex environments. Ph.D. thesis, Swinburne University, Australia 2016—available at https://www.academia.edu/24919250/ Understanding_the_behaviour_of_design_thinking_in_complex_environments.

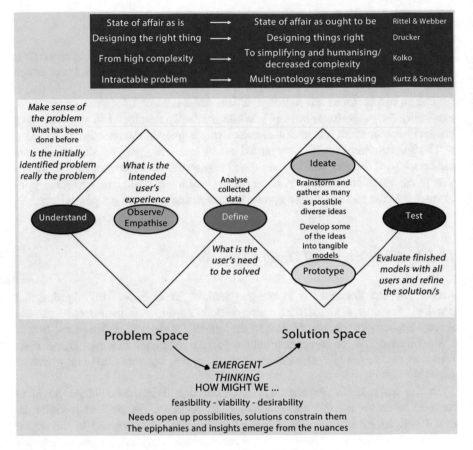

Fig. 13.1 Summary of the philosophy and the practice of design thinking.
Only the full understanding of the problem allows the emergence of the "right" solution. Note that
solutions are invariably temporary; new problems will start the process all over again

- DESIGN (creating feasible "wholes" from infeasible "parts")

in ways that are best suited to find solutions to "wicked problems" [1] in the realm
of uncertainty. In the early 1990s Buchanan [8] asserted that design thinking is
particularly useful in :

> ...the design of complex systems or environments for living, working, playing, and
> learning. ...this area has also expanded and reflects more consciousness of the central idea,
> thought, or value that expresses the unity of any balanced and functioning whole. This area
> is more and more concerned with exploring the role of design in sustaining, developing, and
> integrating human beings into broader ecological and cultural environments, shaping these
> environments when desirable and possible or adapting to them when necessary.

13.1.3 The Process of Designing

As outlined above, design thinking in the first instance reflects a mental approach. Its principle focus is on the outcome, i.e. *how things ought to be* [6]. The link between the philosophy and the processes of design thinking is summarised in Fig. 13.1. The key to successful problem solving is simple—***understand the problem*** without preconceived ideas of a solution, ***let the solutions emerge*** as a result. As Einstein put it: "*If I had an hour to solve a problem and my life depended on the solution, I would spend the first 55 minutes determining the proper question to ask, for once I know the proper question, I could solve the problem in less than five minutes*".

13.2 Health System Redesign: The Principles

As the aphorisms by Max Planck, Michael Sandel, and Chauncey Depew of the previous chapters suggest, redesigning the health system requires a different mindset. A "new look" health and healthcare system requires:

- A willingness to take a different perspective

  – *When you change the way you look at things the things you look at change*

- The articulation of a desired state of the system

  – *The way things are does not determine the way they ought to be*

- A willingness to take the necessary first step of engaging in the necessary dialogue

  – *The first step of getting somewhere is to decide that you are not going to stay where you are*

This book has outlined the rationale and the principles for a redesign of the health and healthcare system based on its complex adaptive properties. It also put to the forefront the need to design a ***health system*** rather than narrower *healthcare systems* that deal with the—evitable or inevitable—consequences of the "***outputs of the health system***". Most importantly, it has highlighted that health and healthcare systems' complex adaptive system dynamics arise from the ***behaviour of its human agents***, thus the success of any redesign effort requires a participatory approach.

Design thinking,[4] viewed as a framework closely linked to the complex adaptive systems framework, appears a useful model to "kick-start" the process facilitating the *necessary adaptive work required* to succeed with the redesign effort.

---

[4]Other approaches include: positive deviance (see, e.g., Positive Deviance Initiative—www.positivedeviance.org/), relational coordination (see, e.g., Relational Coordination—Relationship Centered Health Care—www.rchcweb.com/Relational-Coordination), and appreciative inquiry (see, e.g., The Appreciative Inquiry Commons—https://appreciativeinquiry.case.edu/).

13.3   *"...to get there"*: the Need to Focus on Person-Centredness, Equity, and Sustainability

The thesis of this book is that a redesigned health and healthcare system—for *philosophical, economic*, and *political* reasons—*ought to be*:

Person-centred
Equitable
Sustainable

Based on these foundations it proposes that the "best-adapted" solutions would arise from (Fig. 13.2):

- Understanding the current state of the health and healthcare system
- Engage citizen juries to define a new vision for their health and healthcare system
- Engage all concerned stakeholders to brainstorm possible solutions, and develop promising ones into possible models for "road testing"

A *patient-centred*, *equitable*, and *sustainable* health and healthcare system requires a whole-of-systems thinking approach, and it requires a mindset that views the health of the community as a prerequisite for a successful and economically vibrant society [9, 10]. However, achieving such a health and healthcare system ultimately is a political process that requires professional as well as political leadership—to engage ALL in the design process of the health system and a governance framework to oversee its implementation and running. The WHO [11] proposes that:

> "governance **for** [emphasis added] health" is defined as the attempts of governments or other actors to steer communities, countries or groups of countries in the pursuit of health as integral to wellbeing through both a "whole-of-government" and a "whole-of-society" approach. It positions health and well-being as key features of what constitutes a successful society and a vibrant economy in the 21st century and grounds policies and approaches in values such as human rights and equity. Governance for health promotes joint action of health and non-health sectors, of public and private actors and of citizens for a common interest. It requires a synergistic set of policies, many of which reside in sectors other than health as well as sectors outside of government, which must be supported by structures and mechanisms that enable collaboration. It gives strong legitimacy to health ministers and ministries and to public health agencies, to help them reach out and perform new roles in shaping policies to promote health and wellbeing.

and, similar to Ron Heifetz's notion of "leaders facilitating the necessary adaptive work that needs to be done by ALL" [12], advances five leadership strategies to manage the necessary *adaptive* changes:

> On the basis of a review of case studies of new approaches to governance **for** [emphasis added] health, five types of smart governance for health are proposed for consideration, which should be combined in whole-of-government and whole-of-society approaches:
>
> - Governing by collaboration
> - Governing through citizen engagement

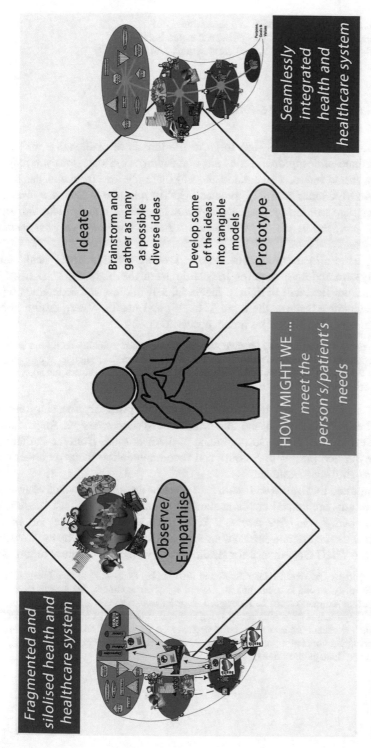

Fig. 13.2 Redesigning the health and healthcare system—summary of the principle steps. Understand the current situation, define what we might want to achieve, envision and test possible models to achieve the defined/desired future state

- Governing by a mix of regulation and persuasion
- Governing through independent agencies and expert bodies
- Governing by adaptive policies, resilient structures, and foresight

13.4   "... and what may stand in the way"

A final thought—unavoidably—has to go to the threats of challenging the status quo. The outlined *philosophical, economic,* and *political* reasons, however, may be contested by vested interests (see Addendum 1) that may lose from changes to the status quo. As McGinnes et al. [13] pointed out "[i]*t takes more than just evidence that social change would improve health to convince the general public that such redistributive investments should be undertaken. These choices are very much about ideology and social values*".

However, as outlined throughout various sections of this book, health and healthcare system redesign requires leadership from the highest levels. Lack of leadership and political will in light of industrial self-interest and economic power are readily evident whenever the topic of health and health system design arises [14]. Just consider Don Berwick's ardent observation:

> It boggles my mind that the same people who cry 'foul' about rationing an instant later argue to reduce health care benefits for the needy, to defund crucial programs of care and prevention, and to shift thousands of dollars of annual costs to people—elders, the poor, the disabled—who are least able to bear them.

It should be unsurprising then to see governments primarily focusing on cost containment rather than real health and healthcare system redesign. Addendum 2 provides an example of advice to Australian parliamentarians from the Parliamentary Library Service [15]; 4 of 5 issues and recommendation focus on either cost saving or cost shifting measures.

Having outlined that health and healthcare systems are complex adaptive systems *ought to stop* any prejudicial condemnation of arguing for or against "*socialised medicine*" or being "*anti-free market*". Economics unreservedly are part of the health and healthcare system, **but** so are social and societal entitlements. Consider the view of the WHO Governance for Health in the twenty-first century report [9]:

> A recent report by the World Economic Forum (2011) [16] notes that, to be efficient and effective in today's complex, interlinked, fast-changing environment, the structures and processes of governments must be redesigned in order to encompass a new set of actors and tools. They must remain relevant by being responsive to rapidly changing conditions and citizens' expectations and must build capacity to operate effectively in complex, interdependent networks of organizations and systems in the public, private and non-profit sectors to coproduce public value (p 14).

13.4.1 Disambiguation: Social

The terms "social" and "socialised" have been afflicted by so many derivations[5] that it requires some clarifications to achieve common ground.

At its most basic SOCIAL[6] as a contrast to *private* in relation to ownership of or access to resources and services refers to the simple fact that humans live together, and that living together is a prerequisite for the survival of the human species. The term links to the notions of interconnectedness and interdependency—two foundational tenets of complexity and networks—and thus emphasises our personal dependency on the behaviours and actions of other members of our "mob".[7]

Health ultimately depends on societal function, and social actions and interactions that improve societal function are conducive to improving health. Government plays a pivotal role in ensuring actions and interactions of its citizens through *social policies* that promote the health and well-being of its constituency. Government has a regulatory function; the implementation of these policies can be taken up by the private, public, or not-for-profit sectors. The provision of health and social service contributes to the *common good* (or welfare[8]/well-being) of society (see Addendum 3 for a more detailed exploration of social policy—kindly provided by Professor Paul Spicker, Emeritus Professor of Public Policy at Robert Gordon University, UK[9]).

13.4.2 Disambiguation: Adam Smith Advocated for the Public Good AND the Free Market

Adam Smith's treatise *An Inquiry into the Nature and Causes of the Wealth of Nations (1776)* [17] emphasised that people are motivated not by their benevolence but rather by their own interest (p 16). However, self-interest risks exploitation, hence competitive markets are needed to keep everyone honest. Smith's economic thought entailed that the market itself would figured out what people wanted, and how to get it to them most efficiently. In other words the market would create its own order without anyone giving orders—resulting in the notion of the *invisible hand*[10]—that has become the core of our economic doctrine.

---

[5](1) the concept of attitudes, orientations, or behaviours that take interests, intentions, and need of others into account, (2) political meaning depends on political orientation—liberal characteristics on the left-wing side, conservative characteristics on the right-wing side, (3) *social* that it requires some clarifications to achieve common ground.

[6]Latin socci - allies

[7]The Australian Aboriginal term for family, kinship group, or more generally group of people.

[8]Old English phrase wel faran—to fare well, get along successfully, prosper.

[9]see also Paul Spicker's website "An introduction to Social Policy"—http://www.spicker.uk/.

[10]Smith used the term only once in 743 pages, and then clearly in a metaphorical way—*By preferring the support of domestic to that of foreign industry, he intends only his own security: and by directing that industry in such a manner as it produce may be of the greatest value, he*

But, Smith was cautious about the market; in particular he was well aware about the failure of markets to provide public goods. As he stated: *I have never known much good done by those who affected to trade for the public good. It is an affection, indeed, not very common among merchants and very few words need be employed in dissuading them from it* (p 350).

Indeed Smith was worried about the concentration of markets in one hand (the big capitalists) as he saw that they were evading the market.[11] Their political power allowed them to push governments to prescribe protective laws, tariffs, and subsidies which would guarantee high profits. What governments overlooked was that these approaches were bad for society at large.[12] Hence it was not government that was dangerous for the "free market" but rather big enterprises coercing governments into protecting their profits. In Smith's own words:

> Their superiority over the country gentleman is not so much in their knowledge of the public interest, as in their having a better knowledge of their own interest than he has of his. It is by this superior knowledge of their own interest that they have frequently imposed upon his generosity, and persuaded him to give up both his own interest and that of the public, from a very simple but honest conviction that their interest, and not his, was the interest of the public. The interest of the dealers, however, in any particular branch of trade or manufactures, is always in some respects different from, and even opposite to, that of the public. To widen the market and to narrow the competition is always the interest of the dealers. To widen the market may frequently be agreeable enough to the interest of the public; but to narrow the competition must always be against it, and can serve only to enable the dealers, by raising their profits above what they naturally would be, to levy for their own benefit, an absurd tax upon the rest of their fellow-citizens. The proposal of any new law or regulation of commerce which comes form this order ought always to be listened to with great precaution, and ought never to be adopted till after having been long

---

intends only his own gain, and he is in this, as in many other cases, **led by an invisible hand to promote an end which was no part of his intention** *[emphasis added]. Nor is it always the worse for the society that it was no part of it. By pursuing his own interest he frequently promotes that of the society more effectually than when he really intends to promote it.* (p 349).

Here Smith alludes to what was not known to him at the time, the *system dynamics of the economy as a complex adaptive system*.

[11]Pitts argues that the *Wealth of Nations* was to alert the public to the hollow arguments of the merchants who had captured policy making in Britain. She contends: *But in contrast to recent scholarship that has rightly moved beyond the older caricature of Smith as an uncritical apologist for capitalism by exploring his anxieties about the corruptions of commercial society, I stress instead his evolving concern that members of commercial society have failed to be properly critical of the violence and exploitation inflicted by the British-led system of global commerce and imperial expansion.* p 142

Pitts J. Irony in Adam Smith's Critical Global History [18].

[12]*Adam Smith has sometimes been caricatured as someone who saw no role for government in economic life. In fact, he believed that government had an important role to play. Like most modern believers in free markets, Smith believed that the government should enforce contracts and grant patents and copyrights to encourage inventions and new ideas. He also thought that the government should provide public works, such as roads and bridges, that, he assumed, would not be worthwhile for individuals to provide. Interestingly, though, he wanted the users of such public works to pay in proportion to their use.*

The Concise Encyclopedia of Economics. http://www.econlib.org/library/Enc/bios/Smith.html

and carefully examined, not only with the most scrupulous but with the most suspicious attention. It comes from an order of men whose interest is never exactly the same with that of the public, who have generally an interest to deceive and even to oppress the public, and who accordingly have, upon many occasions, both deceived and oppressed it (p 200).

Thus, unsurprisingly, Adam Smith favoured what in today's terms is termed societal *equity* and *sustainability*: *No society can surely be flourishing and happy, of which the far greater part of the members are poor and miserable* (p 66).[13]

13.5 When You Change the Way You Look at the Health and Healthcare System the Health and Healthcare System You Look at Change

This book aimed to offer a rationale and an approach to look at the health and healthcare systems in a different way. Five broad concepts underpin the "new look" of a person-centred, equitable, and sustainable complex adaptive health and healthcare system:

- The concept of interconnectedness of people, health professionals, the community, and government
- An appreciation of the distributed powers and responsibilities amongst the system's agents
- A shared understanding of purpose, goals, and values
- An understanding that health is a personal experiential state
- A working focus on *meeting the needs of each person* in an equitable and sustainable fashion

The healthcare vortex as a visualisation of the health system emphasises the layered organisational nature of health care. It highlights that a seamlessly integrated health system arises from the shared focus on *meeting the needs of the person/patient*.

Looking differently at the health and healthcare system also requires a different look at its governance structures. A new governance structure needs to link "the health and healthcare system as a complex adaptive system" with a new look "policy and governance dynamic" embracing *diffusion, democratisation, and "shared values"* (Fig. 13.3). This will not result in a "one-size-fits-all" solution [11];

---

[13]Coker argued: *Even though Smith's economic man acts in his own self-interest, he. never fails to recognise that his behavior should have consequences for others which are beneficial. However strong self-love is, it can never prevail over man's desire for social approbation. With this position, it can be argued that Smith rejected unrestrained individualism and approached an organic view of society.* p 141
Coker EW. Adam Smith's Concept of the Social System [19].

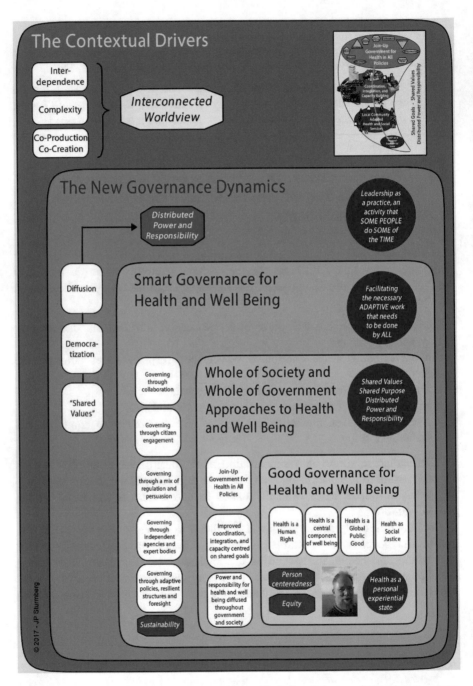

Fig. 13.3 Integrating the conceptual and philosophical foundations underpinning a person-centred, equitable, and sustainable complex adaptive health system with the principles of governance across the health system. Expanded framework based on: World Health Organization Regional Office for Europe. Governance for health in the twenty first century: a study conducted for the WHO Regional Office for Europe. Copenhagen: World Health Organization Regional Office for Europe, 2011

in fact not seeing local adaptations reflecting the uniqueness of local circumstances would be a clear failure of the redesign efforts.

Only shared understandings will allow health system transformation that *meets the needs and expectations of all parties* in the health and healthcare space.

It is time to put ideology aside and focus on what matters—the needs and the health of our current and future patients.

————

The gross national product ... measures everything ... except that which makes life worthwhile.
Robert F. Kennedy (1925–1968)

References

1. Rittel HWJ, Webber MM (1973). Dilemmas in a general theory of planning policy sciences. Pol Sci 4(2):155–69.
2. Weick K (1995) Sensemaking in organizations. Sage Publications, London
3. Weick K (2001) Making sense of the organization. Wiley-Blackwell, Oxford
4. Kolko J (2015) Design thinking comes of age. Harv Bus Rev. 93(9):66–69
5. Archer B (1965) Systematic method for designers. The Design Council, London
6. Simon HA (1969) The sciences of the artificial. MIT Press, Cambridge
7. Papanek V (1971) Design for the real world: human ecology and social change. Pantheon Books, New York
8. Buchanan R (1992) Wicked problems in design thinking. Des Issues 8(2):5–21
9. World Health Organization Regional Office for Europe (2011) Governance for health in the 21st century: a study conducted for the WHO Regional Office for Europe. Copenhagen: World Health Organization Regional Office for Europe
10. Rasmussen L (2010) Making our health system more sustainable: an ideas paper for the Commissioner of Environmental Sustainability, Victoria. Doctors for the Environment Australia, College Park, SA
11. Prowle M, Harradine D (2015) Sustainable healthcare systems: an international study. ACCA (the Association of Chartered Certified Accountants), London. Available at: http://www.accaglobal.com/an/en/technical-activities/technical-resources-search/2015/february/sustainable-healthcare-systems.html
12. Heifetz R (1994) Leadership without easy answers. Harvard University Press, Cambridge, MA
13. McGinnis JM, Williams-Russo P, Knickman JR (2002) The case for more active policy attention to health promotion. Health Aff (Millwood). 21(2):78–93
14. Starfield B (2011) Politics, primary healthcare and health: was Virchow right? J Epidemiol Community Health 65(8):653–655
15. Boxall A-M (2011) What are we doing to ensure the sustainability of the health system? Canberra, Australia: Department of Parliamentary Services, Parliament of Australia, 18 November 2011. Report No.: Contract No.: 4 2011-12. Available at: http://www.aph.gov.au/About_Parliament/Parliamentary_Departments/Parliamentary_Library/pubs/rp/rp1112/12rp04
16. World Economic Forum (2011) The future of government. Lessons learned from around the world. World Economic Forum, Geneva. REF: 010611. Available at: http://www3.weforum.org/docs/EU11/WEF_EU11_FutureofGovernment_Report.pdf
17. Smith A (2007) An inquiry into the nature and causes of the wealth of nations. MεταLibri - digital edition, São Paulo
18. Pitts J (2015) Irony in Adam Smith's critical global history. Polit. Theory 45(2):141–163
19. Coker EW (1990) Adam Smith's concept of the social system. J. Bus. Ethics 9(2):139–142

Addendum 1

Threats to Systems Change—Views from the Insight

- Vested interest—providers, healthcare organisations, external organisations

  - Unscrupulous over servicing of a procedure purely as income generation
  - Medicalisation of daily life
  - Fee-for-Service reimbursement
  - Promotion of consumerism rather than *health service*

- Lack of financial incentives to use less resource

  - Saving money by reducing inefficient resources
  - Fear of reduction of budget in light of savings through more effective resource utilisation
  - Outsourcing—reduces the level of control an organisation retains in the overall running of the organisation

- Questions about current medical practice

  - Is there a difference between physiotherapy and exercise compared with a particular surgical procedure in orthopaedics?
  - Is a widely used drug any different to a placebo?
  - Is a complex, highly invasive surgical operation any better than a less invasive, less resource using one?

- Medical education

  - Current focus on disease-management based on EBM-based guidelines
  - Lack of a humanities curriculum and exposure to the humanities in clinical practice
  - Systems thinking—health and disease in the context of the person's external environment: nutrition, housing, working environment and conditions, education

- General misconception of health and disease

  - Overestimation of frequency of diseases
  - Overestimation of treatment benefits and underestimation of treatment risks
  - Sensationalisation of "medical breakthroughs"
  - Process auditing fails to promote "strategic social decision" making

Addendum 2

What Are We Doing to Ensure the Sustainability of the Health System?—Executive Summary [11]

Health care expenditure has been steadily rising in Australia in recent decades, just as it has in many countries around the world. Increasingly, governments are becoming concerned about how this level of public spending will be sustained. Many are looking for ways to contain the growth in health care expenditure or "bend the cost curve".

Burgeoning health expenditure is a difficult problem to solve because there are a myriad of factors driving up health costs, and most of them are rooted deeply in a complex health system where much of what happens is beyond the reach of government. Simple technical solutions such as imposing tighter constraints on government spending, or using monetary incentives to change health professionals' or consumers' behaviour are unlikely to work on their own because they do not grapple with important political dimensions of the problem. Governments, for example, need to find ways of slowing the growth in health care expenditure without adversely affecting health outcomes, particularly for people who are already in poor health. Governments also need to affect change on the ground where health care services are delivered. This can be difficult because many health care providers operate in the private sector beyond the direct control of governments.

Despite the challenges, most governments use a range of policy tools to help control the growth in health care expenditure. This paper identifies some of the main ones used in Australia:

- deciding which health care interventions will be publicly funded
- changing the way health care providers are paid
- imposing costs on individuals
- constraining the capacity of the health system and
- encouraging competition

The paper assesses how effectively each of these tools is being used in Australia, and it outlines some potential options for reform.

Key policy tools for containing health expenditure

Deciding which health care interventions will be publicly funded

One of the main tools governments use to control health expenditure is to ensure that public funds are used only to fund the most clinically effective and cost-effective health care interventions. Formally, this process is known as Health Technology Assessment (HTA). Currently HTA processes in Australia operate within discrete sectors of the health system rather than across it. The assessment process for new drugs, for example, is completely separate from that for new medical procedures. Currently, most assessments are done on new technologies or interventions; existing ones, even if they are out-dated or ineffective, continue to be funded except in relatively rare circumstances.

To remedy these problems in HTA, policymakers could consider establishing a single HTA agency capable of systematically assessing the clinical effectiveness and cost-effectiveness of all types of new and existing health care interventions. Under these arrangements, it should be possible to compare the effectiveness of different types of interventions for the same health conditions. Some consideration should also be given to implementing mechanisms to "de-fund" or "disinvest" from the least effective interventions.

Changing the way health care providers are paid

The way health care providers are paid also has an impact on health care expenditure. Some payment methods provide incentives to "over-service", while others provide little incentive to deliver high quality care. Australia currently relies heavily on provider payment methods considered by the World Health Organisation to be the least effective ways of curbing expenditure growth: fee-for-service payments and activity-based funding (ABF) both provide strong incentives to increase the volume of care delivered and therefore overall expenditure.

To help contain health expenditure, policymakers could consider supplementing or combining fee-for-service and ABF methods with others that are better able to constrain expenditure growth (examples include fixed budgets and salaried employees). It will be important that these new methods are also accompanied by reforms that strengthen systems for monitoring performance so that they do not have a detrimental impact on the quality of care.

Imposing more costs on individuals

Many governments try to curb health care expenditure growth by imposing costs on individuals; these costs are commonly known as co-payments. Most countries are shifting away from using co-payments as a means of financing health care, but Australia continues to rely heavily on them. Even though Australia has a system of safety nets in place to protect people from excessively high out of pocket costs, evidence is now emerging that the cost of care is stopping some people from using necessary health services. Because this is neither equitable nor efficient, policymakers should consider undertaking a high-level review of Australia's co-payment and safety net policies. As well as considering technical issues such as access, entitlements, and benefit levels, this review should also canvass and debate alternative co-payment policy proposals.

Constraining the capacity of the health system

The overall capacity of the health system has a powerful influence on expenditure growth. Capacity is determined to a large degree by the number of health care facilities and the number of health workers practicing in the system. Reforms to the way health workers are trained and registered in Australia have recently been implemented, but it is too soon to assess their impact on expenditure growth. Australia's health infrastructure decision-making processes, however, have received relatively little attention. There are currently multiple health infrastructure funding processes in operation, which makes it difficult, if not impossible, to monitor the impact of infrastructure funding decisions on health expenditure.

To help control health expenditure growth, governments could consider consolidating the various infrastructure decision-making processes in Australia and making them more transparent. To make further advances in the health workforce area, governments will need to continue to find new ways of working together on areas of shared responsibility.

Encouraging competition Competition is a key driver of efficiency and innovation in many sectors of the economy but it is contentious in the health sector because there are so many areas of market failure. While competition does exist within the Australian health system, in many areas it is limited.

There are many potential options for encouraging competition in health care but past experiences here and overseas demonstrate that competition policies do not always deliver the anticipated benefits. To design and implement effective competition policies in health care, policymakers first must acknowledge the differences between health care and other markets.

Some options in medical services are to encourage greater role substitution (for example, using nurse practitioners or physicians' assistants where appropriate). Another is to give the government a greater role in training medical specialists, and make the process more transparent.

Australia's health insurance system should be considered as a priority for reform because it has an overarching influence on competition between providers and in service delivery. The key issue in health insurance is to resolve long-standing questions about the role of private insurance in the context of Medicare. A number of proposals for insurance reforms already exist, and include options such as: promoting managed competition between insurance funds, re-allocating existing public subsidies for private insurance to other areas such as to patients in the form of vouchers, private hospitals in the form of bed subsidies, or directly to public hospitals.

Addendum 3

Social Policy and Health Care—Paul Spicker
Emeritus Professor of Public Policy at Robert Gordon University, UK

My thanks go to Prof Paul Spicker for providing this addendum.

The study of Social Policy has not, for the most part, been concerned directly with "health". Many issues which are central to people's welfare—love, laughter, leisure, culture, music—play no part in the provision of services. Social Policy is much more concerned with health care—the organisation, management, and delivery of health services. Health care has not always been seen as a distinct category in its own right. It is sometimes seen as part of another system—the Poor Law, which provided medical care along with income, education, and workhouses, or the idea of "social security" in France, which manages the finance of health care along with pensions. Equally, other service systems are sometimes treated as part of health care: the Victorian Board of Health was also responsible for public housing and sanitation, and in the 1920s and 1930s psychiatric hospitals used to deal with mental illness, learning disability, and illegitimacy almost interchangeably. It is conceivable that future generations will look back at our distinctions between health and social care, or health promotion and physical education, with bemusement—or that areas where we fail to distinguish health care from other fields, which has happened with the medicalisation of dying, will prove equally baffling.

Governments and Health Care

Health care does not provide health; it provides care. The main purpose of collective social organisation has been to regulate and manage the provision of care, most directly through providing some guarantees of treatment in the event of need. The "health systems" of continental Europe can mainly be understood as systems of insurance, covering medical expenses for contributors or for citizens. In general terms, nearly all these systems offer reasonably comprehensive cover for hospital care; most cover ambulant care to some extent, and at least some of the costs of medical goods [1]. The insurance principle is also implicit in national systems; the UK National Health Service provides everyone not with health, but the equivalent of universal health insurance, financed through taxation.

In developing countries, specialised medical care tends to be restricted to those with greater resources, with only limited exceptions (e.g. Sri Lanka and Cuba); for general populations, a different sort of model has been emerging. Essential Health Packages, sometimes called Basic Health Care Packages, offer universal provision of selected medical events, such as vaccination or maternity support, while typically

Table Add 3.1 Disambiguation of terms—Social policy, welfare, and the welfare state

Social Policy	Welfare

• Administration of social services
 	
  – Health administration
  – Social security
  – Education
  – Employment services
  – Community care
  – Housing management
 	
• Managing social problems
 	
  – Crime
  – Disability
  – Unemployment
  – Mental health
  – Learning disability
  – Old age
 	
• Addressing social disadvantage
 	
  – Race
  – Gender
  – Poverty
	• Well-being and "utility" (where people's well-being or interests consist of the things they choose to have)
	• Social protection and the provision of services, e.g. for childhood, sickness, or old age (this is the main understanding in Europe)
	• Financial assistance to poor people (this is the main usage in the USA)
	
	Welfare state
	
	• An ideal view of welfare provision, offering the best possible services based on the right of citizenship
	• The provision of welfare by government (the main usage in the USA)
	• The varied social systems which exist to provide services and offer social protection (the main usage in Europe)

Note: For more information see P. Spicker (2014) Social policy: theory and practice [4]

avoiding coverage of both the more expensive, high-tech response to disease and accident, or the coverage of longer-term conditions such as psychiatric care or disability support [2, 3].

The systems which have developed to deliver health and social services are complex. Collective provision is sometimes discussed in terms of the actions of "welfare states", but that term is misleading (see Tables Add 3.1 and Add 3.2 for clarification). In many societies, collective provision has not developed through government or the state; it has begun through mutual insurance and voluntary societies, or even through trades unions [6, 7]. Mutual insurance is intrinsically redistributive: people pool risks in order to be able to cope with changes in fortune, and membership buys security. The experience of several countries has been one of progressive expansion of coverage, mainly encountering difficulties when existing schemes fail to cover people on low incomes or those with special needs. When compulsion has been introduced, it has often been concerned with mopping up the residuum—extending to the poorest the benefits of solidarity and social protection that could only otherwise be guaranteed to those with more resources [7].

Governments and states are not the only way that collective services are organised, then, but they have come to play a major role in service provision. Sometimes this is done to supplement the existing pattern of provision (such as the French *régime général*, or the Affordable Care Act in the USA); in others, more rarely, the state has taken on the role formerly undertaken by voluntary

Table Add 3.2 Some arguments for and against the provision of welfare

	Arguments for welfare	Arguments against welfare
Humanitarian	• Welfare meets needs • Welfare empowers people • Welfare protects individual dignity	• Welfare restricts individual liberty
Religious	• Catholicism recognises a duty of social solidarity (or mutual social responsibility) • Judaism, Islam, and Lutheran Christianity require collective responsibility for one's community	• Collective provision drives out charity
Democratic	• Democratic governments serve their citizens • Social protection has developed in tandem with democratic rights	• Constitutional government must be restricted to avoid tyranny
Humanitarian	• Welfare meets needs • Welfare empowers people • Welfare protects individual dignity	• Welfare restricts individual liberty
Economic well-being	• Welfare is what people choose; self-interested individuals pool risks and take collective action	• Welfare compromises the fundamental rights to property
Economic organisation	• Markets leave gaps	• Markets offer choice and do things better
Social	• Welfare promotes social cohesion	• Welfare leads to dependency

Note: For more information see P. Spicker (2017) Arguments for welfare: the welfare state and social policy. [5]

and mutual aid. The most fundamental argument for government action is that a democratic government is there to do what people want it to do. Government, Edmund Burke wrote, is "a contrivance of human wisdom to provide for human wants." [8] The main restriction on this kind of government action is imposed in constitutional governments where constitutions restrict the legitimate scope of government activity. Governments commonly engage with provision where:

• action protects the public as a whole, such as vaccination to achieve herd immunity, or sanitation and drainage to promote public health

- where other methods (voluntary, mutual, or market) have left unacceptable gaps (for example, the long-term care of older people)
- it is necessary to protect the interests of some people from actions by others (e.g. regulation of food quality or the abuse of antibiotics)
- some element of provision is not voluntary for the patient—for example, in psychiatric care

Sometimes the provision of health care saves other expense; sometimes public provision is just the most practical thing to do. The reason why the Poor Law's Boards of Guardians took on responsibility for public health in the 1850s was, simply, that in much of the country there was no other administrative body around to do it.

Public sector provision has been heavily criticised. It is often characterised as economically inefficient. The free-market Institute of Economic Affairs is critical of the way that the UK National Health Service restricts spending on health; if things were done privately, they argue, people would be free to spend more money as they think fit [9]. The criteria that public services work to are different from those which apply to private firms. They are described by Hood as "sigma type values", emphasising frugality and the reduction of waste; "theta type values", emphasising rectitude, fairness and legitimacy; and "lambda-type values", emphasising resilience, robustness, and security [10]. Some critics object to the public services making different decisions from those that would be made in a market [11, 12], which rather misses the point—that is what they are there to do.

Public and Private: Welfare Pluralism

The main alternative to the public sector is sometimes referred to as the "private sector". That term stands for a range of somewhat different activities. In the first place, it is taken to mean the provision of goods and service by commercial providers working through an economic market. This approach is passionately supported by the "neo-liberals" who have come to dominate much thinking in economics and international organisations. Arthur Seldon argues that the price mechanism leads to choice for the consumer; a service led by the consumer rather than by the professions; more efficient services at lower costs (because this increases profitability); responsiveness to need (because their payment depends on it); and the education of people as to the implications of their choices [13].

Economists make much of "market failure", circumstances where the assumptions that are made in theoretical economics do not apply. Markets have imperfect information (markedly so in the case in health care, where specialised knowledge is one of the principal items being purchased); they are tied to particular locations (especially in the provision of personal services); there may be issues of "moral hazard", where people's needs and claims health care are shaped by their own behaviour. In health care, the normal constraints of demand do not apply; people will spend anything they have to stay alive. The fundamental problems of markets, however, run deeper than the conventional idea of market failure. It is in the nature of a market that consumers are not the only people who have a choice; producers have one, too. People who have complex and potentially expensive needs, who live in remote areas, are uncertain to be insurable. There is a process of "adverse selection", leaving people out; and the public sector is generally left to fill in the gaps [14]. Wherever public services have been left to provide in the last resort, there are issues of equity and maintaining the boundaries; the process of dealing with residual needs is invariably costly and inefficient; and those elements, in turn, have led to relentless pressure to expand the range of provision.

There is no country where services are delivered wholly through the activity of government, or through the commercial market. The provision of medical care in the USA is often represented as "private", but in practice government pays for about half the expenses, through a range of services and finance mechanisms including Medicare (support for older people), Medicaid (support for people on low incomes), State governments (typically paying for long-term psychiatric care), State-based insurance (e.g. in Hawaii and Minnesota), and the service for native Americans. Then there is TRICARE, for military personnel, and the Veterans Health Administration, a system for former service personnel and their families, together dealing with more than 70 million people. When we look into more detail at the "private" sector, it includes voluntary non-profits, charities, mutual insurance, and commercial payment for service. A voluntary hospital may well have both private and public wards.

The distinction of public and private does not, however, capture the full range of services that are commonly found in developed societies—a range variously referred to as a "mixed economy of welfare", or sometimes as "welfare pluralism". The term "private" is sometimes conflated with the "voluntary" sector, but the motivations and approaches of voluntary provision are generally very different from commercial providers. Some voluntary providers are non-profit organisations, formed to advance a social objective. Some are mutual, offering social protection. The boundaries between different classes of activity are indistinct. There are "social enterprises", which combine market practices with communal objectives. Some voluntary organisations guide themselves by the principles of commerce and enterprise. Conversely, some commercial organisations have elaborate systems for occupational welfare or corporate social responsibility.

It is also worth noting the existence of an "informal" sector. Many people receive physical care, not from professionals, but from family members, partners, neighbours, and friends. In a devastating critique of social care provision for people with learning disabilities, Michael Bayley made the case that the care provided by professionals or government services should be seen, relative to the work of informal carers, as marginal—sometimes a complement, often a supplement to the real work [15]. He argued, in consequence, that planning for social provision could only be done if it built around existing social networks—a process he called "interweaving", but which has come to be thought of in terms of a "care package".

Why Health Care Is Not Like a Business

The model of business that dominates economic textbooks is the model of a range of providers, all making choices about what to provide, how to do it, and what to charge. It is a truism to say that health care is not much like that, but that does not get us very far; real-life businesses are not much like that, either. It is difficult to generalise, because there are so many different strands, but in any discussion of health care there are likely to be fundamental departures from the theoretical model.

The first of these departures concerns objectives. One of the primary characteristics that defines an activity as a public service—whether it is based on government, voluntary activity, charity, mutualism, or other independent—is that it acts to further public aims [16]. The primary test for any public service is whether it is effective in doing so—"effectiveness" being defined in terms of the extent to which the service meets its aims. Most public services equally attempt to do this without wasting resources, aiming for cost-effectiveness. Some will "target" their activities, aiming to choose the areas where they will have the maximum effect; some will ration services, applying criteria about eligibility and service allocation in order to achieve their objectives more effectively. Cost-effectiveness is a very different test from the idea of "efficiency" found in economics textbooks. Productive efficiency is achieved when firms produce goods or units of service at the lowest possible cost per unit. Cost-effectiveness is achieved when the aims of a service are achieved to the greatest extent at the lowest cost. The difference between the two is straightforward: it is a matter of how much a producer should do. Businesses become efficient by deciding how much to produce; they will limit the scope of their activity to the level which maximises their returns. I referred earlier to the issues of adverse selection. It makes perfectly good sense on economic grounds to refuse to treat people with burns; burns are expensive to treat. This kind of selection is implicit in the market process—if commercial firms are choosing which activities they should undertake, they are only doing what they are supposed to do. Public services, when they try to avoid these consequences, are not trying to be "efficient"; they are trying to do something else.

The second key issue concerns commoditisation—an ugly piece of jargon, for which I must apologise, but there is no real substitute. The sale of goods works most efficiently when it is clear just what is being sold and what it costs to produce. This is more difficult with personal services, but some personal services (such as hairdressing or hotel rooms) can be commoditised—that is, turned into saleable products—in the same way. There are certainly elements in health care which can be treated on this basis—the sale of medical goods, laser eye surgery, specific tasks in dentistry. Arguably insurance can be sold in this way, though it offers more security if it does not. However, the attempt to extend commoditisation more widely, for example, to parcels of time for the care of elderly people, has been controversial; something is lost in continuity, personal relationships, and trust. Objectives such as holistic response, emotional support, or continuing care are likely to be disrupted by commoditisation. So it should not be surprising that much of the work of public services, voluntary organisations, and charities is "decommodified"—taken out of a market régime altogether.

The third difference concerns service integration. Commercial markets do not need to be coordinated or integrated; they have the "invisible hand". Each individual chooses what they will receive from a range of options that is offered. However, that approach has serious limitations—providers have choices, too. The patchy and selective approach of markets imply a landscape of fragmented and partial provision from the outset. That has been exacerbated by the complex, restricted, and sometimes residual development of public services.

There has been increasing emphasis in public services on issues of integration: providing holistic care, engaging a range of stakeholders, breaking down barriers between "silos". There are reservations to make about some of those attempts: professional differences reflect differences in training, expertise, and purpose and the delivery of complex services requires a division of labour to be effective. A strong emphasis on partnership can have negative effects on a service—blurring professional boundaries and diverting attention from core activities to peripheral ones. When several services are all trying to be holistic at the same time, they can duplicate effort and end up dancing on each other's toes. None of that detracts from the reasoning which has led to the emphasis on integration: a desire to ensure that people do not suffer when responsibility for them is passed between services, to avoid gaps, to reduce duplication (which is wasteful), and to make it possible for each service achieves its aims to the greatest possible extent. Cooperation and partnership are only part of that process; the other part is the engagement of the service user [17]. Personal services cannot be delivered effectively without the presence, and in some sense the engagement, of the service user. The idea that services are "co-produced" by professionals and service users is a call to take into account the role of the patient as well as the health professional. As the contemporary slogan puts it: "Nothing about me without me".

References

1. Paris V, Hewlett E, Auraaen A, Alexa J, Simon L (2016) Health care coverage in OECD countries in 2012. OECD Health Working Papers, No. 88. OECD Publishing, Paris. http://dx.doi.org/10.1787/5jlz3kbf7pzv-en
2. World Bank (1993) World Development Report 1993: investing in health. World Bank, Washington DC
3. http://www.who.int/healthsystems/topics/delivery/technical_brief_ehp.pdf
4. Spicker P (2000) The welfare state: a general theory. SAGE, London
5. Spicker P (2014) Social policy: theory and practice. Policy Press, Bristol
6. Baldwin P (1990) The politics of social solidarity. Cambridge University Press, Cambridge
7. Yanay U (1990) Service delivery by a trade union - does it pay? J Soc Policy 19(2):221–234
8. Spicker P (2017) Arguments for welfare: the welfare state and social policy. [7]. Rowman and Littlefield, London
9. Burke E (1790) Reflections on the revolution in France. Holt, Rinehart and Winston, New York 1959.
10. Niemitz K (2016). Rebuttal: "The NHS is wonderful, just underfunded", Institute of Economic Affairs. https://iea.org.uk/blog/rebuttal-the-nhs-is-wonderful-just-underfunded

11. Hood C (1991) A public management for all seasons? Public Adm. 69(1):3–19
12. Wolf C (1978) A theory of non-market failure, Rand Corporation, Santa Monica
13. Winston C (2006) Government failure versus market failure. Brookings, Washington DC
14. Seldon A (1977) Charge. Temple Smith, London
15. Barr N (2004) The economics of the welfare state. Oxford University Press, Oxford
16. Bayley M (1973) Mental handicap and community care. RKP, London
17. Spicker P (2009) The nature of a public service. Int J Public Admin. 32(11):970–991
18. Osborne S, Radnor Z, Nasi G (2013) A new theory for public service management? Am Rev Public Admin 43(2):135–158

Index

Printed in the United States
By Bookmasters